THE WORD

THAT WHICH IS WRITTEN AND SHOULD BE KNOWN

By
RAY C. M. HARRIS

Published by
Research Associates School Times Publications/
Frontline Distribution Int'l Inc.

CHICAGO•JAMAICA•LONDON
REPUBLIC of TRINIDAD and TOBAGO, CARIBBEAN

Research Associates School Times Publications/
Frontline Distribution Int'l, Inc.
5206 S. Harper Avenue
Chicago, IL 60615
Tel: (773) 288-7718
Fax: (773) 288-7528
Email: info@frontlinebooks.net

Published 2006 by
Research Associates School Times Publications/
Frontline Distribution Int'l Inc.
and
Miguel Lorne Publishers, Jamaica
P.O. Box 2967
Kingston 8, Jamaica
Tel/Fax: (876) 922-3915
Email: Headstartp@hotmail.com

ISBN 0-94839-088-3

Edited and typeset by:
Dorothy M. Johnson

Illustrations by:
Omari Harris
Liz Dangleben
Aisha Cruickshank
Dinnia Joseph-Peter

ABOUT THE AUTHOR

RAY C. M. HARRIS, LL.B., LL.M. (U.W.I.), LEC (NMLS), was born in the nature island of the Caribbean, the Commonwealth of Dominica. He received his education from the St. Mary's Academy in the Commonwealth of Dominica, the Law Faculty of the University of the West Indies in Barbados, and the Norman Manley Law School in Jamaica. Mr. Harris is an Attorney-at-Law and a Legal Consultant, who specialises in legislative drafting, law revision and law reform. He has held the posts of Parliamentary Draftsman, Chief Parliamentary Draftsman, Law Revision Commissioner, Director of the Law Commission, and Legal Adviser — Law Revision and Law Reform in the Commonwealth of Dominica. He has also served as Law Commission Adviser to the Southeast African State of Malawi under the auspices of the Commonwealth Secretariat. Mr. Harris has been the Chairman of both the Law Revision Commission and the Law Reform Commission of the Commonwealth of Dominica. He has also served as a member of the Commonwealth of Dominica Constitution Review Commission set up by the Government of the Commonwealth of Dominica to review the Constitution on the 21st Anniversary of Dominica's Independence. Mr. Harris, who has also served as a member of the Drafting Committee of the CARICOM Inter-Governmental Task Force, is presently a member of the Dominica Bar Association, the OECS Bar Association and the Commonwealth Association of Legislative Counsel.

Ray Harris or "Roots", as he is lovingly referred to, is a brother with a difference. Despite his accomplishments, he is amazingly unassuming and humble. To many grassroots brothers and sisters, he is known as an elder, a Caribbean sage, who is never too busy to assist. He explains both mundane and esoteric matters with a clarity and simplicity that can only be described as outstanding. This capacity to explain complex matters in a simple yet clear manner is aptly reflected in this outstanding work. This work of devotional service can only be described as essential reading for all people dedicated to Truth.

CONTENTS

PREFACE

In this book, I have not written anything new, as the saying goes: 'there is nothing new under the sun'. What I have attempted to do, however, is to give the golden thread: the spiritual cohesive link that connects our lives on Earth to the lives of our ancestors, our children, as well as to the lives of those souls yet to be born.

That we are consciously aware of it or not, all of our lives are journeys "in search of Truth"; this is dealt with in chapter 1. And those who live lives dedicated to Truth realise "the Will and the Way," which is dealt with in chapter 2. The Will and the Way, in a nutshell, is understanding and living in harmony with God's Spiritual or Natural Laws, so that the Christ or Divinity in you can be realised here on Earth. Of necessity, those living Souls who want to realise the Will and the Way must know Self; and to achieve this they must know their past, their history. However, in this decadent time of veiled history and blatant untruth, to realise one's true history, one needs to go "beyond the veil of history". This is dealt with in chapter 3. Here, man's veiled history of antiquity, relating to high cultures (civilisations) in places such as Africa (Alkebulan), Asia, Lemuria and Atlantis, is dealt with and linked to events and people of today.

And, finally, in the hearts and minds of those conscious Souls who have gone beyond the veil of history, the pendulum-swing through the modality of time will correspondingly bring them forward in time — so that they will have a sensitivity to, if not a perception of, the future. Hence, they will live in "the Eternal Now", in that their view of the present will be blessed by an understanding and knowledge of the past as well as an attunement to the future. This is dealt with in chapter 4, where living in "the Eternal Now" is explained and prophecy relating to our immediate future is summarised and presented to the reader. *Om peace — And so it is.*

ACKNOWLEDGEMENTS

Many people have assisted me in completing this work. I will merely mention with gratitude a few who immediately come to mind. Merlyn Charles and Rosie Warrington who kindly typed the first few pages of this work many years ago. Although I eventually did a great deal of the typing myself, Dinnia Joseph-Peter assisted me in this regard throughout the exercise. She also helped me with the initial proofreading and editing, as did my mother and my wife. I am also grateful to my wife for assisting me in finalising this work.

Many people over the years have encouraged me to complete this work and have eagerly awaited its completion. A few of them that immediately come to mind are: my friends Bobby Olivacce, Lumumba, Nyriah, Disciple Caesar, Ras Bobby, Kabinda (Desmond Trotter), Errol, Peter, Ras Popo, Sister Nathalie, Adama, Wayne, Paul, Earl, Curtis and Dexter. I say heartfelt thanks to those whom I have mentioned as well as many others whom I have failed to mention. I would also like to express my gratitude to Fred White, who made it possible for me to share this work with readers via the Internet. I also express my sincere gratitude to Ras Sekou Tafari and Frontline Distribution International Inc. for publishing this work. Finally, I thank my family for their support through the years, and ultimately I thank God, the Almighty for the will and the way to complete this work. This is a work of devotional service to all those who can make use of it to better their lives.

CHAPTER 1

IN SEARCH OF TRUTH

We are children of the Universe. No less than the trees and the stars. We have a right to be here and whether or not it is clear to us, no doubt the Universe is unfolding as it should. Therefore, let us be at peace with God, whatever we conceive Him to be, and whatever our labours and aspirations in the noisy confusion of life let us keep peace with our souls. With all its sham, drudgery and broken dreams, it is still a beautiful world. Be careful, strive to be happy.[1]

Introduction

Each one of us strives to be joyful and content, but are we really? All of us struggle whether we like it or not, but are we really happy and at peace with ourselves? Or, on the contrary, don't we find ourselves buried in the mire of clay, filled with sadness, gloom, bitterness, self-doubt and regret?

If this is so, then why is this? Haven't we learnt the lessons of time? The world has been blessed with spiritual guides, prophets, avatars and messiahs who have incarnated on Earth at times of irreligion and decadence to guide and elevate us in our quest for Self-realisation, harmony, peace … that divinity within. Despite this, however, we don't seem to be adhering to the truths taught by the great Masters, be it Confucius, Buddha, Krishna, Noah, Elijah, Isaiah, Moses, or Jesus the Christ, the Messiah, with whom we are most acquainted, or for that matter, the Prophet Mohammed or Baha-ulla, who both came after Jesus the Christ.

The Science of Truth

Accepting the premise that there is nothing without a cause, it is clear that the root cause of our lethargic response in realising this harmony, strength and Truth within ourselves, is intrinsically linked with our error of superficially reading or listening and saying we believe, instead of thinking over, internalising and living those teachings in our daily lives; anything short of this must lead to frustration, pain and failure. *We must totally and devotedly live those truths as we struggle along the path of life,* so that we shall gradually realise this joy and contentment within ourselves, thereby transmuting those beliefs into *living knowledge.* Hence, *living becomes a life science of Truth, and our bodily temples, the test tubes within which the experiments and results of the life science are monitored and realised.*

In the Holy Bible, Jesus the Christ declares in John 17:11-19: "And now I am no more in the world and I am coming to you. But they are in the world, Holy Father, preserve them in your name, those whom you have given me so that they may be one even as we are one. While I was with them, I kept them in your name which you gave me. I guarded them, and none of them perished except the son of perdition, so that the scripture might be fulfilled. Now I am coming to you and say these things while I am still in the world so that they may have my joy made complete in their hearts. I have given them your word. And the world has hated them for they are not of the world just as I am not of the world.

"I do not pray that you may take them out of the world, but that you may preserve them from the evil one. As I am not of the world, so they are not of the world. *Sanctify them by the truth. Your word is the truth.* As you have sent me into the world, so too I have sent them into the world and on their behalf, I consecrate myself so that they too may *be consecrated by truth*".

The Principle of Truth is Within Us

The principle of Truth of which Jesus spoke is within each man. It is opposed to all falsehood, evil and error. Truth is a vital force and one must live by its dictates or else one will soon lose hold of it.[2] We are told: "You shall seek me and find me, when you shall search for me with all your heart"; "Abide in me...."; "Come unto me ... and I will give you rest"; "In quietness and in confidence I shall be your strength".[3]

The promise of rest, confidence, stability and strength is not based on mere inactivity, but on a constant effort to know self, the Truth and divinity within. As Owens puts it: "Truth is based ultimately on self-knowledge and is related inextricably to morality. It is opposed to ... (trickery and deception) and becomes manifest through being 'used' or put into practice".[4] Hence, he that says: "I know him and keepeth not his commandment is a liar and *truth is not in him*".[5] But like the psalmist, our innermost feelings and exclamations should be: "*O how I love your law, it is my meditation all the day*".[6]

By Truth alone will man be released from the shackles of his carnal mind, thereby gaining true freedom and peace as he treads the path of earthly illusion and fleshy desires, because we are advised: "*Walk not after the flesh, but after the spirit*".[7]

The term "conscience" is generally understood, though *this inner whispering spirit* designating good as against evil, right as against wrong, truth as against falsehood, has become unfortunately dullened, if not atrophied with disuse and abuse in lots of us. True, we may walk around and people may think the world of us, but in the final analysis, what is important is what we really think and know about ourselves. Man may therefore be said to live in the 'closet of his mind', and when that closet is filled with the junk and cobwebs of our corruption and lies, stifling true living by the tensions of our disharmony, then life can be an experience of genuine hell and the term "the living dead" an apt description. In the Holy Bible we are advised: "have a good *conscience, and* in all things *be willing to live honestly*".[8]

The Path of Truth

The word "Dharma", which is said to have its roots in the Sanskrit language, is of supreme importance to Buddhism. It means to support a moral law, a spiritual law of righteousness — the eternal Law of the Universe — Truth. In Christian terms, it corresponds to the will of God. "Pada, ... in Sanskrit ... means 'foot, step' and thence...", means "the Path".[9] Hence, "Dhammapada" to the Buddhist indicates the Path of Truth, the path of light, the path of love; to the Christian initiate the Path of Truth, the path of Christ, the will of God.[10]

Some, in their negativity, may be inclined to say that they cannot walk this Path or that they cannot achieve this degree of Christ-like perfection; but it is submitted that even if we do not realise the ultimate Crown of Glory, the joys of the Path are ours. *The Path of Truth is the gem of life that cannot be bought with money.* However, by honest, devoted effort, it can become the path of perfection, the development of talents, both latent and apparent, the realisation of self, the manifestation of the eternal Christ Spirit in the temple of flesh. We are exhorted by none other than Jesus the Christ to "be perfect as" our "Heavenly Father is perfect".[11]

The Longing for Truth is the Gradual Unfoldment of the Divinity Within

The longing for Truth in every one of us reflects the yearning of the Soul; it is the gradual evolutionary unfoldment of the divinity within, the inner essence of our being. *Some of us may concentrate our minds on the finding of facts in the 'material', physical world around us, that is, the outer world, whereas, others may by introspection, meditation and a dedication to true living, find truth within their own being; their 'mind's eye' is concentrated within and becomes centred in the inner "Eye" or eternal "I" of their being.* In the Bible we read: "Your eye is the lamp of your body; when your eye is sound, your whole body is full of light; but when it is not sound, your body is full of darkness. Therefore be careful lest the light in you be darkness".[12]

The above does not in any way detract from "the Everywhereness of God" or the fact that God is the ultimate Truth of all existence, the underlying essence of all creation: what was, what is, and what shall ever be.[13] However, never forget that *God is forever within you* because that is the cornerstone of all truth to be known on Earth. He is the underlying Divine Essence of your being.

We can take solace therefore in knowing that *God is found within* when sought with devotion and selflessness (which, incidentally, is the opposite of selfishness), just as cream is found in milk, and oil in the castor oil fruit. *The search and realisation of Truth is in essence the story of life* — the most marvelous and joyous 'search and find' story there is. It cannot be overemphasised here however that *our search for Truth and relationship with God*, in other words *our religion*, must not be mere attendance at Saturday or Sunday Mass or service or a time when we clap and sing in our congregations, but it *must be everything that we think, feel, say and do.* It must be *our lives. Knock on the door of the temple and enter: Christ, the anointed of the All-Father dwells therein.*

The Way of Truth is Not Based on Blind Submission

The way of Truth or of God is not founded on ignorance or unreasoning blind submission, because the Creator's invitation to us is "Come now, let us reason together".[14] God does not force His will upon His children because that would be contrary to the whole idea of free will, but accepts respect and love given willingly and intelligently. We are advised, "Peace be still",[15] that life's turmoil may be quieted, because when tired we exercise our will by saying and doing things we tend to regret afterwards. Therefore rest, be still, and in that stillness wisdom and strength will come; so too spiritual understanding and light will permeate your whole being. Thus we read: "He that dwelleth in the secret place of the Most High shall abide under the shadow of the Almighty".[16] So remember always, "draw near to God and He will draw near to you".[17]

Most of us never take the time to be silent or to sit quietly and pray to God. Most of us find it very difficult to sit still for a moment without carnal or worrying thoughts running uncontrollably through our minds. We must learn to be at peace in our temples of flesh, instead of restlessly rushing to and fro in neurotic activity. Some of us are like jittery little birds, nervously hopping from branch to branch, so restless we are within ourselves. We relentlessly look here and there for excitement and always seek happiness outside ourselves when the whole fountain of joy, the whole fountain of happiness and truth is within us. 'Be still and know thyself'. Incidentally, such inscriptions are to be found above the doors of many ancient temples of Egypt.[18]

Religious Experiments

Ignorance is bliss. Hence, world-renowned scientists once thought, albeit erroneously, that water was a single element; but by experiments they came to realise that two invisible elements, namely, the gases hydrogen and oxygen, come together in a certain combination to make water that is not only different in its manifestation but visible to the optic senses.[19] Likewise, *religious experiments prove wonderful spiritual truths.* For example, when you sit in silence and your mind's eye is concentrated within, your Indwelling Divinity[20] will communicate with you. You will become attuned to God the All-Father, and your true Self, the Christ Spirit that must be realised in you.

It is submitted that to the initiate on the Path the results of religious experiments are absolutely convincing, as convincing as chemistry or physics experiments; if anything, more so. Religious experiments are also enjoyable and worthwhile, because they do not take place outside ourselves in a glass test tube but within our own body (test tube). We all know of the peace and the feeling of well-being that overwhelms us when we get away from the hustle, carnality and noise of the city or town and avail ourselves of the harmony, beauty and solitude of nature; for example, in the forest, by the sea or the riverside. The invigoration we feel after being blessed by nature may be likened to the charging of a depleted car battery, which prior to the charging, could not even start the engine that is necessary to propel that iron box we call a car, along 'the road of life'.

Sitting in silence with your mind directed to God may seem to some people a waste of time, but in reality it is 'value time', a time of great activity in your inner-life. Because by gaining control of the self and building up the energising forces of life, you will become a more disciplined and powerful force in the furtherance of your more mundane, material pursuits in the society of which you will be an integral part.[21]

All is of Divine Substance

As indicated above, God is the Divine Essence or Substance of all creation, and in consequence, all we think, say, and do forms part of an indivisible, (w)holistic vibration or motion within the underlying Divine Essence or Substance of Creation. God, or this Divine Essence or Substance manifesting as motion or action is called force. God is therefore not only the Original but the Ultimate Force; force is inherent within Him, having made all creation and knowing all forces. All creation that is perceived by the physical senses (of sight, hearing, smell, taste and touch) is but atoms or substance in motion or vibration; and the Eminator or Begetter of all matter (substance) and motion is the self-same God or Divine Essence or Substance.[22]

Man, as he becomes conscious of this *Divine Essence or Substance inherent in all life*, like the budding plant or flower, progressively manifests the innate, vibrational potentiality of truth and divinity within. Hence, it is important that we view all of our 'budding' ideas, opinions and 'so called' convictions 'on the path of life', as attempts at manifesting something of this *Divine Essence or Substance* within ourselves and our lives. The realisation of truth and perfection is an ongoing process; it is progressive and with faith will be realised in time. Hence, we must be understanding and patient with ourselves and more so with others, because as we tread the path of life we realise that good and evil are not constant, but shifting qualities as time and circumstances vary; as some people would say, 'good and evil' are not 'black and white', neither is the distinction between the two always crystal clear. For that matter, there is usually a vast grey area, especially considering that we tend to judge situations by external events, whereas God judges by the heart.

What is considered evil today in a particular circumstance may be considered at another time or in another circumstance, necessary, helpful or even good. For example, electricity is a force that may be used to destroy the lives of convicted criminals, as is still practised in some states of the United States of America; however, on the other hand, it gives us light in our homes, power in our factories and is used to treat rheumatic pain and other ailments.[23] Some would say that this tends to lend weight to the idea that no force is inherently good or bad.

At the spiritual level, we must realise that in all things there is utility and purpose even if that utility and purpose may not be clear to us struggling Souls. The Omniscient Creator, you can be assured, transmutes all things if you put your faith in Him, into useful purpose. That which we perceive today as evil, may be the good of tomorrow and vice versa. A seemingly bad occurrence today sometimes turns out to be as they say a 'blessing in disguise'. Hence, our failure today may be the foundation of tomorrow's victory. The lives of all so-called geniuses and great inventors reflect this; their greatest achievements came after years of failure. Faith and determination or faith and one-pointedness, if you prefer, were the miraculous ingredients of success.

We therefore would be well advised not to become too emotionally attached to what we perceive to be 'our opinions', no matter how right or good we may think them to be; we must always be open-minded enough to reject all that is false in what we initially thought to be right or good. We must accept only the true and divine, asking God constantly for spiritual light, guidance and strength on the Path. It is written: "If any of you lack wisdom, let him ask of God, who gives to all men generously and without reproach, and it will be given to him".[24] For God gives those who are good in His sight wisdom, knowledge and joy.[25]

On the path of life, we must endlessly praise God in advance for granting us the spiritual light and flexibility to realise that some of our conduct that seemed acceptable may be questionable and should be improved. With such flexibility we suffer no loss, but lose only some of our ignorance and narrow-mindedness; we will progress morally and may be endowed with the capacity to be in harmonious empathy with all struggling and stumbling Souls of the world. We can be assured that the more we vibrate the good, the harmonious, the Divine in our lives, this sublime force permeates every plane of our consciousness.

Despite the Constraints on the Path, Man Has Been Given a Priceless Gift

Man's search for Truth or conduct thus far on Earth, however, has developed within certain constraints. He has what is considered his personal needs, preferences and fleshly desires.[26] This he struggles with literally from birth. He also has to contend with the constraints of the family that he loves and tends to become attached to; his struggles, successes and failures within the family in some way reflect what his social interaction will be in the larger society; as he gets older he also has to contend with the laws of man and with concepts such as 'the good of the collective whole'; *and finally, he has to deal with the overriding divine laws of nature, which just cannot be fooled.*

Remember, we are all Spirit-Souls incarnate in flesh, and in our quest for full spiritual maturity, we express a gradual manifestation of our true Self, the Infinite Essence, the immortal "I", the Christ or divinity within. We must imbibe this basic truth of life which has been explained by all God's prophets, holy men and avatars, because whether we are consciously aware of this or not, that does not negate Truth and God's laws. Despite our ignorance of God's laws and consequent pain, God's divine plan within the framework of His Laws will not be frustrated. Our struggles are organised for our benefit and if we persevere with patience and faith, we will conquer; as long as we live in harmony with God's laws, a glorious victory shall be ours. Unfortunately, however, down here on Earth, man's temple has become his mire of clay in which he struggles totally immersed in material fantasy. The animal in man or the passions and desires of his dense, physical body tend to obscure the inner reality of life.

Man is bought and sold by his so-called needs and constant stirrings of desire. He lives half-crazed and befuddled by his desires; those desires become habitual and in time possess him. Man thus, like a donkey, with the proverbial carrot before him, strives to satisfy and in many instances satiates his physical, emotional and mental cravings.[27] But for every driving force, there is a balancing force or overriding force. Therefore those who ask humbly to be reconciled to the will of God, with contrite hearts, prayer and meditation will realise Truth, happiness and success; they will realise mastery over self through *the Christ or divinity within,* which is *the ultimate, priceless gift of God, the All-Father.*

Conclusion

We must surrender to the Divine will by the immersion of our separated egos into the One who is All. We must become joyous, harmonious, Divine Sparks, immersed in the inspired movement of Omniscient Light and Wisdom. Guidance shall be ours, replacing the stumbling and suffering of the ignorant ego. That blessed prospect of eternal life will fan the quickening energies of the innermost Spirit, the Christ within, setting alight the path of faith and devotion to God. We must exhort each other unceasingly to keep steadfast on the Path of Truth. As taught by the ancient Masters, we must desire Truth like a drowning person desires air; we must desire the Truth with all our heart, soul, mind and strength.

Remember the words of Jesus/Yashua: "If you continue in my word, you are truly my disciples, *and you will know truth, and the truth shall make you free*".[28] Let the Spirit of Truth, whom the world (materialistic people) cannot receive, dwell with you and in you always.[29] Never forsake the Path of Truth, devotion and love, for remember: "*the world is passing away, and so is its desire; but he that does the will of God remains forever*".[30]

Then and only then shall the whole 'Garden of the Earth' — the 'Garden of God' — radiate true happiness. When the way of the world (that is, the way of carnality and materialism) has passed away, the remnants of humanity shall realise heaven within their beings, within their temples, within their families, within their societies and on Earth. The finite or carnal mind will be replaced by the Infinite, Divine or Christ mind, the supreme light shall replace the receding darkness of human ignorance and, finally, immortality shall replace mortality. This is the will of God, the All-Father, who is the epitome of patience, grace and love.[31] The rivers and streams of Zion, as prophesied, shall sparkle with fresh, pure, spiritual water so that the children of the Kingdom of God shall be able to drink deeply thereof and '*the Will and Way*' of the All-Father' shall reign supreme.[32]

CHAPTER 2

THE WILL AND THE WAY

Introduction

It must be understood from the very outset that the 'will and the way' referred to in this chapter is the 'Will and the Way' of the All-Father, GOD, the Generator, Organiser, and Destroyer of all that there is.[1] This 'will and way' of life is flawlessly demonstrated by the life and teachings of Yashua or Jesus the Christ of the Holy Bible; it shall be presented as the ultimate science, the esoteric or spiritual science of life.

From the very beginning the Omniscient, Omnipotent, Omnipresent Creator in His wisdom, had willed into activity and motion, by the power of the Word, a perfectly ideated and evolving creation. Of the four basic elements — *fire, air, water,* and *earth* — He created this planet that we call Earth; a creation incidentally that must eventually realise the Creator's ultimate design, because His will cannot be frustrated. The 'will and the way' for man to overcome this Earth Realm or Earth School was ordained by the Infinite Consciousness of the All-Father from the time of Creation. God made no mistake, as some would have us believe.

Besides the Messiah, Yashua or Jesus the Christ* of the New Testament, who represents the way whereby the will, power and activity of the All-Father are manifested in and through man, the way has also been demonstrated in the Bible by the High Priest Melchisedeck of the Old Testament, who saw not death.[2] The Christ-man or Divine man is God's ultimate plan for man; the Christ-man overcomes sin and sickness as well as death, the last sting of this Earth Realm or kingdom. There always have been doubting Thomases, like Thomas of the Bible, but even they may satisfy their doubts by reading, understanding and most importantly endeavouring to live the life science, with faith, as presented in this chapter. This chapter represents a synthesis of esoteric teachings that are dealt with at length in other books relating to Truth and the esoteric laws of life.

The Seven Realms or Mansions of Creation: The Macrocosm

"In My Father's house are many mansions".[3] So said the Messiah, Yashua or Jesus the Christ. All that exists, both in the visible and invisible realms or mansions, is of substance. Our Universe is divided into seven different planes or realms of substance as illustrated in Diagram I: the mansions or realms of the All-Father's House. The realms or mansions may be described as follows:

(1) First Realm or Mansion — This is the realm or mansion of the Absolute substance, which is formless and limitless; the realm of God, the Absolute, Omniscient, Omnipotent, Omnipresent One;

(2) Second Realm or Mansion — This is the realm or mansion of the God substance, which is formless and limitless; the realm of the Virgin or Christ Spirits, the Sons of the Absolute, "the Begotten of the All-Father";

(3) Third Realm or Mansion — This is the realm or mansion of the universal Christ substance or Divine spirit substance, which is formless and limitless, referred to as "the bread of life";

(4) Fourth Realm or Mansion — This is the realm or mansion of the Life spirit substance, which is formless yet limited, as the Absolute substance has undergone

---

* Also referred to as Yeshua or "Yeshai"; see R. W. Bernard, *The Dead Sea Scrolls and the Life of the Ancient Essenes* (Mokelumne Hill, CA: Health Research, 1990), p. 4.

a great degree of modification whereby there has been a slowing down of the motion or vibration of the Absolute substance;

(5) Fifth Realm or Mansion — This is the realm or mansion of the Mind spirit substance or the realm of the spirit substance of thought. The upper part of this realm is formless but limited and the lower part is formative and limited;

(6) Sixth Realm or Mansion — This is the realm or mansion of the Desire spirit substance, which is formative and limited, the realm of the First Heaven, Catholic Christians' Purgatory as well as what is generally referred to as Hell;

(7) Seventh Realm or Mansion — This is the realm or mansion of the Physical spirit substance, which is formative and limited, the upper part of which is made up of etheric spirit substance and the lower part comprised of dense spirit substance. This is the realm of our dense material Earth where gases, liquids and solids are made manifest.[4]

DIAGRAM I – THE REALMS OF CREATION*

1. Absolute Substance	The Realm of God: The All-Father and Originator of all that there is		
2. God Substance	The Realm of the Virgin Spirits or Sons of the All-Father: the Begotten of God		
3. Universal Christ Substance	The Realm of the highest spiritual power and influence in Man whilst on Earth	Divine Spirit	The Three-fold Spirit
4. Life Spirit Substance	The Realm of the second aspect of the three-fold Spirit in Man	Life Spirit	
5. Mind Spirit Substance	The upper region of this Realm is Formless: the lower is formative	Human Spirit	
		Mind	Mind-link
6. Desire Spirit Substance	The Realm of Attraction, Indifference & Repulsion	Desire Body	The Three-fold Body
7. Physical Spirit Substance	The Earth Realm is comprised of an Etheric region & Chemical region: Gases, Liquid and Solids	Vital Body	
		Physical Body	

*The Universal Christ Substance of Realm 3 is said to be the only spiritual substance that has access to the Absolute Substance Realm as well as to the lowest vibrating Realm, which is Realm 7. This Christ Spirit Substance is said to continuously descend to Realm 7 only to return to Realm 3 in a figure 8 fashion; hence the Christ Spirit Substance constantly drifts into and becomes the substance of Realm 7 only to change back to the Christ Spirit Substance of Realm 3. In light of this the Nazarene Jesus the Christ/Yashua said "I lay down my life that I may take it up again" and "I am the Bread of Life". The Christ Spirit Substance of Realm 3 is the "Bread of Life"; spiritual substance that we on Earth can feed on. Remember: "Faith is the substance of things hoped for, the evidence of things not seen". And so it is. As regards Diagram I see Hodges n. 4, pp 58, 108 and 120; also Heindel n. 4, p 54; and Leadbeater n. 4.

It should be noted that there is no arbitrariness in the divisions of the Seven Realms in that the substance of each of these realms "is amenable to laws which are ... inoperative in" other realms.[5] In the Physical Spirit Substance Realm, for example, especially in the lower part, that is, in the dense spirit substance that forms our Earth, "matter is subject to gravity, contraction and expansion"; by contrast, in the Desire Spirit Substance Realm concepts such as heat and cold, contraction, expansion, distance and time are almost non-existent and are of no relevance. In the Desire Spirit Substance World or Astral Realm "forms levitate as easily as they gravitate".[6]

The substance of those Seven Realms of necessity varies in density, the Etheric or Physical Spirit Substance Realm being the densest, the most crystallised, the slowest in vibration. Gaseous, liquid and solid substances (in that order) are the three densest substances of our Etheric or Physical Realm. In that there are seven Realms and each Realm is subdivided into seven subdivisions, then, that makes solid substance the forty-ninth modification of God's Absolute substance (7X7=49). Solid substance is therefore the densest of all substances.[7]

From the above, it is clear that all creation came about by God, the Creator, ideating and differentiating the various realms or mansions within His Infinite Ocean of Spirit Substance, that is, as He in His Omniscience knew was necessary for the perfection and realisation of His evolutive scheme.[8] Hence, during the creative process, immutable laws were promulgated by the Infinite Consciousness of the All-Father to this end.

In order to give the reader a greater sensitivity to those Realms and hopefully in time a working knowledge thereof, the following short explanation is given of the Seven Realms mentioned above:

(1) The First Realm or Mansion or the Absolute Substance Realm

All that will be said of this Absolute Substance Realm, besides what has been said earlier, is that it is the Realm of God, the Realm of the All-Father and All-Mother. From this Realm all things come.[9] This Realm consists of seven subdivisions or regions. From the lower subdivisions of this Realm comes the highest aspect of the Christ Spirit.[10]

(2) The Second Realm or Mansion or the God Substance Realm

In our day of creation, God the All-Father, the Primordial Builder of the Cosmos, felt the creative urge and ideated what He desired and the ultimate results. Having done this, He projected the Word — rhythmic sound and tone carrying the particular rate of vibration, activity and motion — that would cause the differentiation of Centres of Energy or Force within "His Absolute Substance", in the form of a matrix or pattern ideated.[11] It must be remembered that the Bible states that "God was the Word", and the word was life and the life became the light of man and the world.[12] The initial differentiated vortices or centres of God are the Virgin, Christ or Divine Spirits, the Divine Sparks from the Infinite Flame, "the Begotten of the All-Father and Creator". These Christ Spirits, "Begotten of the All-Father", begin from this Realm to extend their consciousness downward through the various Realms of Creation, eventually to descend into the Etheric or Earth Realm or plane of Physical Spirit Substance.[13]

(3) The Third Realm or Mansion or the Universal Christ Substance Realm

This Universal Christ Substance Realm or Divine Spirit Realm is the Realm that has the highest spiritual effect on man.[14] It is the spirit substance that pervades, interpenetrates and thereby correlates the planets of all solar systems including ours. It must be realised that this perfect, Universal Christ Substance Realm, with all its attributes of universality, is the last Realm within which the differentiated Divine Sparks or Christ Spirits on their descent to the Etheric or Earth Realm will so easily realise this natural, perfect, universality and love because they are still in and of this Universal Christ Substance Realm.

Although the Divine Sparks are differentiated from the All-Father they are still unconscious to a great extent of this differentiation and separateness.[15] In that Realm the Christ or Divine Spirits, although filled with universal consciousness, are not conscious of their separateness; for that matter, they are not self-conscious or aware of their separateness from the rest of creation.[16]

It must be remembered that God makes no mistakes and therefore made no mistake then, now, nor shall He ever. Hence, by Divine Ordination, the Christ Spirits, Divine Sparks of the Infinite Flame, descended to the lower and more consolidated Realms of God whereby consciousness, and a free and wise exercise of divine will, power and activity could be experienced by the Immortal Christ Spirits throughout all the Realms of the Father's Creation; and most importantly experiencing life on Earth, esoterically known as the Earth Schoolroom or Realm.[17]

Incidentally, the substance of the Universal Christ Substance Realm is the only substance continuous throughout space, for that matter, throughout the Cosmos. It is 'the bread' or 'substance' of life; the building-block substance of all creation. It is the only substance that is intimately connected to all the Realms below as well as to those above.[18] It is the substance upon which the Sons and Daughters of the Light can feed; the Cosmic Fire of God; the Infinite Light which kindles the Divine Fire within us; the Living Flame that spiritualises our body-temples, creating immortality from that which was mortal; bringing back home to God (the Absolute One, the Infinite Consciousness, the All-Father of all that there is) another prodigal son or daughter. This is a very potent Realm in the process of our development and eventual evolvement into divinity; we would do well to think about, attune to, and consciously imbibe this substance into our very being; let it nourish our Souls and sustain our bodies.

(4) The Fourth Realm or Mansion or the Life Spirit Substance Realm

It is in this Life Spirit Substance Realm that the vibration of the Absolute substance has become slow enough or dense enough to allow the Virgin or Christ Spirits to feel the differentiation brought about by the Will, Power and Motion of the All-Father. Hence, although they still feel that universality or consciousness of the Universal Christ Substance Realm, they are endowed in this Realm with a sense of separateness, of 'self', of individuality; it is in this Realm that the seed of the enduring Divine Life Spirit was born. The seed of the Divine Life Spirit is the vitalising essence that organises, sustains and vitalises the sheaths or bodies of the Christ or Divine Spirits through the ages as they descend into the lower, slower vibrating, formative Realms of Creation, such as our Earth Realm.

However, although self-consciousness is experienced by the Christ Spirits in the Life Spirit Substance Realm, this Realm is a universal one and there the Divine or Christ Spirits still feel a "oneness" or universality with all things.[19] The Life Spirit Substance Realm is said to be "common to and interpenetrating all the planets of our solar system".[20] This vitalising life sustaining substance Realm is important because it allowed the Christ Spirits to realise two aspects of their 'being', the 'universal' and the 'individual'.[21] They were still aware of their universality but pleasantly conscious of their individuality. The Divine Life Spirit is said to be the centre of divine, altruistic love, which is the most potent 'cure-all' substance, the most powerful energising force by which all problems are overcome and all things are sustained and harmonised.[22]

(5) The Fifth Realm or Mansion or the Mind Spirit Substance Realm

The Realm of Mind Spirit Substance is subdivided into seven modifications of mind spirit substance. It is in the three lower subdivisions of this realm that the Infinite Spirit Substance becomes formative. The first three upper subdivisions of this Realm are formless.[23]

This Realm of mind substance or thought substance is a pulsating flow of mind and spirit substance, wherein, more specifically in the subtler, formless, upper three subdivisions, the germinal ideas of all form originate; be it in the form of mineral, plant, animal or man. It is the soil within which all ideas germinate, be they good or bad; all seeds of desire and emotions originate here.[24]

As indicated above, the Absolute God substance has been modified sufficiently to make form possible. Hence, the archetypes of all desire, passion, emotion, energy, thought and all forms of material phenomena that we perceive are ideated and in fact take shape here.[25] The matrixes or archetypes of all creation take place here.

It should be noted that the first three upper subdivisions of this Realm, comprised of formless, mind spirit substance, are referred to as the region of abstract thought; the region of the most refined mind spirit substance. The fourth subdivision of this Realm is referred to as the "Great Divide" or "Record of Nature".[26] This subdivision of the Mind Spirit Substance Realm is aptly called "the Great Divide" as all above this region is formless while all below is formative. Here the formless substance world meets and flows into the formative substance world in a lemniscate or figure 8 fashion; the forces and currents of life cross over and run into each other. This subdivision, which represents the centre or meeting place of the upper and lower vibrating currents of the Spirit World, is also, as indicated above, referred to as "the Record of Nature" or "the Akashic Records": the substance upon which all the imprints of life are stored like film transparencies. This subdivision is said to be the focusing point or lens through which the Spirit World mirrors itself into the formative or material world.

The lowest three subdivisions of the Mind Spirit Substance Realm, as indicated before, are the real region where the archetypes, matrixes or moulds of all form created by God or man take shape;[27] the realm of concrete thought.

The beauty and power of this Mind Spirit Substance Realm cannot be overstated. All desire seeds or seed ideas of man planted in this field in time must bear fruit. Hence, plant good thoughts with faith, and good results are yours in visible, material form.

(6) The Sixth Realm or Mansion or the Desire Spirit Substance Realm

This Realm or Mansion of God, the Desire or Astral Realm, is one of great activity, relevance and influence at this juncture of man's development. Our desires, which gain their substance from this spiritual Realm, tend to hold sway and dominate our intellect, soul and heart. Our heart centre always influences us to live love, not carnal love, but altruistic love. Hence, when we do not always do right in any given situation; when we fail to do what we ought to do; when we fail to live love, it is our carnal, selfish, fearful, hateful, egotistic desires that gain their substance in the three lower realms of the Desire or Astral Realm that dominate our will, power and activity.

Like all the other Mansions or Realms referred to above, the Desire Spirit Realm is subdivided into seven (7) subdivisions. The first three higher subdivisions are crucial to man's Self-realisation. They are referred to as Organic or Soul-Power spirit substance, Light spirit substance and Life spirit substance.[28] Hence, the organic power substance is the seventh or highest subdivision of this Desire Realm; the organic light substance is the sixth subdivision and the organic life substance is the fifth subdivision of this Desire Realm. These three upper subdivisions are referred to as "The First Heaven". In those three subdivisions, all is positive and cohesive: the place of attraction, cohesion and construction. Everything in this First Heaven is imbued with abundant life, love, harmony, joy and peace. If anyone wants to be filled with these God-like virtues, one must feed on these three upper subdivisions of this Desire Realm.[29]

More will be said later of these three upper subdivisions in relation to the Soul's experience in the afterlife in the World of the Unseen, that is, after what we call death. After the first three subdivisions of this Realm, to wit, Organic Power, Organic Light and Organic Life (the First Heaven), there is the "Great Divide" or "Borderland" sub-realm or region.   This is the region of indifference and inaction or interest and action.[30] Considering there can be no manifestation without generating interest in the object of your desire, one must be aware of this Great Divide or "Borderland"; this sub-realm or region is the battleground of interest and indifference, action and inaction.   There will be no creation and success without generating interest and right desire.   It is useful to remember that generating interest and desire (emotion) increases the mind's power to transmit thoughts as well as to receive them (thought waves); whatever knowledge that is required is magnetised to anyone that seeks it with all his or her heart, soul and mind: 'seek and you shall find,' 'knock and it shall be opened unto you'.

As intimated above, the three lower subdivisions are the sub-realms of lower desires, fear, turmoil, sickness, pain, selfishness, greed, hatred, suffering, phantasmal and demoniac spirits and the desires that satisfy the relentless reaper, death.   Here, the battle of Armageddon is fought daily within the temples of all initiates on the Path of Truth.

It must be understood that in this Realm, depending on whether the initial impulse for an idea was from the Christ mind or the mortal (carnal) mind, the final result will be good or bad, constructive or destructive.   If it originated in the Christ Spirit mind, it will gain its desire substance from the three higher subdivisions of this Realm, and the manifestation will be imbued with organic Power, organic Light and organic Life, the substances of the First Heaven.   The result of this manifestation will therefore be positive and enduring; it will assist you in realising your true Self, the Christ within you, the Eternal "I".[31] If the thought or idea originated in the mortal or carnal mind, the idea will gain its desire substance from the three lower subdivisions of the Desire Realm where all is discord and confusion; where the Law of Repulsion and Dissolution holds sway.   In that the idea is from the mortal or finite mind, which is limited and by and large carnal, the idea or materialised manifestation of it will be one of limitation and degradation, and therefore must ultimately be destroyed and dissolved into primal spirit substance.   In time, better use may be made of the substance when and where required.

Incidentally, it is in the three (3) lower subdivisions of the Desire Realm where one finds the proverbial hell and purgatory.[32] This will be elaborated on later.   Hence always remember, if interest is engendered in something and such interest has flowed from the mortal or carnal mind, the action or end-product will ultimately be evil or deleterious to your well-being; whereas, if the interest engendered has come from your Christ Spirit or mind, then the action or ultimate product will be good, uplifting, beneficial to your well-being, putting you steadfast on the path to God.[33]

(7) The Seventh Realm or Mansion or the Physical or Etheric Spirit Substance Realm

This Realm is the one that grants vitality to all chemical life forms.   It may be referred to as the Etheric or Physical Realm; some of it can be seen and some of it cannot be seen by the optic senses.   Our Earth and its atmosphere are comprised of the substances that make up the fifth, sixth and seventh subdivisions of this Etheric Realm.   The subdivisions of this Realm from the highest vibrating substance to the lowest vibrating substance are as follows: (1) reflecting ether, (2) light ether, (3) life ether, (4) chemical ether, (5) gaseous substance, (6) liquid substance, and (7) solid substance.   The denser substances, such as solids, liquids and to a certain extent gases, are all visible to the optic senses; whereas the more subtle substances such as reflecting ether, light ether, chemical ether and life ether are all invisible.

Obviously, we humans feel most comfortable with the substances numbered (5), (6) and (7) namely, gases, liquids and solids.   Our physical bodies that we see and identify with are comprised of those three substances.

It is noteworthy that the highest vibrating substance of this Realm, the reflecting ether, is a secondary memory of nature.   All ideas are imprinted in this etheric subdivision and can be seen reflected in this fluidic substance by those who have eyes to see. This is the substance-medium whereby thoughts are transferred and imprints or impressions are made on the brain. Many a medium gains his information from this reflecting ether; all that we think about is reflected here. It must be remembered however that the ultimate true Record of Nature is in the Mind Substance Realm, more specifically, the fourth subdivision thereof, "the Great Divide", mentioned earlier.

The next in line is the light ether. This etheric substance is directly related to the five basic senses of sight, taste, touch, smell and hearing. It is also directly related to regulating the temperature within any material form and controlling the colouring in all life forms. Light ether is crucial in promoting the circulation of fluids or sap in plant, animal and human life.[34]

The life ether is the next etheric substance. This substance is directly related to reproduction, propagation and the sustenance of all life forms in the physical world that we live in. It is closely related to certain substances of the Life Spirit Substance Realm.[35]

After the life etheric substance comes the chemical etheric substance. This substance is the force behind the basic elements of the physical world.[36] It is directly involved in the assimilation of nutritive elements from food and the elimination of waste.[37]

The three remaining subdivisions are comprised of the substances that we human beings are most accustomed to, that is, gases, liquids and solids. Gas, which is a substance like air, neither solid nor liquid, makes up the next subdivision of the Etheric Realm. In the air that we breathe, there are several gases: oxygen, hydrogen and nitrogen to name but a few. After this subdivision comes liquid substance. The majority of our planet Earth is comprised of this substance; so too are our bodies, which seem to be quite solid. Finally, there is solid substance — as solid as rock. Solids, as indicated before, are the slowest vibrating God substance of creation; the slowest vibrating substance of the Etheric or Physical Realm.

Having explained the subdivisions of the Physical or Etheric Realm, it must be understood that although the Realm has been subdivided, those substances interpenetrate each other. For example, air and gas interpenetrate water or liquid, and liquid can be placed into a solid like a glass, or made to interpenetrate solids like limestone and wood, limestone and wood being quite porous. Likewise, etheric spirit substance is interpenetrated by all the more subtle substances, such as desire spirit substance, mind spirit substance, life spirit substance and Christ spirit substance.

The Seven Realms or Mansions of God Within Man: The Microcosm

The above was a brief, but hopefully understandable, explanation of the seven Realms or Mansions of the All-Father's House.[38] Having dealt with the Macrocosm, that, is the Seven Mansions of God's Creation, we will now deal with the Microcosm, that is, the human body-temple and its seven inner realms or chakra centres; that body within which the Eternal Christ Spirit dwells. Hence, we read: "Know you not that you are the Temple of God, and that the Spirit of God dwelleth in you?";[39] also, "behold the Kingdom of God is within you".[40] With that in mind, being temples of "the living Christ Spirit of God", the interrelationship of what we call "the Spirit", "the Soul" and "the Body" should be understood and therefore will now be explained.

In esoteric parlance, God's Creation called 'man' is made up of a three-fold Spirit: that is, the Divine Spirit (the Heavenly Father), the Life Spirit (the Son) and the Human Spirit (the Holy Spirit or Holy Ghost). That is the Triune God that must be realised 'in man'. That Spirit, collectively called the Christ or Virgin Spirit, sustains man and makes man's whole life possible; it links man to the Messiah, Christ Jesus/Yashua, as well as to the Absolute One, the All-Father, the God of all creation.

This three-fold Christ Spirit via the mind lives and experiences life in a three-fold body. From the interaction of the three-fold Divine Spirit on the three-fold body, the Divine Spirit extracts as pabulum a conscious Soul from the Dense or physical body, the Life Spirit extracts an intellectual Soul from the Vital body, and the Human Spirit extracts an emotional Soul from the Desire body. Hence, succinctly, a three-fold Spirit begets a three-fold body and this fusion by the grace of God begets a three-fold Soul. To this effect, see Diagram II below.[41]

More will be said later of this interaction between the Spirit, Soul and Body, but what is important at this juncture is that the terms and inter-linkages are understood. Before we deal with the bodies of man, to wit, the physical or Dense body, the Etheric or Vital body and the Astral or Desire body, it should be noted that each of those bodies is linked to a person's three-fold Spirit by what is referred to as 'seed or permanent atoms'. For example, a seed atom links the Dense body to the Divine Spirit or Father aspect of the Triune Christ Spirit; a seed atom links the Vital body to the Life Spirit or Son aspect of the Triune Christ Spirit; and a seed atom also links the Desire body to the Human Spirit or Holy Ghost aspect of the Christ Spirit. More will be said later about the location of each seed atom and its importance.[42]

<u>Diagram II</u>

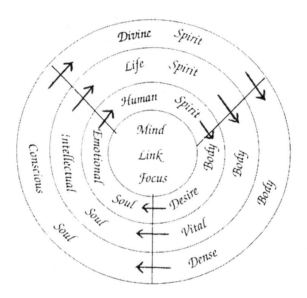

(1) The Bodies of Man

(a) The Physical or Dense Body

Briefly, from the exterior, the human temple or Dense body is comprised of a head, torso, arms, hands, legs, and feet. The head, which is the potential 'realm of heaven' in man, is the foremost or upper part of the body containing the brain, sense organs and the mouth. The torso is the trunk of the human body, apart from the head and limbs. The arms are the upper limbs and the legs are the lower limbs, the lower limbs being basically for support and locomotion.

The body described is the body we perceive with the five basic senses of sight, hearing, smell, taste, and touch. Those five senses belong to the physical body or temple. It is of interest to note that the physical description of the human body in the paragraph above does not seem very different from any animal creation of God, although on closer scrutiny, even physically there are serious differences. The major difference, however, is the divine potentiality of the human being; this will be thoroughly discussed below. Before moving on, it is important to note that all that we perceive as our physical body is comprised either of gaseous, liquid or solid substance.

In esoteric parlance, as indicated before, 'the gaseous, liquid and solid substance body' is known as the "Dense body".

Inside that physical exterior, which is covered by skin and hair, there is an endocrine system, a nervous system and an array of organs, a skeletal structure to assist us in walking upright, meridian lines of energy, nadis (not seen by the optic senses), and seven centres or vortices of electro-magnetic energy called chakra centres or padmas (also not visible to the optic senses). These seven centres or realms within the human body (the microcosm) correspond to the seven Realms of God's Creation (the macrocosm). Hence, the esoteric saying: 'as above, so below'. Before delving further into the seven realms or centres of force within the human body (the chakra centres), we will deal briefly, first, with the endocrine system and then with the nervous system.

The endocrine system is described by some as 'the power behind the throne'.[43] This ductless gland system is closely linked to our nervous system and the seven chakra centres within our temples of flesh. The glands of the endocrine system starting from the head and going downwards are as follows: the pineal gland, the pituitary gland, the thyroid and parathyroid glands, the thymus gland,[44] the pancreas, adrenal or suprarenal glands and the gonads or sex glands.[45]

If one wants to enjoy good health, the proper functioning of the endocrine glands is essential, and by and large, they can be said to control our growth, size, metabolism, emotional balance and vitality.[46] The proper functioning of the endocrine glands or system is also essential for realising mental balance and in time transcendence of the mind.[47] As can be seen in Diagram III below,[48] the pituitary and pineal glands are in the head; the thyroid, parathyroid and thymus glands are in the area of the neck and chest; the adrenal/suprarenal glands, the pancreas and the spleen are in the area of the abdomen or solar plexus; and the gonads, ovaries or testes, as the case may be, are to be found in the pelvic area.

<u>Diagram III</u>

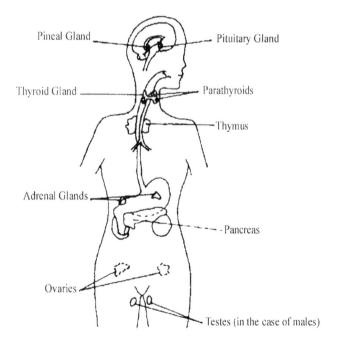

The endocrine system and, by extension, the more subtle seven chakra centres, are closely related to the body's nervous system. For example, both the endocrine system and the nervous system assist the body to adjust and deal with external stimuli in our environment. The nervous system works through nerve impulses or stimuli similar to electricity; and the endocrine system works through hormonal secretions that are transported throughout the body via the blood. The electrical nerve stimuli are quick and short-lived, but the hormonal influence is slower, more all-embracing and enduring.

What may be seen as an intriguing link between the body's nervous system and the *Seven* Realms of Creation, with its *forty-nine* subdivisions of the Absolute substance of God, is reflected in the sympathetic nervous system; this system has a cluster of nerves in the area of the heart consisting inter alia of a chain of nerve ganglia on either side of the spinal or vertebral column. From the chain of nerve ganglia, fibres are distributed throughout the body-temple: for example, to the heart and larynx, to the heart and thyroid, to the heart and lungs, to the stomach and abdominal organs, and finally, to the pelvic organs. These ganglia, from the head downwards, are said to be forty-nine in number, seven of them being of special importance.[49] The consistency of the numbers in italics with the *Seven* Realms or Mansions of God and the *forty-nine* subdivisions of the Absolute spirit substance reflects yet another similarity between the microcosm (the human body) and the macrocosm (the Realms or Mansions of God, the Cosmos).

Incidentally, the sympathetic nervous system and the para-sympathetic make up the autonomic nervous system; this system is entirely involuntary and is concerned with the automatic regulation of certain internal organs in the body and their functions. The cerebro-spinal or central nervous system, on the other hand, consists of the brain and spinal cord and can be viewed as the voluntary nervous system. Before moving on to the seven chakra centres, it should be noted that the voluntary nervous system is closely related to the desires of man.[50]

We will now deal with the seven chakra centres or vortices of force within the human body. These centres have been referred to in most religious and arcane writings; usually reflected in allegory and symbolism, their existence was understood and taught by all high cultures (civilisations). With reference to the seven vortices of spiritual-electromagnetic-energy oscillating within the human body, the Bible indicates: "Wisdom has built her house, and she has hewn out her seven pillars".[51] Similar symbolism is used in Solomon's temple. The temple itself is equated to the central pillar or tree; while its two pylons Yakhin and Boaz, on the right and on the left, "represent the tree of good and evil", the positive and negative forces of life.[52]

The seven centres are also referred to in the Bible as the book with seven seals (Rev. 5:5), the seven lamps (Zech. 4:2) and the seven eyes of the Lord (Zech. 4:10). There are other references to those seven centres of light in the Christian Bible. There are also many references to the more complete idea of the proverbial tree and serpent, which represents the spine (the bony serpent), the cerebro-spinal (voluntary) nervous system, its electro-magnetic (spiritual) counterpart, the seven chakra centres and the kundalini or the Christ Fire or Light in man. To this effect, one should read Genesis 3, where the 'serpent' and 'the tree in the midst of the garden' are first mentioned; read too Num. 21:9, where Moses made a brazen serpent, which he set on a pole; as well as Num. 17:8, where the seven centres are referred to as buds on the rod of Aaron, which bloomed blossoms and almonds. The budding and blossoming referred to the opening of the chakra centres by illumination or the realisation of Christ-consciousness.[53] This is when the Mystic Marriage referred to in the Bible takes place.[54]

The references to 'the tree in the midst of the garden', and to 'the fruit and the serpent' all relate to the spine, the chakra centres and the Christ serpentine force or fire within man; this fire or flame of life is all-pervasive and eternal throughout all creation. This was the same eternal flame or fire that encircled the bush on the Mountain of God, but did not consume it; that engulfed Moses, but did not harm him; that not only purified Moses but exhilarated him; that inspired him to take off his shoes so as to place his feet firmly on "holy ground".[55]

In Eastern Philosophy and Yoga, those seven centres of force or chakra centres within the human body-temple are commonly referred to as the Muladhara Chakra (Root Centre), the Svadhisthana Chakra (Pelvic Centre), the Manipura Chakra (Solar

Plexus Centre), the Anahata Chakra (Heart Centre), the Vishudha Chakra (Throat Centre), the Ajna Chakra (Brow Centre), and finally the Sahasrara Chakra (Crown of the Head Centre).

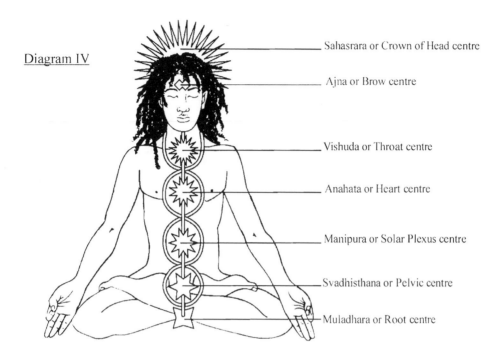

Diagram IV

Sahasrara or Crown of Head centre

Ajna or Brow centre

Vishuda or Throat centre

Anahata or Heart centre

Manipura or Solar Plexus centre

Svadhisthana or Pelvic centre

Muladhara or Root centre

The Muladhara Chakra (Root Centre), which is located at the base of the spine, is generally portrayed as a lotus with four petals. The Christ serpentine force or kundalini lies dormant there and the positive and negative currents that run on either side of the spine, known as the Ida and Pingala Nadis, also meet the central Sushumna Nadi here at the base of the spine. Its symbolical element is the earth (soil) and its colour is golden-yellow.

The Svadhisthana Chakra (Pelvic Centre), which is located close to the sexual organs, is portrayed as a lotus with six petals. This chakra is within the Shushumna Nadi. Its symbolical element is water (liquid) and its colour is milky white like a conch shell.

The Manipura Chakra (Solar Plexus Centre), which is located in the area of the navel or solar plexus, is portrayed as a lotus with ten petals. Its symbolical element is fire and its colour is crimson red.

The Anahata Chakra (Heart Centre), which is located in the area of the heart, is portrayed as a lotus of twelve petals. Its symbolical element is air and its colour is a mild smoky colour. Incidentally, the seed atom of the Dense body, which links the Divine Spirit to the Dense body, is said to be located in the left ventricle of the heart.[56]

The Vishudha Chakra (Throat Centre), which is located in the area of the throat, is portrayed as a lotus with sixteen petals. Its symbolical element is ether and it is a play of colours like the sea, but is mostly perceived as blue.

The Ajna Chakra (Brow Centre), which is located in the area between the eyebrows, is portrayed as a lotus with two petals. Its symbolical element is mental or mind substance and its colour is silvery white. This chakra is really within the Shushumna Nadi and represents the "Third Eye" centre.

The Sahasrara Chakra (Crown of Head Centre), which is located at the top or crown of the head, is said to be the seat of the positive pole; the realm of Vishnu,[57] or in Christian parlance, the Realm of the Heavenly Father, the Christ or Solar Being in the human temple. This chakra centre is portrayed as a lotus with a thousand petals. When this centre is reached by the Christ or kundalini force, the individual will realise Christ-consciousness or super-consciousness; in yoga parlance — nirvana: a state of wisdom, understanding and bliss that is only experienced when one's consciousness is voluntarily immersed into God's Infinite Sea of consciousness. This is brought about through the purifying fire of prayer and meditation, which centres one's heart and mind on God. By the means of prayer and meditation, one's desires are washed clean and one's dedication to God is made complete.[58]

Before dealing with the other, finer or subtler bodies of man that interpenetrate the Dense or physical body, it would be remiss of me not to point out two things. One is that the Caduceus of Hermes, represented by a rod or staff and two entwined serpents, is yet another illustration of the symbolical tree and serpent; the Caduceus of Hermes is mentioned as it is often used today as an emblem or insignia on many medical vehicles and pieces of medical equipment throughout the world. The other is that although we have been brought up to think of the Dense body as a biochemical mass, we must consciously realise its electro-magnetic nature as well. For example, it is intriguing to note that although we tend to think of food as either proteins or vitamins or minerals, at the end of the day, the cells of the Dense or physical body select from the blood the ions necessary to replace those ions used in the living process.[59] As we all know, "an 'ion' is an electrically charged particle, consisting of one or more atoms carrying a unit charge, or a multiple";[60] and ions are referred to as the carriers of the electricity of life.[61]

As a natural corollary of the above, the blood or liquid light or fire (as it is referred to in esoteric law) that feeds the cells of the physical or Dense body, must be kept pure by frugal eating, fasting, the use of herbs and exercise, especially breathing exercise.[62] Hence, all on the Path of Truth are humbly advised to do the exercise called "the Complete Breath" on a daily basis. It is done as follows: Sit erect and quietly so that you can consciously put your mind on breathing deeply, completely and rhythmically. Start the cycle of breathing exercise by consciously exhaling as slowly and completely as you can through your nose. It should be noted that your diaphragm should lift upwards and your stomach should sink in slightly as you complete your exhalation. After your exhalation there will be a natural pause before you inhale slowly, filling the lower portion, then the mid- and upper portions of your lungs. Initially, as you inhale your diaphragm should relax downwards and your stomach should bulge out slightly.

This slow, complete inhalation and exhalation described above should be consciously continued for 10 to 20 minutes. This can be done every morning and afternoon or whenever required. If your mind drifts as you do your breathing exercise, 'seed' your mind with the thought of exhaling "fear" and inhaling either "health", "strength", "confidence", "power", "Christ Spirit" or whatever you so desire.

(b) The Vital or Etheric Body

There are some that are of the view that the seven chakra centres described earlier are really an aspect of man's Vital or Solar body, as distinct from his biochemical Dense body. This view is certainly correct; however, those centres of energy are undeniably an integral part of the electromagnetic make-up of the physical or Dense body. The Vital body should therefore be seen as the 'electrical' or 'solar' power source that enlivens our nervous system and vitalises our Dense bodies.

The Vital or Etheric body realises complete organisation and vitality in the seventh year of one's life. It interpenetrates the physical or Dense body, and if one has 'eyes to see', or with the use of a Kilner Machine, named after the doctor who created it, one can see the etheric lines of energy emanating through the pores of the skin.[63] Those initiates who may want to develop the ability to 'see' their Etheric or Vital body, as well as that of others, should read *The History and Power of Mind* by Richard Ingalese; *The Vital Body* by Max Heindel; *Man Visible and Invisible* by C. W. Leadbeater; *You Forever* by Lobsang Rampa (especially pp. 27-28); and *The Celestine Prophecy* by James Redfield.

One's state of health can also be ascertained by means of the Vital or Etheric body: if an organic part is not healthy, the etheric lines in that area of the body are weak and bent, as distinct from being vibrant and straight.[64] Incidentally, the etheric substances working within the body assist in converting food into blood, which is aptly called 'the liquid fire of life'.[65]

The Vital body, like the Etheric Realm of the Macrocosm described above, is comprised of the following substances: chemical ether, life ether, light ether and reflecting ether. It must be remembered that the highest vibrating etheric substance, the reflecting ether, is a rudimentary record of nature. Hence, your thought imagery can be seen imprinted in your reflecting ether; these imprints form part of your "aura", which will be discussed below.[66]

Your next highest vibrating etheric substance is your light ether. The light ether is crucial to the functioning of the physical senses, the circulation of liquids and the regulation of temperature in the body. The life ether substance is next, and as reflected in its name, is involved in ensuring the propagation of life through reproduction.

Finally, the slowest vibrating etheric substance that completes the Vital body is the chemical ether; the chemical ether is intimately related to the elements of the earth. The Etheric or Vital body, which interpenetrates the gases, liquids and solids body, is essential to the life and vitality of the Dense or physical body.

The reflecting ether and the light ether are referred to as the "Marriage Garment" or the "Ghost body" in esoteric parlance. They are called the "Marriage Garment" because this is 'the garment' used when the 'Spirit-Soul' moves around in the higher Realms above the 'material world', the 'material world' being the gaseous, liquid and solid substance world. On the other hand, the "Ghost body" idea came about because the reflecting and light ether of a deceased person are what people see when they see the 'ghost' of someone. The reflecting ether and light ether, which are emitted from a person, are the exact image or replica of the physical or Dense body; hence another reason for the term "Ghost body".

Although whole books have been written about the Vital or Etheric body, only certain essential facts will be presented here. Hopefully, they will be sufficient to give the reader an understanding of the importance of the Vital body. In esoteric law, it is taught that true development on the Spiritual Path must begin with an understanding and strengthening of one's Vital body. It is the foundation upon which the physical temple for the Christ Spirit is built. In a person who is more earthbound, the chemical and life ether form the bulk of that person's Etheric or Vital body; whereas, in a person who is more dedicated to Truth and spiritual matters, the light and reflecting ethers form the bulk of that person's Etheric or Vital body. Usually such an individual is quite indifferent to material wealth and extravagance.

Besides referring to the two higher ethers as the "Marriage Garment" and "Ghost body", some refer to these two higher ethers as the "Soul body". These two important etheric substances are closely related to the conscience of a person and, by extension, the virtue exhibited in that person's life; this will be elaborated on later when dealing with the cycle of life.[67]

Incidentally, before making some closing comments about the Etheric or Vital body, it should be remembered that a child's Etheric or Vital body is not organised (although it is present) until the child is seven years of age. Until that time, the child draws from the Etheric or Vital Substance Realm of the Macrocosm.[68] As life progresses and the child matures into an adult, and the adult in turn matures into an initiate, work must be done on purifying and spiritualising the Vital body.

This spiritualising or purifying process is greatly assisted and enhanced by living love, altruistic love: doing for others, being of service to others without expecting anything in return; or at least 'doing unto others what you would have them do unto you' — a theme which is to be found in the teachings of all the leading religions of the world. This adds lustre to the Soul.[69]   Other effective ways of advancing your cause on the path of life are to purify the Vital body through consistent prayer, the use of lofty, ennobling affirmations, harmonious chants, fragrant incense and spiritual rituals — even rituals as simple as making the sign of the cross.

It is taught that the best times to effectively use affirmations are just before you drift off to sleep and just after you awake; although when you have learnt to use affirmations, that is, by using them consistently over a period of time, they can be used at any time of the day with tremendous positive effect.[70]   An example of a simple ancient affirmation worthy of repetition by Christians or followers of Yashua, which will purify the Vital body, is as follows: 'Oh †(my Christ/Yashua), I am blended with You so that forever I go forth in Thy Light. Thanks and Praises!'

The seed or permanent atom that links the Life Spirit to the Vital body is said to be located in the solar plexus. However, the solar energy from the sun that feeds the Vital or Etheric body enters the physical body via the etheric counterpart of the physical spleen. Some teach that the object of life in this time is oneness or union with Christ through purification of the Vital body.[71]

(c) The Desire or Astral Body

The Desire or Astral body of a person is comprised of desire spirit substance. This spirit substance is the spirit-force behind all activity and motion in one's life; this desire substance manifesting positively as organic Power, Light and Life is said to be "God in action".[72]   The seed atom of the Desire body that links the Human Spirit to the Desire body is said to be located in the vortex of the liver and by extension the blood.[73]

The Desire or Astral body of a person becomes completely organised and strong around the fourteenth year of life; some say the fourteenth year signals the birth of the Desire body.[74]   The Desire or Astral body, comprised of desire spirit substance, interpenetrates the etheric or vital substance body as well as the physical or dense substance body. After seven years of rapid physical growth, when the etheric or vital substance body held sway between the ages of seven and fourteen, the desire substance body comes into its own between the ages of fourteen and twenty-one. From then on personal desires dramatically increase and puberty takes its course.[75]

An intense drama of life takes place in those formative years of maturity. It is a period when you are usually wild with desires, yet filled with utopian thoughts of purity, perfection and idealism — an idealism that unfortunately fades, and in many instances dies, with age. This period of fourteen to twenty-one is also the beginning of strong physical attraction to the opposite sex. During that period the pituitary and thyroid glands become more active and the sexual glands in both males and females mature; the circulation of blood is said to increase in the pelvic region during this period, allowing for easy sexual arousal.[76]   This is a period of intense emotional development and social interaction. Those years are 'the foundation years' in the development of a person's Desire body; crucial years when a person magnetises, according to his thoughts and desires, the desire spirit substances of either the higher region of the Desire World or Realm, or the lower vibrating substances of the lower regions of the Realm.

Throughout a person's life, his Desire body is dominated either by the higher substances of the Desire Realm or World, that is, the spirit substances of organic power, light and life, or the lower substances of that Realm or World. A person, who through his hard-earned experience has purified his thoughts and desires, tends to reflect this improvement by his words and deeds. Hence, in that person's Desire body, the more subtle, refined desire spirit substances of the higher regions of the Desire Realm or World replace the lower vibrating desire substances that had formerly prevailed in that person.

---

† Use what is in accordance with your faith.

The Desire body of any person who goes through bad experiences in his life, as we all do, tends to impress the idea of revenge in the form of memory upon the Vital body of that person. During a person's life, this must be overcome. One must learn — as the Lord's Prayer (the "Our Father") dictates — to forgive our debtors (which purifies our Vital bodies), and to stay out of temptation. Desire is the great allurement or tempter of humanity. Hence, we must gain control of our Desire body if we are to successfully purify our Vital and physical bodies.

The best methods recommended to conquer the relentless ebb and flow of desires, especially the warped and degrading ones, are said to be the art of prayer, concentration and meditation. In the Holy Bible we read the following: "pray that you may not enter into temptation; the spirit indeed is willing but the flesh is weak".[77]

Some prefer concentration upon high ideals or the use of mantras in meditation or Yantras, as those methods tend to be cold and unemotional, whereas, prayer tends to be emotional. Be that as it may, emotion is not inherently bad, because emotion and desire are the vortices of force behind all thoughts and actions. If those thoughts and actions are wholesome and in harmony with God's will (which is love), then a great degree of positive power and activity will be generated by them. If those thoughts or actions, on the other hand, are degrading to the higher nature in man (the Indwelling Christ/the divinity within), then emotion will just increase the negative and detrimental effect of those thoughts and actions.

At such times it is wise, as indicated above, to pray relentlessly, with faith, that we 'be not led into temptation'; this is the part of "The Our Father" taught by Christ that is dedicated to the purification of the Desire body.[78] Incidentally, for those who do not know what a mantra (referred to in the paragraph above) is, it is a sound vibration (with a specific meaning) based on the sounds of the Universe and the chakra centres within man. And a Yantra is said to be a "machine" or tool in a specific form or shape, which when concentrated upon, has a tremendous calming, purifying and strengthening effect on the mind and Desire body.[79]

If constant prayer is the method of choice, it should preferably be prayers to do the will of God and devoted to high ideals and not merely for personal gain, fame, material wealth or power; because as valid as those prayers are, they will not purify the Desire body of the individual. That is why some people prefer concentration and meditation to effectively purify the Desire body, as distinct from prayer, which is emotional and often involves personal desires. However, as indicated above, prayers filled with emotion to do God's will ("Thy Will be done") are excellent in tempering and balancing the Desire body of an individual.

On our path of life, our desire for love must eventually move beyond the type of love that is a mere yearning for physical attachment or control and possession of another person's body (lust), to true altruistic love, which is to do good for others without expecting anything in return. Our desire for wealth and power should be to better serve others and for ensuring the general upliftment of all humanity.

The wisdom of antiquity and esoteric law teaches that the Desire body is ovoid in shape and luminous in appearance; it encircles the Vital and Dense bodies like the albumen encircles the yolk of an egg.[80] The Desire body grows as one develops on the Path, and those of saints are said to be truly beautiful, radiant and luminous.

As indicated before, as one progresses the purer, brighter substances of the higher subdivisions of the Desire Realm prevail in one's Desire body, as distinct from the murky substances of the lower subdivisions of the Realm.[81] The Desire body possesses important centres of perception, which manifest, when active, as vortices within the Desire body. In most people, those centres are latent; in an advanced initiate on the Path of Truth, the vortices or centres rotate from left to right or clockwise.[82]

It should always be remembered that the desire substance body is the counterpart of the Emotional Soul and the Human or Holy Spirit within the human (body) temple;[83] and further, as pointed out earlier, we humans are comprised of a three-fold Christ Spirit that is infused into a three-fold body, which in turn realises and enlivens a three-fold Soul. All of us have to eventually purify our Desire body and perfect our Emotional Soul. When that 'washing of the feet', or 'washing of the carnal desires' takes place, we become illumined or enlightened by the Human or Holy Spirit.

This unity with the Holy Spirit is well portrayed in the Christian Pentecost, with the 'tongues of fire' on the heads of the apostles; the heads and faces of the apostles shone with light as they spoke so that all could understand them. The race and language differentiation melted away when unity with the Holy Spirit was realised by the apostles.

The complete religion or path as taught and demonstrated by Yashua or Jesus the Christ taught unity with the Higher Self within man, that is, the Triune Christ Spirit within: the Father (the Divine Spirit), the Son (the Life Spirit) and the Holy Ghost (the Human Spirit) within the body-temple. The Triune Christ Spirit is represented within the 'vestal cup' (the skull or head of the physical body), by the 'Third or Inner Eye' centre (located between the eyebrows), the pituitary gland and the pineal gland, respectively.

Our vestal cup (cranium/skull) overflows when the Triune Christ Spirit is realised in the heavenly sphere within us (the head) whilst we are here on Earth. As Paul the Apostle said: "Christ must be formed in you".[84] As an assistance on the Path, we must affirm good and illumined desires and always visualise that which we affirm; make all affirmations in the name of Christ. That way, the will, power and activity of the Christ Spirit will be stirred into action and all base or carnal desires will be overcome.

Accepting that our physical body (our gases, liquids and solids body, which is but a vibration of substances kept together by the Christ Spirit) has a particular sound or tone according to our mental, physical and spiritual state of being, it must be realised that every time one overcomes a desire that would have led to eventual death of the physical body, a higher energy, tone or vibration is realised in the body. If that higher note or tone is struck and maintained, the warped desire or sin is overcome, never to return. 'The last Trump' in the Bible refers to your last keynote to desires and things of the 'world'. Sin after sin is overcome until death is swallowed up in defeat.[85]

A great deal more could be written about the Desire body, but suffice it to say that enough has been said to give you, the reader, the Seeker of Truth, an insight and attunement to your Desire body, as well as, hopefully, a greater ability to direct your desires in a more positive way that will certainly hasten the realisation of God's grace.[86]

Having dealt with the three-fold body of man — that is, the Dense or physical body, the Vital or Etheric body and the Astral or Desire body — it must be reiterated that the three-fold body only enjoys and experiences life through the power, love and Spirit-essence of the Christ or Divine Spirit. The (three-fold) Christ Spirit infused into and enlivening the (three-fold) body produces an evolving (three-fold) Soul (the Persona). That Soul or person treads the path of life, evolving to perfection daily, until what we call death takes place. At that juncture, the essence or seed atoms of the Christ Spirit and Soul depart from the body and the silver cord is severed. When this happens, the dead physical body is thereafter entombed in the womb of Mother Earth, where it is usually encircled by flowers and moistened by tears. We will now deal with the cycle of life.

The Cycle of Life

Earlier in this chapter, the Realms or Mansions of God's Creation were simply explained and illustrated. In our present stage of development, the more crystallised aspects of the Etheric or Earth Realm are perceived by our optic and other senses, but there are other Realms or Mansions of God in what is called 'the Unseen World'. In the Holy Bible we read: "look not at the things which are seen, but at the things which are not seen: for the things which are seen are temporal; but the things which are not seen are eternal".[87]

Unfortunately, most of us, once we get a name-tag, fall prey to seeking wisdom, happiness and success outside of ourselves. We become ensnared in satisfying our five basic senses; that is, the senses of sight, smell, hearing, taste and touch. This we do with the able and game assistance from our five motor organs, to wit: our hands, feet, vocal chord, sexual and excretory organs.[88] We forget very quickly that we really belong to and ultimately are the Divine Sparks or Christ Spirits that manifest on Earth in temples of flesh made up of the sap of earthly parents. When we realise this in every fibre of our human form, we will know the fullness of God's grace in our lives by overcoming this earth as Christ Jesus/Yashua did almost two thousand years ago. However, until this conscious awareness becomes common place, the norm will be to manifest in a very limited way as Mr. A, Miss B or Mrs. C for some seventy years, and due to sin (living contrary to God's way or Laws), go through a physical death.

(1) Life Beyond Physical 'Death'

We will therefore deal with the cycle of life beyond physical 'death' through the various Realms or Mansions of God until "rebirth into the physical world for a new life experience".[89] I know that the last ten words may come as a surprise for some of you because you may not know of or accept rebirth or reincarnation of the Spirit-Soul, but this will be dealt with immediately after dealing with the Spirit-Soul's 'life' after 'death'.

When one has through physical, mental and spiritual abuse of the physical body or through trauma or accident brought an end to his or her physical life on Earth, one is said to have 'died'; somatic death is said to have taken place. As indicated above, in most cases we earthbound Souls, in our present state of non-being, destroy our dense, physical temples in seventy years; and amazingly, some of us even destroy them in less time, that is, despite God's perfect physical design.

At the time of death, the Spirit-Soul leaves the gases, liquids and solids Dense body: the biochemical-physical body. After leaving the physical body, the Spirit-Soul (along with the higher vibrating, subtle bodies: the Vital body, the Desire body and the mind) hovers above the dense, physical body connected by the silver cord for about three days.[90] During this time the consciousness of all that transpired during that life is absorbed from the Etheric or Vital body and stored in the seed atom of the Desire body. Hence, it is advised that the Dense body should not be buried or otherwise disposed of prior to three days after its death so that a proper record of past experiences or 'record of life', as it is called, can be made. This is necessary if one is to benefit fully from his or her life experiences and the 'purgation' process, which will be discussed below.

In the Bible, Eccles. 12:6-7, we read of "the silver cord" as follows: "Or ... the silver cord be loosed, or the golden bowl be broken.... Then shall the dust return to the earth as it was: and the spirit shall return unto God who gave it". The silver cord is said to have "a glistening silvery appearance".[91] The silver cord connects the Spirit-Soul to the dense, physical body throughout life and, as indicated above, up to three days after somatic death.

The silver cord is similar in many ways to the umbilical cord that attaches the baby to its mother until it is severed and the baby's separate existence on Earth begins. Likewise, when your silver cord is snapped, the Spirit-Soul begins a journey or another form of life in the Unseen World of God. Before dealing a little more with the record of life, it should be noted that whenever the Spirit-Soul and the more subtle (Etheric and Desire) bodies hover outside the Dense body, like when one becomes unconscious (be it by electrical shock or otherwise), the body can be resuscitated. Consciousness is regained because there is a re-entry of the Spirit-Soul and the more subtle bodies into the dense, physical body. This has happened many times when accidents have occurred or when people go into a coma, but the important thing to remember is that in all those cases, the silver cord has not been severed. Those people who go through these experiences usually have interesting stories to tell about their 'out of body experiences', as they are called in common-day parlance. In considering what has been said above relating to the silver cord, Diagram V should be looked at.

DIAGRAM V –TRANSITION TO THE UNSEEN WORLD

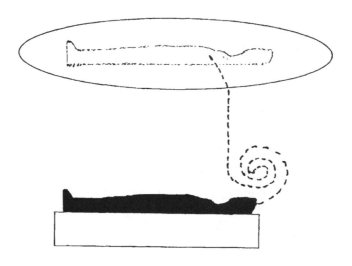

In the Diagram, the Spirit-Soul is seen leaving the physical body at death with the silver cord fitted together like two sixes. The silver cord snaps where the two sixes join. When this happens, the physical body cannot be resuscitated. See Hodges n. 4 supra – illustration on p. 127.

Incidentally, the record of life, referred to in the text above, begins to be imprinted on the reflecting ether and seed atom of the Vital body from the first breath of life and only ends when the last breath is taken. During life, we get impressions from around us via the air and etheric substances we breathe, even if we are not consciously aware of it.

Around three days after the somatic death of the Dense or physical body, the silver cord weakens and then snaps. At that point, the spiritualised aspects of the two higher vibrating elements of the Etheric body (that is, the reflecting and light ether referred to earlier as "the Ghost body"), the Desire body, and the Spirit-Soul depart from the denser or physical body. The Spirit-Soul, with the subtle, Solar body, moves quickly to the lower regions of the Astral or Desire World or Realm. This is the Region referred to as "Hell" and "Purgatory".

Before dealing with the purgation process, a few words are in order about the Dense or physical body that lies entombed in the elements of the earth as well as the two lower elements of the Etheric body — that is, the chemical and life ether. Those two lower elements of the Etheric body hover just above the grave for those who have eyes to see. The deterioration of the entombed Dense body is said to be reflected by the degeneration of its chemical and life etheric substances. Both the 'dead' (gases, liquids and solids) Dense body, as well as the chemical and life etheric substances related to it, degenerate and lose their organisation by returning to their original elements from which they came. Years after burial of the Dense body, there is sometimes little left to reflect that a body was buried there.

We can now deal with the Spirit-Soul's journey through the three lower regions of the Desire Realm. Here, the Spirit-Soul starts to go through a panorama of his or her life, more specifically of all the "wrong" that was committed whilst alive on Earth.

Without the ensnarement of flesh, the Spirit-Soul's sense of "right" and "wrong" is much sharper and clearer. The 'panorama' of life's unloving or wrongful thoughts, words and deeds, which caused suffering and distress, flows like a film before the Spirit-Soul; the last wrongful act is seen and dealt with first, and the first wrong action is dealt with last. All the pain and suffering caused is felt; great lessons are learnt here from past wrongs; the anguish and even hidden hurts inflicted are felt by the Spirit-Soul that inflicted them. If your wrong actions caused suffering to many, your suffering shall be great.

Fortunately, events take place in the Desire World with great rapidity. Those 'sins' or 'transgressions of God's laws' are purged from the Spirit-Soul. Of necessity, those painful experiences leave an indelible mark on the conscience or mind substance of that Spirit-Soul. The Spirit-Soul moves on to the First Heaven after a thorough purgation process, akin to going through the 'fire' so to speak in the lower three regions of the Desire Realm. It must always be remembered that all people that die, even those referred to as saints (as good as they, undeniably, were), die because of 'sin' (transgression of God's laws); 'the wages of sin is death'.[92]

Before dealing with the First Heaven, it must be understood that the Spirit-Soul, after being purged of 'sin' in the lower regions of the Astral or Desire Realm, passes through the 'Borderland' region of the Desire Realm.[93] Usually, little time is spent in this Borderland region in transition to the First Heaven. The only Spirit-Souls that are said to spend considerable time here are materialists who did not necessarily hurt many or any people whilst on Earth, were maybe quite honest, but thought little or not at all of spiritual things or of God; and others, who did not accept the reality of life after physical death. All those Souls tend to wander around here aimlessly, some in a very confused state, until they gradually realise their folly.

The First Heaven has been dealt with much earlier.[94] Hence, it is sufficient to remind the reader that this Heavenly Region is comprised of three substances: Organic Power, Light and Life; and all is positive and harmonious here. The Spirit-Soul's Desire body tends to be smaller and more refined here because it has been purified by the purgation process. The purging process in the lower regions of the Desire Realm effectively etches indelibly onto the permanent seed atom of the Desire body the sufferings caused and also imparts the quality of right feeling, which acts as a deterrent to similar misdeeds in the future.[95]

All is joy and peace when the Spirit-Soul reaches the three upper regions of the Desire Realm because, again, the Spirit-Soul's panorama of life experiences is rolled back. In contrast to the purging process — of being shown all the pain and suffering caused — the experience of seeing and feeling the joy and happiness you caused to people whilst on Earth is beyond comprehension. Any kind look, gesture or act of benevolence and love shown during one's earth life will be felt here; nothing is missed, all the energy and exhilaration generated will be felt.[96]

Hence, you are advised, when on Earth to live clean because your benevolence and good works shall follow you.[97] Obviously, those selfish Spirit-Souls, who were miserly with their love and gave very little, experience little joy here. It should be noted that one does not have to possess a great degree of material wealth to give. Further, giving a person money, for example, is not bad, but this may just make the person dependent upon you. Hopefully, your assistance should help the individual in time to help himself or herself, as the case may be. However, all of us can give a kind look, a sympathetic or empathetic ear to a person's problems, or can give good, loving advice, or an expression of confidence or loving helpfulness when another is in need.[98] This is crucial as you tread the path of life. Remember, there is great spiritual power in giving.

Due to the plasticity of the desire stuff of this Realm, any beautiful thing envisaged is an instant reality. Incidentally, children who die before the birth of the Desire body (around the age of fourteen) usually await rebirth here; they go through no real purgation process. Usually they are met by Spirit-Souls who were related to them in their last life on Earth, or failing this, by others who loved to "mother" children. Even on Earth we all know many people like this.[99] Before moving on to the Second Heaven, which is located in the Realm of Mind, it should be remembered that the Desire Realm is known as the Realm of Colour.[100]

The Spirit-Soul now moves on to the Realm of Mind, which is known as the Realm of Tone; it is the ultimate Realm of music and harmony, a musician's paradise. It is interesting to note that when many materialistic Spirit-Souls depart from their physical bodies (at the time of physical death), many of them are said to go through a time of total unconsciousness. When semi-consciousness returns, it takes some time for them to realise that they no longer have physical bodies and have very little of their vital-substance bodies remaining. Hence, there is said to be a kind of sleep or unconscious stage when materialistic Spirit-Souls make their transition from Earth to the Desire Realm.

In contrast, when Spirit-Souls make their transition from the First Heaven in the upper regions of the Desire Realm to the Second Heaven in the lower regions of the Mind Substance Realm, this is done in an ecstatic state of complete consciousness and tranquillity. This conscious transition, and the attendant "peace and silence", is called "The Great Forever" or "The Great Silence".[101] The feeling of being completely alone yet unafraid fills the consciousness of the Spirit-Soul. No longer possessing a physical body, a Vital body, or a Desire body, the Spirit-Soul moves about in the sheath of mind, which includes the seed atoms of the three discarded bodies.

The Second Heaven, also referred to as the region of concrete thought, is located in the region of the formative mind substances. Here, the symphony of sounds and tones, with each tone having a colour, gives the Spirit-Soul an intimate awareness of the link between sound, tone and colour. Every tone creates a colour, and it is the variety of tones that create all physical forms and manifestations; the archetypes of those forms are eventually crystallised into gaseous, liquid and solid manifestations. Here, too, the Spirit-Soul becomes acutely aware that the formative process is directly related to sound and tone referred to in the Bible as the "Word".[102] Having no mouth, the Spirit-Soul also realises with great certainty that every thought is a vibration with an attendant tone, which is in itself accurate and formative.[103]

The Second Heaven is the region where the third attribute of the All-Father — "Activity" — manifests in all its glory; here, there is an incessant ebb and flow of sound, tone, colour and activity. The Spirit-Soul is said to do a great deal of preliminary work with the archetypes of force on the environment to be used in its next sojourn on Earth. The good deeds of the past life are permanently incorporated into the mind as "right thought". The seed atom of the Dense body transmits all the consciousness that it appropriated from the Dense body to the Divine or Universal Spirit; the seed atom of the Vital body transmits all the consciousness and data appropriated from the Vital body to the Life Spirit; and the seed atom of the Desire body transmits all the emotional power that it managed to appropriate from the Desire body to the Human Spirit. It is therefore in the Second Heaven that the seed atoms of the three-fold body transmit all the consciousness or data from the last life to the three-fold Spirit. The Spirit-Soul is now ready to move on to the Third Heaven.

The Third Heaven is located in the higher region of the Mind Substance Realm — the region of abstract thought and formless mind substance. Here, the Spirit-Soul is formless, because even the sheath that encircled the mind in the Second Heaven no longer exists. The Spirit-Soul in this formless Realm becomes "one with the Universal life of the All-Father".[104] Here, the seed atoms of the Dense, Vital and Desire bodies become imbedded in the Divine or Universal Spirit, Life Spirit and Human Spirit, respectively. The three-fold Christ Spirit, the true child of God, has come home with the quintessence of his physical experience and consciousness on Earth; through that means the Christ child has accumulated first-hand experience and knowledge of this sphere of the All-Father's Creation.

Here, the Spirit-Soul or Christ Spirit-Soul is indelibly blessed by the All-Father and rests for a period to gather strength for another earth life, when as Mr. A or Miss B, he or she will hopefully overcome that Earth Realm by the realisation of the Mystic Marriage. The mystic union or marriage of the Christ Spirit and Soul must be realised while living in a Dense body on Earth; that is the ultimate "Crown of Glory". When that happens even the Dense body is spiritualised and vibrates at the level of the Vital body. It is said that the essence of right thought and right feeling from past experience is infused into the Spirit-Soul for future right thoughts, words and deeds. The Spirit-Soul will be much more au courant with the laws and forces of life and so should do much better in overcoming in the next life.

Before dealing with the return journey back to the Earth Realm, when a Spirit-Soul incarnates in the temple of flesh (when a baby is born), it is now necessary to deal with the reality of what is referred to as "reincarnation" or the doctrine of "rebirth".

(2) Reincarnation

Reincarnation refers to a Spirit-Soul's return to the etheric or material world from the Spirit World for experience and consciousness that can only be obtained and realised in the material world on Mother Earth. Mother Earth, it must be remembered, represents the most crystallised of the spiritual substances of God. The Spirit-Soul, known as a human being or person when incarnated on Earth, goes to Earth in the same way that a person goes to school, returning home every day or at the end of every term or academic year, as the case may be.[105]

Usually, in the educational institutions of this world, if a student fails to "fight the good fight" by passing the required exams, he or she is given another opportunity to repeat the exams, sometimes more than once, if necessary; and further, all those students who passed the required exams for a particular class also return to school but to be promoted to a higher form or class to be further educated. This promotion, as we call it, continues until the student has 'fought the final good fight' and has passed the final exams of that institution and graduates from it. If that person ever returns to that institution, he or she may return as a teacher but certainly not as a student. Nevertheless, that person may go to another institution of higher education to learn certain lessons that the previous institution could not teach.[106]

Similarly, the Spirit-Soul comes to Earth and keeps returning until all the lessons of time have been learnt: the Spirit-Soul having fought "the good fight" on Earth realises the "Crown of Glory".[107] A human being receives the "Crown of Glory" when the Mystic Marriage of the Christ (the Bridegroom) and the Egotistic Self (the Bride) takes place on Earth.[108] Then — and only then — is this Earth Schoolroom and its final 'sting', death, overcome. Death can only be overcome here on Earth, not as a 'duppy' in the sky. Having passed his or her final exams, so to speak, that Spirit-Soul can be said to have graduated from this Earth Realm, and from then has access to the other Mansions or Realms of the All-Father's House or Creation.[109]

The truth is, although many people of the Western world may know very little about reincarnation, most leading religions have taught reincarnation. For example, if you read the writings of some Jewish authorities, such as Moses Gaster, Ph.D., who was once Chief Rabbi of the Jewish Congregation of London and vice president of the Royal Asiatic Society, reincarnation is reflected as an accepted principle of life on Earth. The cycles of life, or reincarnation, was the acknowledged process of purification culminating in the perfection of the Spirit-Soul on Earth.[110]

Reincarnation has been the acknowledged means of human evolution. Millions of people know the truth of reincarnation and of the Law of "Consequence" or karma ('as you sow so shall you reap'),[111] and they have been greatly assisted in understanding life and its seeming inconsistencies. It also assisted them in doing what they ought to do in any given situation, which is living love — that which is from the heart. The early Christian Church acknowledged and taught the doctrine of reincarnation. This is not surprising in that the Christian religion is an outgrowth or flowering of Judaism, the Jewish religion. The early church fathers, such as Clement of Alexandria and Origen, both of the third century, accepted reincarnation. So did St. Augustine and St. Jerome of the fifth century.[112]

The church eventually decided, however, that the doctrine gave too much time for the realisation of salvation, and further it did not enhance the doctrine of divine atonement, a doctrine that must be grasped and accepted by all good Christians in one 'quick' lifetime. Because, according to church dogma, if you are not blessed by knowing Jesus Christ/Yashua as your Messiah and Saviour in the one (in some instances very short) life afforded you, you are unfortunately doomed forever (sorry, lad/lass). Some may say: 'Not very loving or illumined to say the least'.[113]

Incidentally, as a matter of historical interest, Empress Theodora, the powerful and some would say notorious lady of Europe,[114] also had tremendous influence on de-emphasising the knowledge of reincarnation in the Western world. She influenced her husband, Emperor Justinian, to ensure in A.D. 553, at the Fifth Council of Constantinople, that the doctrine of reincarnation was dropped from Orthodox Church doctrine.[115] The equitable doctrine of "Divine Justice" or "karma" was too much for her. She certainly did not want her just deserts: she did not want 'to reap what she had sown' — not in this life or in any future life for that matter. There was then a vain effort to expunge the doctrine from the Bible. I say vain effort in light of the following abundantly clear references that still remain in the Bible: Mal. 4:5; Matt. 17:10-13, 11:1-15; Luke 7:27-28; and, as regards karma, one should read Gen. 9:6; 2 Cor. 5:10 and Rev. 13:10. Some of these citations are discussed below.

For excellent presentations on the subject of reincarnation, one can read *Mansions of the Soul*, by Spencer Lewis, Ph.D., F.R.C., as well as the chapter entitled "Reincarnation" in *Teachings of the Secret Order of the Christian Brotherhood*, by Edward Lewis Hodges, M.A., M.D., Ph.D.,[116] and the chapter entitled "Rebirth and the Law of Consequence" in *The Rosicrucian Cosmo-Conception or Mystic Christianity*, by Max Heindel.[117]

Despite the fact that some of us who think of ourselves as Christians have not been made aware of the biblical references to reincarnation cited above, it must be remembered that the doctrine of reincarnation was accepted by the Jews.[118] It existed from time immemorial, before the coming of Yashua/Jesus the Christ. Hence, there was no need for him to belabour the point or criticise it, as it did not detract from the main principle of his teaching, which was and is the energy and life force engendered by "selfless love". The doctrine of reincarnation enhances the spirit of understanding and love.

For those who have 'eyes to see and ears to hear', some of the passages cited above are now elaborated upon. In the Old Testament, we read in Mal. 4:5: "Behold, I will send you Elijah the prophet before the coming of the great and dreadful day of the Lord". Hence, John the Baptist (the returned Elijah) was sent "before the coming ... of the Lord", as the forerunner of Christ Jesus/Yashua, the Messiah or Massu.[119]

To prove the above, one merely has to read Matt. 17:10-13: "And his disciples asked him (Jesus/Yashua), saying, why then say the scribes that Elias must first come? And Jesus answered and said unto them Elias truly shall first come, and restore all things. But I say unto you, that Elias is come already and they knew him not! Then the disciples understood that he spoke unto them of John the Baptist".

Further, Matt. 11:7-10 indicates: "And as they departed, Jesus began to say unto the multitude concerning John. What went ye out into the wilderness to see? A reed shaken with the wind? But what went ye out to see? A man clothed in soft raiment? Behold, they that wear soft clothing are in kings' houses. But what went ye out ... to see? A prophet? Yea, I say unto you, and more than a prophet. For this is he of whom it is written, "Behold I send my messenger before thy face, which shall prepare the way before thee". That chapter states further: "And if ye will receive it, this is Elias, which was ... to come. He that hath ears to hear, let him hear".[120] For a further reference to John the Baptist being the reincarnation of Elijah, one should also read Luke 1:13-17. It should be noted that the original spelling of "Elijah" and his disciple "Elisha" is used in the Old Testament, but was changed by the Greek translators in the New Testament into "Elias" and "Eliseus", respectively.[121]

An intriguing insight into an individual's conscience is given by an understanding and appreciation of the doctrine of reincarnation. The conscience of each individual is said to be "the fruit of mistakes in past earth lives, which in the future guides the spirit aright and teaches it how to avoid similar missteps. Virtue, being the essence of all that was good in former lives, ... acts as encouragement to keep the spirit ardently upon the path of aspiration".[122]

Certainly Jesus the Christ/Yashua did not and would not expound the unloving, bigoted view that by dint of one sometimes very brief or long lifetime, a Soul is either condemned or blessed for eternity; that is, regardless of the cultural, environmental and other variables relating to opportunity that exist. There always have been many paths to God, all narrow but existent, from the beginning of time. Arguably, to the Christian and followers of Yashua, the path of Christ is the easiest because it is open to all and he takes the yoke from off your back if you just allow him; this atonement comes about by faith (substance) in his Divine sacrifice for your sins. According to your faith (substance)[123] in his name, his life and resurrection, a quickening of 'the Christ Spirit in you' takes place. When, as indicated earlier, the "Bride" (the Ego or Persona that you identify with by a name tag given to you at birth) by faith submits to and becomes one with the "Bridegroom" (the Christ/divinity that must be realised in you), then you will be 'one with your Christ within' (the "Door" to the All-Father), and, simultaneously, one with your Messiah, Christ Jesus/Yashua (Yeshai). From then you will be a realised son or daughter of the All-Father and will have access to all mansions of the All-Father's Creation. There will be no need for rebirth (reincarnation) to overcome this Earth Schoolroom. In the words of a modern-day prophet and Nazarene, Bunny Wailer, "changing names fool the innocent".[124]

The essence of life is to know what the purpose of life is. If one does not understand the purpose of life, one is like an individual walking aimlessly in circles. If one accepts that life is a spiritual journey in the temple of flesh, one quickly realises that to live love is the only way to overcome this school called Earth; the only way to realise one's divine potential; the only way to realise that peace and happiness we desire so badly. One has to become centred in the eye of his or her being, wherein dwells the Christ or Divine Essence within[125] — 'the doorway' to the All-Father.

When one accepts the spiritual nature of the purpose of life on Earth, a purpose that culminates ultimately with conscious attunement with God, one is then influenced in his views of law, politics, economics, education, development and life in general. One who is thus conscioutised ultimately judges all things by the principle of love, be it in the realm of politics, economics or law; one always is influenced by what is just, fair and equitable in any given situation. All things must be seen and developed in a way to assist all humanity to be victorious in overcoming this Earth Realm. Morality, ethics and doing that which you ought to in any given situation should be taught as the basis of this victory in life. People must see this and understand why this is so.

It is important, therefore, that in the education process, besides teaching people English (and other languages), history, mathematics, biology, geography, chemistry, physics, physiology, sociology and other worthwhile subjects, they must be taught the truth about God's laws, including the fundamental laws of "love" and "as you sow so shall you reap" and "doing unto others as you would have them do unto you". That form of education is essential if people want to develop a viable and enduring society.

It is noteworthy that most great civilisations or high cultures, at their zenith, had developed great spirituality and devotion to God as well as a conscientious work ethic and a moral code to guide their daily lives; this seems to be the recipe for wholesome development and success. As soon as a reversal of those values set in, so did decadence, decay and rapid decline. It must be realised that moral codes that have evolved in all cultures of humanity have usually been based on God's spiritual or natural laws: eternal truths that can be found in every leading religion of the world.

(3) The Spirit-Soul's Incarnation on Earth and the Spiritualisation of the Temple

Having dealt with the cycle of life and reincarnation, we can better appreciate the physical birth of a 'living Soul' on Earth. When Mr. A or Miss B decides to continue their spiritual journey on Earth so as to overcome that schoolroom or Realm by realising the fullness of God's grace (the Christ or divinity within), the Spirit-Soul finds an environment most conducive to working out his or her destiny, as the case may be. The environment of necessity includes the parents and country where the Spirit-Soul hopes to incarnate.[126]

With the above having been decided, when the prospective parents are joined in sexual union, just prior to conception, the seed atom of the Dense body, which is part of the incarnating Spirit-Soul, enters and quickens a sperm cell, a positive nucleated element of the potential father. This quickened sperm cell in turn fertilises the negative ovum of the potential mother. The operation of the Christ or Divine principle in the seed atom of the Dense body is crucial in successful conception; for that matter, the life-giving principle in the four seed atoms of the Christ Spirit makes the life of Mr. A or Miss B possible, as will be elaborated on below.[127]

Undeniably, the biological or earthly parents contribute significantly to the gases, liquids and solids, biochemical body, which is the flesh, blood and bones body: the physical temple of the Spirit-Soul. But, as indicated above, even in creating the physical temple the seed atom of the Dense body, which is an atom of the Christ Spirit, must quicken the male seed. Otherwise, conception and ultimate birth of a human being would not occur.

Likewise, it is the seed atom of the Vital body, the Desire body and the mind that allows the three other vehicles or bodies of the Spirit-Soul to be developed and perfected on Earth. As indicated before, the Dense or physical body is complete at birth, the Vital or Etheric body is born at age seven, the Desire or Astral body at age fourteen (puberty), and the mind substance vehicle or sheath at age twenty-one. Each one of us, if we honestly observe our own lives, will notice or would have noticed, as the case may be, those changes in vitality, desire and intellectual maturity around those times in our lives, each change occurring seven years apart.

From the above, it is clear that we truly belong to the Christ or Divine Spirit from birth.[128] However, in the noisy confusion of life, we lose track of this; but when as adults we eventually, consciously become aware of this in every fibre of our human form, by the grace of God, the "Mystic or Spiritual Marriage" takes place. Perfection and union with the Infinite Consciousness of the All-Father becomes a living reality through the realised Christ within the holy temple of flesh; spiritualisation of the molecular or Atomic structure takes place here on Earth, and you are thus 'translated'.[129]

As indicated at the beginning of this chapter, the doctrine or science of spiritualising the physical temple through the Christ within was not only taught but also demonstrated by Yashua or Jesus the Christ. He taught his disciples and close associates that the seed or permanent atom of the Dense body dwells in the left ventricle of the heart like a tiny flame of life.[130] Each time the heart beats, according to the purity of a person's blood[131] and thoughts,[132] the fire or flame of life is transmitted throughout a person's physical body. By this method, ordained incidentally by the All-Father, the physical temple is quickened and spiritualised,[133] achieving a similar vibration to that of the Etheric or Vital body, and death loses its sting. The molecular structure, having been spiritualised, can be re-assembled by the Spirit-Soul whenever it is necessary to manifest itself on Earth to do God's will. A realised son or daughter of God has access to all the mansions of the All-Father's House. This is the All-Father's plan for all of us — not some of us. And so it is! Praise God. Hence, we read: "My little children, of whom I travail in birth (again) until Christ be formed in you".[134]

Keys to Realising the Will and the Way

(1) Sacred Writings and the Bible

All who require light on the path of life have an earnest desire for "the Word", be it the spoken or written word; spiritual nourishment via the word is always necessary to the initiate on the Path. The Bible, for example, is considered by Christians and other adherents to be the inspired Word of God. Others consider the Osirian Text, the Coming Forth by Day, the Torah, the Talmud, the Upanishads, the Vedas, the Bhagavad Gita, the Holy Quran, the Kitab-i-iqan (and many other sacred writings that are deserving of the utmost respect and admiration) as their sacred book of divine guidance.

Most of the great messengers, Masters, prophets and avatars taught the inner esoteric truths of life via symbology and allegorisms (parables).[135] True, most of the Bible can be taken literally, referring to historical happenings and personalities as well as future events (prophecy); however, to the initiate on the Path, esoteric truths of the Will and the Way are presented in symbology and allegorisms (parables) throughout the Bible. To the initiate on his spiritual journey on Earth, gaining an understanding of the inner meaning of the Bible, the inner mysteries of life, is light and nourishment on the Path: sustenance for the Soul. Some would say that seeing the Bible as merely historical events, personalities and prophecy is the crude understanding, the outer layer of the Bible; whereas, seeing the eternal truths reflected in the symbology and allegorisms in the Bible about realising the Inner or Eternal Self, the Christ, the Elohim, is the subtle understanding or inner essence of the Holy Book. These priceless truths are for every man or woman 'who has eyes to see and ears to hear'; all those who desire with all their heart that their will becomes one with God's will. To those people all things will become possible. We are therefore humbly advised to keep our Bible or other sacred book enshrined in a special yet accessible place in our home so that we can nourish our Soul on a daily basis.

Since ancient times, the distinction between exoteric Christianity and esoteric Christianity has been made. Certainly, the Alexandrian School of Northeast Africa made such a distinction and so did Origen, himself an African. Origen, born in A.D. 185, was one of the most distinguished theologians of the ancient Christian Church. Although Origen was eventually disowned by Christendom during the Middle Ages, when the world was plunged into a spiritual abyss (the "Dark Ages"), the Encyclopaedia Britannica describes Origen's character as "blameless", indicating that "there are few church fathers whose biography leaves so pure an impression on the reader".[136] St. Augustine, another African, was the only other church father and theologian who may have been as distinguished and influential in developing the theology and religious science of the early Christian Church.[137]

(2) An Esoteric Insight into the Holy Bible

We read in the Bible: "Unto you it is given to know the mystery of the kingdom of God; but unto them that are without, all these things are done in parables".[138] We also read: "And with many such parables spake he the word unto them (the multitude), as they were able to hear it. But without a parable spake he not unto them: and when they were alone, he expounded all things to his disciples".[139] Similar statements can be seen in many other areas of the Bible, such as: Matt. 13:11; Luke 8:10; Rom. 11:25, 16:25; 1 Cor. 2:7, 4:1, 13:2, 14:2, 15:51; Eph. 1:9, 3:3, 3:4, 3:9, 5:32; Col. 1:26, 1:27, 2:2, 4:3; 2 Thess. 2:7; 1 Tim. 3:9, 3:16; Rev. 1:20, 10:7, 17:5 and 17:7. The word "mystery", when used in the Bible, did not mean some strange occurrence, but "that which is known only to the initiated".[140]

The first esoteric key to the initiate is that, although stories in the Bible may refer to historical events, nations, races and personalities, at the same time they can relate to happenings within our being on the path of unfoldment. The Apostle Paul not only understood this but also reflected this in his teachings. To Paul the Nativity of Christ was not merely an event that occurred in Bethlehem, but the experience of humanity as well as the individual initiate who gradually awakens to the reality of the redemptive power of the Christ within. Thus, he wrote: "... I travail in birth again *until Christ be formed in you*", and also "... this mystery ... is *Christ in you,* the hope and the glory".[141]

Incidentally, the need for veiling the esoteric truths in narratives of history, places and personalities was to prevent the premature awakening of certain innate powers within "uninitiated" people (hard-hearted, carnal materialists), who would merely use those powers for selfish purposes to the detriment of others and, eventually (by dint of the Law of Karma), to the detriment of themselves.[142]

The second esoteric key to the initiate is that places (e.g., "the Red Sea", which symbolises salt, matter, a material problem,[143] and "Egypt", which symbolises spiritual bondage, unless we are referring to the story of the flight of Jesus to Egypt, which refers to his visit to the Mystery School of Egypt for Initiation and Mastership)[144] and personalities (e.g., Mary the mother of Jesus and Mary Magdalene, whose personalities are dealt with below) in the Bible represent states of consciousness or qualities of character.[145]   By extension, clashes between personalities represent the struggle between the Christ, Divine mind (the higher mind and intuitive nature) and the arrogant, carnal mind (the lower, base, animal mind); or simply put, between the higher spiritual nature and lower physical nature in man. An epic example of the foregoing is the struggle between the shepherd boy David (the higher, spiritual, intuitive mind that shepherds our thoughts: our sheep)[146] and the giant Goliath (the excessively arrogant, carnal mind that eventually must be destroyed). Those states of consciousness, qualities of mind or character-types as reflected by personalities in the Bible do not only relate to the internal struggles within the individual initiate, but sometimes also refer to humanity generally in a certain era of development, when that state of consciousness, quality of mind, character-type or behavioural pattern was exemplified.

When the central personality being portrayed in a story is a normal human being, the usual, slow spiritual evolvement of everyday (materialistic) humanity is being described. When the personality and events relate to a semi-divine being, the hastened or enhanced progress of the initiate on the Path of spiritual Self-realisation is being described. Finally, when the experiences of an avatar are spoken of, or those of Divine Conception or descent, this refers to humanity in the later phases of God's human evolutive scheme, when humanity will go through certain inner experiences and realise perfection as divine beings. Or it may refer to individual initiates who are advanced Souls within whom "the Mystic Marriage" (Mastership) takes place during their sojourn on Earth. Those keys are not only relevant to the Bible but to many eternal parables and allegories in other sacred writings.[147] It must be remembered that God is the underlying Essence of all religious thought and the Eternal Truth underlying all religion; the spiritual or golden thread to be found throughout all sacred writings.

States of consciousness or qualities of character are well reflected in biblical personalities, such as Mary, the mother of Jesus (Yashua), whose virtues of selfless love, devotion and humility are an example to all of us; Mary Magdalene and Peter, in whom the potential for transmuting human frailty into ultimate sainthood is exemplified; the two sisters Martha and Mary, representing both sides of the coin or character-types: the busy (materialistic) Martha, who was filled with the cares of the world, and Mary, on the other hand, who was more interested in pursuing the Word, the Spirit, the contemplative nature within herself. The comment of the Messiah to Martha, on the face of it, may look to some as an unfair rebuke, but in fact it merely reflects an esoteric truth that one must seek first and foremost spiritual truth — wisdom — and all material things requested, as long as it is for a wholesome purpose required by you,[148] shall come to you to bless and sustain you; not to whip, worry and destroy you, as some ill-gotten, material possessions do when obtained by greed, selfishness, or by some other clearly immoral means. All these attributes of character seen in the biblical personalities referred to above can be found in each individual or can be seen emphasised more in one individual than another.[149]

The accounts in the Bible of Christ and the twelve disciples refer esoterically to the twelve major character-types, attributes or potentialities exemplified in the astrological zodiac Signs as well as within each living Soul on Earth. The closeness of the twelve disciples to the Divine Teacher reflects a high state of spiritual evolution or refinement of character. When the twelve disciples or qualities of character are disciplined (discipled) by the Centrifugal Figure, Christ Jesus (the Messiah), or the Indwelling Christ realised within one's bodily temple, the Christ Spirit in the disciples of the Bible or within the true devotee or initiate, as the case may be, will be awakened from sleep, as reflected in the ship in Galilee, when a great storm arose and Christ was awakened by the disciples;[150] or will be born, as reflected in the Mystic Nativity, when "Christ" is said to "be formed in you".[151] When this discipleship (discipline) is realised, the initiate is perfected "unto the measure of the stature of the fullness of Christ".[152]

The third esoteric key to the initiate is that each narrative reflects a graphic description of the stages of the Spirit-Soul's evolutionary journey to the Promised Land (Christ or Cosmic Consciousness). In using this third key, each narrative can be interpreted from at least two perspectives.[153] The first is the normal process of evolution along the wide and heavily used way or path of the majority, and the second is the 'straight and narrow way' or path of the minority. Hopefully, the 'straight and narrow path' will become the path of the majority, that is, if those living Souls of the present era have ears to hear.[154]

The parable of the sower who encountered various soil and environmental conditions is a beautiful example of the above. As explained by the Messiah to his disciples privately, the environment and soil conditions and the results that followed from the sowing can be related to the spiritual receptiveness or lack of it, as the case may be, of individual Souls or of humanity generally at certain stages of development.[155]

The biblical narrative of the ten virgins spoken of in Matt. 25:1-13 refers on one hand to those living Souls on the path of life (the five foolish Virgins), who are not sufficiently evolved to respond to and receive the higher spiritual impulses from the Higher Self, the Bridegroom or Christ within (these Souls show little interest in spiritual matters); and on the other hand, to those other living Souls (the five wise Virgins), who are sufficiently evolved and disciplined to respond to the higher spiritual stirrings of the Christ Spirit, culminating in the Mystic Marriage of the mortal and immortal natures in man. Mortality is thus raised to immortality through the grace of God, which is the Divine Essence or Christ Spirit within the body-temple. When this is fully and consciously realised in the hearts and minds of all of us living Souls, then God's grace in us will be fulfilled. All marriages referred to in the Bible relate to the same Mystic Marriage; this will be elaborated on further below.[156]

The fourth esoteric key to the initiate is that certain physical objects, words, actions and numbers have specific esoteric or symbolic meanings that can be applied throughout the Bible according to the context. A few examples are as follows:

(a) "Water" and its associations at a macrocosmic level esoterically refers to all-pervading life, Universal or Cosmic space; and at a microcosmic level, according to the context, to the emotions within a living Soul,[157] or when referred to as "wells of water, rivers of water, still waters, pools of water, springs and brooks",[158] to spiritual refreshment or the life force to the Soul;[159]

(b) "Air" generally refers to the intuition and "fire" to the mind. However, quite often fire also refers to the creative life force of "the Word", "the Logos", as well as the creative Christ or serpentine force within man, which is frequently represented as a serpent or dragon in some ancient sacred writings;

(c) "City" represents a state of consciousness in man, and reference to "mountain" or "mountains" means spiritual ascent, an elevation of consciousness. This is in keeping with the second esoteric key, above, which indicates that references to places reflect a state of consciousness;

(d) "Feet" refer esoterically to the desires of the initiate: by a man's desires you know him. We read of the Master Jesus washing the feet of his disciples, which symbolically means that the disciples' grosser attributes and desires (their desires of the world) were washed clean by the Massu, and their desires were therefore no longer of this world but one-pointed on God. Hence, you are said to be in this world, but not of this world;

(e) "Flesh" (which is sometimes referred to as "meat") of a Divine Being esoterically refers to "spiritual truth and God's natural law";

(f) "Blood" symbolises the eternal outpouring of "Divine Life by which the Universe and man are spiritually sustained".[160] It always symbolises life in its divine sense; the eternal Christ substance of life; the wholesome eternal life force that cannot die, for there is no death in life: only evil can be destroyed.[161] Hence, the sprinkling of the blood on the door posts represents the sprinkling of the Christ blood or Christ life at the doorway of our consciousness whereby the angel of death (evil, destructive thoughts and actions, sin, which bring about death) cannot enter our minds and lives;

(g) "The act of the eating of such flesh and the drinking of such blood" signifies the initiate's conscious absorption of Eternal Truth as well as the "conscious coalescence with the one life of the Universe ... unity with its Source";[162]

(h) "Seven" is the spiritually perfect number: The sacred wisdom is said to have seven layers; there are seven Realms or Mansions of Creation; there were seven days of creation ("And on the seventh day God ended his work which he had made; and he rested on the seventh day..." (Gen. 2:2)); Solomon's temple was built in seven years;[163] there are seven chakras or vortices of force in man. In Revelation, there were seven stars and seven churches; the dragon had seven heads and seven crowns; there were seven angels; seven golden vials; seven Mighty Spirits before the Throne; and seven mountains. In Daniel the furnace was to be heated seven times ... before Shadrach, Meshach and Abendego were joined by a fourth, who appeared like the Son of God.[164] Likewise, the walls of Jericho were encircled on the seventh day for seven times before they came tumbling down. Man is said to have a sevenfold nature, and esoterically, the number seven is symbolised by the square and the triangle. The Triune Christ or Divine Spirit enters the square or "four-sided city of Jerusalem" (the lower self and physical body) and spiritualises it into New Jerusalem: the three-sided triangle merges or marries the four-sided square and becomes seven. The Egyptians expressed this sacred number in the structure of their pyramids: a pyramid was built with triangular sides on a four-sided base, with the apex or 'eye' of the pyramid pointing to the heavens.[165] The Bible is replete with the use of the number seven in this esoteric manner;[166]

(i) "Forty" is another of the many esoteric numbers utilised throughout the Bible and means a time of probation, preparation, waiting and purification. The flood is said to have lasted forty days, and Moses and the Israelites were in the wilderness for forty years; Joshua had to wait until he was forty years before he was fit to become leader of Israel, and the children of Israel were delivered to the Philistines for forty years; Mary and Joseph waited for forty days before Christ was presented in the Temple, and Moses, Elijah and Jesus the Christ (Yashua) fasted in the wilderness for forty days.[167]

We will now deal with a few biblical narratives in Genesis, Exodus and Revelation reflecting the esoteric or inner meaning to all initiates of the Mysteries of the Kingdom of God. To my mind, there is no better place to start than the Adam and Eve story.

In Genesis we read: "Male and female created He them; and blessed them, and called their name Adam, in the day when they were created". The Mesopotamian word ADUMAH, ADAM or ADM in Hebrew represents the number 9 and means "of the ground"[168] or "child of black clay".[169] Hence, we read in Genesis that God "formed man out of the dust of the ground" (the rich, black soil of Mother Earth, which is filled with heat and electro-magnetic energy from the sun and all the necessary chemical elements), "and breathed into his nostrils the breath of life; and man became a living soul".[170]   Esoterically, as the name relates to humanity, Adumah or Adam (ADM) symbolises the original human family when humanity, in keeping with God's creative evolutionary impulse, was in its infancy, totally pure and unconscious of things of the flesh.   This period of innocence represents the time before the separation of the sexes when human beings were said to be passionless, androgynous beings who were self-reproductive.[171]

The Adamic era, and even for some time after the separation of the sexes (reflected by the story of God causing a deep sleep to come over Adam whereby one of his "ribs" — more accurately one of his sides with the more feminine attributes — was taken), can be seen as a period of innocence similar to the period between the birth of an individual to the time just before puberty. This is reflected when we read that God "closed up the flesh ... thereof. And [with] the rib, which the Lord God had taken from man, made he a woman, and brought her unto man. And Adam said, this is now bone of my bones, and flesh of my flesh: she shall be called Woman, because she was taken out of Man.... And they were both naked, the man and his wife, and were not ashamed".[172] Their lack of shame at their nakedness reflects an innocence and purity of mind: the carnal or lustful aspect of sexuality had not yet taken hold of humanity. Humanity is said to have performed the act of fecundation (sex) within a natural cycle of life influenced by the positioning of planets around the sun.   For some time this innocence and attunement with natural law continued and human beings were almost unconscious of the sex act; some may say they were so attuned to the higher spheres and laws of life that they lived like automatons under God's immutable, natural laws.[173]

In that the story of Adam and Eve is dealt with in chapter 3, to wit, "Beyond the Veil of History", suffice it to say here that the temptation of the more intuitive, sensitive Eve (the female) and the eating of the proverbial apple represents a lowering of spiritual consciousness to a lower plane of physical consciousness (esoterically, this can be taken to refer to the individual initiate or to humanity generally during that era). This was brought about by self-willed, physical indulgence, which reflected behaviour outside the natural rhythms or cycles of the spheres and contrary to the natural laws of human existence. After the abuse of the creative force, the eating of the forbidden fruit, they realised their nakedness, and lost their power of divine attainment and their gift of eternal life.[174] Hence, by the sweat of their brows they thereafter lived to sustain and support the offspring, in some cases, of their indulgence, who incidentally carried within them the ignorance (lack of right knowledge and attitude) of their 'flesh and blood' earthly parents.[175]

The Cain and Abel story as reflected in the Bible may seem quite unfair to some people, if taken at its face value. But like many stories throughout the Bible, besides the historical or prophetic aspect, there is also the dual esoteric understanding that refers to the spiritual and psycho-physical development of humanity at a certain period in time, as well as to the spiritual and psycho-physical development of the individual on the Path of Self-realisation; the path that leads to the conscious realisation of the Christ or divinity within: Christ-consciousness, the door through which you must pass to get back to God, the All-Father. Incidentally, this is the same door through which Jesus the Christ passed to become one with his All-Father whilst here on Earth.

With the above having been said, "Cain", who is represented as the tiller of soil, refers to the more physical, masculine, sons of fire type, the head or mind type: those who were and those who still are more influenced by reason and materialism. That nature or emphasis can be seen in individual character-types or experienced within each individual, to a lesser or greater extent.

Relating the name Cain to humanity generally, it represented humanity's total immersion into the material, physical world when they lost their attunement to things of the Spirit; when they lost their birthright to eternal life; a time when humanity developed the concrete mind at the expense of the heart, or the spiritual side of their nature. As indicated above, "Cain" represents the 'head' or 'reason', the sons of fire;

whereas "Abel" on the other hand represents the 'heart' (the feminine), or spiritual side, the sons of water.[176]

"Abel", it must be remembered, was a "keeper of sheep" like David, and keepers of sheep in the Bible always represent purity of thought, innocence, pertaining to the heart, the more feminine or intuitive nature. Hence, the offerings of the heart (Abel) given in faith and love were acceptable to God, whereas the offerings of the head (cold intellect, reasoning and materialism — Cain) were not acceptable or pleasing to God.

It should be noted that Cain, the head, the cold, selfish intellect, kills Abel, the heart, and great misery sets in.[177] When the selfish, reasoning mind dominates the heart (the love nature) in an individual or humanity generally, misery is the result. Hence, Cain and Abel represent types of humanity at different eras of time as well as qualities of character to be found in each of us.[178]

The idea of the voice of Abel crying from the ground represents the unhappy heart or spirit being engulfed by the earth or ground (the physical body) whereby the heart or spirit is dominated by the 'heartless' mind or intellect; the heart or spirit therefore cries out for release from such materialistic bondage. Eventually, the heartless intellect or intellect without heart always brings pain and suffering until one realises the futility of putting one's faith in materialism and carnality, that is, as distinct from things of the heart, the Spirit or of God.[179]

Cain's movement in consciousness to the land of Nod, as distinct from a mere physical movement of Cain to a place called Nod, means a time of mental and physical unrest and trouble. As indicated above, 'the head without the heart' brings about spiritual and physical imbalance and trouble; as a consequence, going to the land of Nod means that one's consciousness is lowered. But suffering and pain always follow such lowered states of consciousness, and suffering and pain tend to assist us in changing our evil ways. Hence, Cain (the head, the intellect) started to cultivate the more feminine aspect (the heart), and began to nurture the spiritual and altruistic aspect of his nature. Thus, we read that Cain knew his wife who bore him a son called Enoch, a name that represents wisdom, a state of high consciousness; hence we read that Cain built a city, and as indicated before, "a city" means a state of consciousness.[180] From the foregoing, we learn that through experience and suffering, wisdom can be realised within the very centre of our being. It is what we make of experiences that counts, what we get out of them. Do we learn from our mistakes and become better people for those experiences? At the end of the day that is what will give us the Crown of Glory: the faith (which is of substance) in good over evil and in love vanquishing hate. That is what will make us rapidly move forward in our glorious journey in realising God's will 'within us' on Earth.

Remembering always that all sacred writings, like an onion, have several 'layers' (meanings) and that all narratives must be understood and realised within our own beings, the Adam and Eve and Cain and Abel saga of the Bible can be esoterically internalised and summed up as follows: Adam represents within the initiate, the pure Monadic Ray or Christ Spirit; Eve, the Soul or Ego encased in the Solar and physical body; Cain, the intellect, reasoning, the brain, body consciousness, carnality and materialism; and Abel, spiritual awareness, the heart, the intuitive nature, faith substance and spirituality. Incidentally, for those who have ears to hear, the mere incarnation of the Spirit-Soul in the mire of clay (the dense, physical body) symbolises a burial in the ground (an entombing) until the deadening effect is overcome and the Spirit re-attains his spiritual glory, bringing home with him to the Almighty (the All-Father) the pristine, perfected Soul (the Bride).[181]

Another narrative we will deal with briefly is the biblical story of the patriarch, Noah. Besides reflecting the history of the descendants of Adam and Noah, chapters 5 to 10 of Genesis reflect the epochs of man. Each "begat" or generation indicates a principle or phase of human development, a state or quality of consciousness. The basic character or principle exemplified by the patriarch is the key to what was the emphasis of human development during that epoch.[182] Hence, Noah and those like him represent the pioneers of the human race who managed to conquer the carnal or lower nature by building "the Ark or Soul Body of the initiate",[183] the "Marriage Garment" or "Solar body" of the Indwelling Christ (Divine) Spirit. Over time, those pioneers or "Sons of God" eventually married "the daughters of men". This reflects marriage (merging) with the more carnal-minded flesh, blood and bones consciousness, which resulted in the gradual decline spiritually of the human race. Noah and those like him, however, represented those dedicated to the Path that did not yield to carnality and abject materialism. Noah is said, therefore, to have walked with God.[184] By building an "Ark", a Marriage Garment or Solar body,[185] by pure living, the initiate cum Master rises above the flood waters of passion and emotion; hence, the "Ark" comes to rest on Mt. Ararat. The door of the "Ark" to the initiate is the spleen (or more specifically, the etheric double of the spleen), where solar energy from the sun enters the "Ark" (the Solar body); and the window of the "Ark" is in the head, more specifically, "the parietal occipital suture, where the Ego (Soul) enters and leaves the body in sleep and at death".[186]

A helpful, yet easy to remember esoteric insight into Noah and the flood is that it also refers to the spiritual evolution of mankind. The "animals" in the Ark represent the lower, animal, or carnal nature in man that must be transmuted to the higher, divine, immortal nature or Self represented by "Noah and his family". The "Ark" represents the Solar body or Marriage Garment of the perfected Soul that successfully rides "the flood waters covering the Earth" (the earthy, animal passions). This is accomplished by sublimating and transmuting those forces, whilst on Earth, into high spirituality and mental illumination represented by "the Mountains of Ararat".

Another insight into interpreting an aspect of Noah and the flood story is that the "raven" represents the intellect and reasoning, and the "dove" represents the intuition and the will (the divine or spiritual aspect in man). Incidentally, the concept of doves and the like flying through the air reflects that the Soul is pursuing, or experiencing, a higher state of spiritual consciousness. By using the intellect and reasoning alone (the raven), one will not attain or experience Truth and spiritual awareness; one needs to also use the intuition and the will (the dove) for one to realise, whilst on Earth, spiritual truth, life and illumination within one's being (Mastership or Christ-consciousness). The intuition and the will go beyond the intellect and become one with the universal life force (symbolised by the dove eventually returning with the olive branch — which signifies "peace" that passeth all understanding).[187]

The Noah narrative also represents to all who have eyes to see the life cycle or, some may say, 'the afterlife experience', starting from the Spirit-Soul's conscious experiences immediately after physical death until rebirth on Earth in another temple of flesh. For example, when the Spirit-Soul takes leave of the physical, Dense body, the Spirit-Soul spends some time in the Astral or Desire Realm, where as indicated earlier in this chapter,[188] there is a precipitation or flood of one's past deeds and experiences — so-called good and bad karma. This part of the cycle is represented by the flood waters; it is a rapid, intense, emotional experience.

Fairly soon after physical death, but for the desire seed atom (the pure, spiritualised, desire essence), the Spirit-Soul is basically purged of its desire substance. Thereafter, the Spirit-Soul experiences a unity and peace (a loving dispassion) in the subdivisions of the Desire Realm described earlier in the chapter as the First and Second Heavens. Here, all is peace, an ecstatic calm. This represents the period in the Noah story when the rain was restrained and the waters were abated[189] — a state of mental and spiritual equilibrium.

The period of the Spirit-Soul's journey in the Third and final Heaven (which is located in the three higher subdivisions of the Mind Substance Realm) is represented in the Noah story by the Ark coming to rest on the Mountains of Ararat.[190] Here, remember, the Divine, three-fold Spirit imbued with the essence of the seed atoms of the Soul, becomes one with the Universal Spirit of the All-Father. The eventual emergence of Noah from the Ark and the descent from the mountains to lower ground represents the Spirit-Soul's descent to Earth for rebirth. This cycle of life is continued until perfect Christ or Divine Consciousness is realised whilst the Spirit-Soul is in the temple of flesh on Earth.   Incidentally, the rainbow in the Noah story represents the bridge or link between the two lives, as well as a covenant between God and humanity to unite the mortal self with the immortal, spiritual Self: the Christ that must be realised in you by the grace of God, the All-Father of all creation.

Finally, in esoteric ethnology and history, the Noah epoch also represents the time of the Atlanteans spoken of in chapter 3. Some refer to them as the Fourth Root Race, who abused both their psychic and material powers for selfish and aggressive ends. Eventually, this behaviour of necessity brought about their own end via the proverbial floods referred to by all ancient cultures.[191]   As reflected later in chapter 3, the remnants of ancient Atlantis can still be seen via the mountain ranges that peak as islands in the Caribbean Sea and Atlantic Ocean.[192] Noah and those individuals saved by the grace of God were chosen as the progenitors of the next generation or Root Race of humans to live and enjoy God's Earth.[193] A great deal more could be said about Noah and the flood, but enough has been said for one to get a true feel of the inner or esoteric meaning of not only this Bible story, but for that matter, many of the stories of the Bible.

We shall now briefly deal with a few excerpts from Exodus and Revelation. In the Exodus story, man's spiritual development is also reflected. The country "Egypt", in Judeo-Christian esoteric teaching, is said to represent a state of consciousness, whereby the individual or Soul is still in bondage or slavery to the material senses, evil and carnality.[194] "Jerusalem", on the other hand, represents the ultimate goal or end of the spiritual journey. To be in Jerusalem is to be in the purified holy body–temple wherein the Divine One dwells and spiritual or Christ-consciousness is realised.[195]

As indicated earlier, characters in the stories of the Bible represent thoughts generally or thoughts of a certain type or quality, and countries reflect states of consciousness; "countries" (states of consciousness) within which we sometimes dwell or stay for a while (until we overcome those thought patterns or habits) and subsequently move on to another country (a higher state of consciousness and behavioural pattern).[196]

It will be noticed that "Moses kept the flock of Jethro, his father-in-law, the priest of Midian: and he led his flock to the backside of the desert, and came to the mountain of God, even to Horeb".[197] This is consistent with earlier guidance that indicated inter alia that men who tend sheep represent the regenerated, the chosen of God, the Davids, the Isaacs, the Abels, those of pure, wholesome thoughts related to things of the Spirit, whereby the mountain, which represents an elevation of consciousness or spiritual awareness (spiritual and mental illumination), is reached. The "flame of fire" out of the midst of the bush, which strangely did not consume it, refers to the Light of the Spirit, the Christ within man that engulfs the initiate cum Master, who submits his desires to God. "Feet", remember, refers to one's desires and "shoes", especially leather shoes, represent materialism; hence, the reason for God's communication with Moses to remove his shoes to "stand on holy ground". Moses, therefore, did away with his material desires to realise the fullness of God's grace and light, and his feet (his desires) were engulfed and purified by the flame of Light (of Truth).[198]

Pharaoh, the king of the Egyptians, represents the alluring, ensnaring power behind the lower thoughts and tendencies in man. Hence, we are told in the story that Pharaoh held the "Israelites" (who represent 'spiritual thoughts that aspire to Truth and godliness') in a vice grip, demanding bricks without giving them straw. The eternal esoteric battle within man, between his Divine and carnal mind, continues; a stalemate ensues until Moses, the leader of the "Israelites", decides to put an end to this ensnarement or bondage.[199] True to life, when Moses (Divine mind and will) tries to lead the Israelites (aspiring spiritual thoughts) out of Egypt (a state of consciousness where base, carnal and material thoughts hold sway), there was a fight literally to the death by Pharaoh and his legions (the carnal mind and base habits) against Moses and the Israelites.[200]

Consistent with what has been said and explained earlier in paragraphs (f) and (g) concerning "the fourth esoteric key to the initiate", "blood" symbolises Divine Life, Truth, the Christ life substance. Hence, the Angel of Death destroyed the Egyptians but not the Israelites, who "sprinkled blood 'on two sides of the posts' and on the upper door" of their houses ... "for in life there is no death, and it is only evil that can be destroyed".[201]

As related in the story, although the Israelites began their journey with confidence, they soon came upon their Red Sea: "old (material) thoughts, fears, habits, appetites, crying wildly" to be satisfied.[202] They had to be exhorted by their leader Moses to "Fear ... not, stand still, and see the salvation of the Lord, ... for the Egyptians (material allurements) whom you have seen today, you shall ... see no more".[203]

The words "Fear ... not, stand still, and see the salvation of the Lord" do not reflect spiritual stagnation, but on the contrary, reflect the means by which spiritual progress and communion with God is realised. In similar vein, one reads, "Be still, and know that I am God".[204] In other words, on the Path of Truth one must go fearlessly ("fear not"), because the only thing to fear is fear itself; to fear evil is to fear ignorance, because wherever Truth is, ignorance is dispelled. Also, besides walking the Path fearlessly, one must be still (one must go into the silence), which means one must stop those carnal and material thoughts, so that in that quietness of mind God, the All-Father, can commune with the devotee, the spiritual aspirant or initiate.

As pointed out earlier in paragraph (a), we should always observe the difference in the Bible between salt water (material, selfish or carnal thoughts, passions and desires) and fresh, pure waters from rivers and wells (which means spiritual refreshment or life force to the Soul). The colour red is also significant; the sea was not only salt but also red. Red is said by the physicist to be the lowest colour vibration that is perceptible to the naked eye, whereas on the other hand, violet is produced by the highest vibrations in the ether. Hence, red in this context also represents the lower animal thoughts: angry thoughts, thoughts of rage. That is why when people are overcome by temper, some say 'he or she saw red'.[205]

It was indicated above that only evil can be destroyed, as distinct from good, but to this may be added: evil destroys itself.[206] This is well demonstrated in Exodus, for example, chapter 10 verses 14 to 19, where one reads that the terrible locusts not only went all over the land of Egypt, but they covered the face of the whole Earth, so that the land was darkened. They ate herb and fruit and left nothing green on the trees, and "a mighty strong west wind ... took away the locusts and cast them into the Red Sea; there remained not one locust in all the coasts of Egypt". "East" in esoteric law represents, amongst other things, spiritual light, spiritual thoughts. Our spiritual thoughts are said to emanate from the eastern or left hemisphere of our brain (consciousness); also, the physical sun that brings life and light to the earth rises in the East. "West", on the other hand, represents the opposite of life and light, to wit, death and darkness. Hence, the locusts (evil or error) were taken away by a mighty strong west (symbolising death, darkness or error) wind and they were destroyed in the Red Sea (the sea of error).[207] So, too, in Exod. 14:21-28 one reads of a strong east wind that divided the waters and made the sea dry land. The children of Israel went through safely, but the story relates that the same fate befell the Egyptians as the locusts: they perished in the Red sea. Hence, in Judeo-Christian biblical symbology, evil destroys evil because in reality evil is out of sync with the vibration of love and harmony.

We shall now move into the New Testament, more specifically, to Revelation where we will deal with the esoteric meaning of a few passages, that is, as they relate to the inner life of the true Israelite or initiate on the Path: the true child of the Kingdom of God. Undeniably, Revelation, it must be remembered, also has a prophetic or visionary aspect, but this will be dealt with later in chapter 4 of this book.

In Revelation, chapter 6, we read: "And I saw when the Lamb opened one of the seven seals, and I heard, as it were the noise of thunder, one of the four Beings (some Bibles say 'living creatures', others, 'beasts') saying: Come and see. And behold a white horse appeared. And he that sat on him had a bow; and a crown was given him: and he went forth conquering, and to conquer".[208]

For those who have eyes to see and ears to hear, the opening of "one of the seven seals" refers to the opening of the pelvic or Svadhisthana Centre or Chakra, mentioned earlier in this chapter. This chakra (vortex of energy) belongs to the generative region, where the pingala (positive) and ida (negative) currents flow strongly; it is at the base of the somatic division. It is said to represent Sagittarius in the ancient science of solar biology or astrology; hence, the biblical reference to the horse and man with a bow. In that he rides a white horse, the being is said to represent the Conqueror, who is starting off on his (spiritual) journey of conquest; hence, the words "he went forth conquering, and to conquer".[209] This interpretation, like in all the other paragraphs to follow relating to the seals, must also be internalised in the microcosm, that is, in each human being or initiate on the Path of God.

"And when he had opened the second seal, I heard the second Being (living creature) say: Come and see. And there came out another horse that was red: and power was given to him that sat thereon to take peace from the earth, and that they (men) should kill one another; and there was given unto him a great sword".[210]

The above refers to the opening of the solar plexus or Manipura Chakra. Its colour is red or crimson, like the red horse, which "symbolises the abdominal somatic division," and the horse in conjunction with the rider epitomises passion, aggression, war (violence). This seal is also referred to as "the epigastric chakra"; its sign is Scorpio and its planet Mars, the ruler of war.[211]

"And when he had opened the third seal, I heard the third Being say, Come and see. And behold a black horse came out; and he that sat on him had a pair of balances (scales) in his hand. And I heard a voice in the midst of the Beings saying: A measure of wheat for a penny, and three measures of barley for a penny; and see that you do not hurt (damage) the oil (olive trees) and the Vine (yard/wine)".[212]

The above refers to the opening of the heart or Anahata Chakra. It is quite clear that it corresponds to the sign Libra with the balance or scales; the ruler of this somatic division is said to be the "parsimonious weigher", the lower mind or lower intellect that is tainted by emotions, selfish motives and carnal desires.[213] The lower mind is said to be able to achieve admirable advancements in science and conventional knowledge, but this superficial, material advancement will be devoid of spiritual attunement or insight.[214] The result of this spiritual deadness or dormancy: chaos, because our culture, science, and social behaviour will not be consistent with God's natural laws of life on Earth. This lower mind eventually has to be conquered by the Higher/Divine or Christ mind, which imbues the heart with love and compassion, and the body with life. Eventually, the heart and mind work in unison and in a balanced manner, as God planned it.

"And when he had opened the fourth seal, I heard the voice of the fourth Being say: Come and see. And I looked and behold a pale horse: and his name that sat on him was Death, and Hell (Hades) followed him. And power was given to them over the fourth part of the earth, to kill with sword (war), and with hunger (famine), and with death (disease), and with the beasts of the earth".[215]

The above refers to the opening of the throat or Vishudha (laryngeal) Chakra. This is the highest chakra that belongs to the sympathetic nervous system (the chakras above the throat chakra are said to belong to the brain). The throat chakra is ruler of the highest of the somatic divisions, the lower 'sky' (the cerebral region, incidentally, is referred to as the mid-sky or the First Heaven within man, the ultimate abode of the Christ Spirit and mind within the temple of flesh). The vocal chord is the mystical organ of creation: the word (Logos), activity and motion.[216] However, until this mystical organ of creation is perfected, when man shall create as God planned it by the power of the word, this throat chakra works in conjunction with the lowest somatic divisions of generation (the higher generative organ and the lower generative or creative organ). In that the sex force (drive and energy) exists only in the physical and psychic realms,

Death and Hades reflect the effect of the abuse of the creative force at the physical (material) and psychic levels.[217] The abuse of the creative force therefore brings death by war (violence), famine and disease not only within the individual initiate, but to the broader society that indulges itself in such abuse.

"And when he opened the fifth seal, I saw under the altar the souls of them that were slain for the word of God, and for the testimony which they held. And they cried with a loud voice, saying: How long, O Lord, Holy and True, does Thou fail to judge and avenge our blood on them that dwell on the earth. And white robes were given to them; and it was said to them, that they should rest for a season (keep still for a little while) until their fellow-servants and brothers, who are to be killed, were killed, as they were".[218]

The above refers to the opening of the Ajna Chakra that is said to correspond to the sign Cancer.[219] This chakra is closely connected to the pituitary gland, one of the two key glands of great power that are dormant and to be awakened within the brain centre (the heavenly sphere). The seventy plus (the mystical three in one) centres of the brain, taught of in phrenology, are said to remain dormant (dead so to speak) by the typical unspiritual, materialistic life, until 'their brothers' (the other chakras) are first brought into activity then 'killed' or put in abeyance, while the cerebral centres (the pituitary and pineal centres) are awakened. Those seventy plus one brain centres referred to above are then said to receive "white robes" as currents of the celestial Flame begin to suffuse through the brain due to the gradual awakening of the two cerebral chakras aforementioned.

"And I saw when he opened the sixth seal, and behold, there was a great earthquake; and the sun became dark and the moon became as blood, and the stars of the sky fell to the earth, even as figs drop their untimely fruit (unripe fruit) when shaken by a mighty wind. And the sky was removed as a scroll being rolled up; and every mountain and island was moved out of their places. And the kings of the earth, and the great men etc. ... hid themselves in the dens and in the rocks of the mountains. And said to the mountains ... hide us from the face of him that sitteth on the throne, and from the wrath of the Lamb. For the great day of his wrath has come; and who shall be able to stand".[220]

The opening of the sixth seal in Revelation refers to the opening of the Root or Muladhara Chakra or seal, thereby releasing tremendous spiritual and electro-magnetic energy up the Sushumna, the principal nadi in the human temple (the closest physical counterpart of the Sushumna is the spinal chord). Nadis are like tubes of energy and life force that flow through the Astral or Solar body of each human being; they are akin to the peripheral nervous system in the physical body. This electro-magnetic, spiritual body interpenetrates and electrifies or vitalises, so to speak, the physical body via the chakras ('seals') and peripheral nadis. However, as indicated above, this release of life force and electrical energy flows from the base of the spine right up the brain stem into the brain; this gives the mind and body an overwhelming experience.

'The darkening of the sun' refers to 'the blanking out of the mind' by this surge of electro-magnetic, spiritual energy into the brain; 'the falling of the stars' refers to the falling away of thoughts.[221] The 'fig tree dropping her untimely or unripe fruit as if shaken by a mighty wind' refers to the awakening of the spiritual fire before the carnal or lower mind has submitted to the Christ mind (before the 'fruit'/individual is ripe/mature and ready for Christ-consciousness). This is reflected in the words of pandemonium and fear when we read of 'the removal of the sky, mountains and islands and the panic and hiding of the earth-dwellers (lower mind and faculties)'.[222] The 'ripeness of the fruit'/initiate is directly related to the re-orientation of mind and the transmutation of the sex force; a fact that most organised Christian religions do not bring to the fore, because it is a hard 'pill to swallow' in our hard-core sex-oriented societies; a fact that would certainly not make them popular. It should be noted that the Roman Catholic Church demands celibacy from its priests, some may say with varied success. The direct link between the sex-force or sexual energy and spiritual development will be dealt with briefly later.

Before moving on to Rev. 8:1-6, when the seventh seal is opened, a few words are in order about chapter 7 of Revelation. In symbology, it reflects the final preparation of the Soul for the mystic fusion or marriage with the Christ Spirit or Lamb, who is in 'the middle of the throne' to guide those Souls that have fought the good fight and gone through the ordeals of the Path of realising him (the Indwelling Christ that must be realised in you), the gift of the All-Father. Each of those Souls' 'scroll of life' (every thought, word and deed coupled with the relevant emotion) is brought to the fore and the final conflict of cause and effect within the initiate (Soul) takes place. The Lamb (the Christ Spirit/the Logos) will then "shepherd them (the Souls) and guide them to springs of life-giving water, and God will wipe away every tear from their eyes".[223] In symbology, the lower principles in each Soul on the Path are chastised and purified and the higher faculties and principles receive the seal of the All-Father's approval.[224]

As indicated above, the opening of the Sahasrara Chakra is reflected in the words of the first six verses of Revelation, chapter 8: "And when he (the Lamb) had opened the seventh seal there was a silence in the sky (heaven) for about half an hour. And I saw seven Angels that stood before God; and to them were given seven trumpets. And another Angel came and stood at the altar, having a golden censer (incense holder); and there was given to him much incense that he should offer it with the prayers of all the saints (devotees) upon the golden altar which was before the throne. And the smoke of the incense, which went up with the prayers of the saints (devotees), ascended before God out of the Angel's hand. And the Angel took the censer and filled it with fire from the altar, and cast it into the earth: and there were voices, and peals of thunder and lightning and an earthquake. And the Angels who had the seven trumpets prepared themselves to give the trumpet-calls".[225]

As indicated above, these verses of Revelation relate to the opening of the seventh chakra centre, which incidentally corresponds to the sign of Leo the Lion, the domicile of the sun. This centre or chakra is directly linked to the pineal gland or the proverbial "third eye", which is said to be the focal point of the nerve system and the aura of the individual. When the forces of the aura and the nerve system realise an equilibrium in this seventh chakra or pineal gland centre, a great 'silence in the sky or heaven' (esoterically, the head, the brain or mind) prevails before the great changes take place within the mind (the sky) and body (the earth) of the individual; the calm before the storm, so to speak.[226]

During this mystic silence or meditation, each chakra that has been opened becomes fully awakened. Leo is said to be the fixed fire sign of the zodiac and thus the reference to the Christ 'fire of the altar' that was cast into the earth (the body), with tremendous purifying and internal effect, both psychic and physical. The Christ fire or flame of life flowing up and through the seven chakra centres makes the body vibrate (earthquake), and each chakra centre produces a vibrant sound, referred to as trumpet-calls.[227] Each trumpet-call or keynote of each chakra (from the base of the spine to the head) reflects a higher tone or vibration, which in real terms means that a higher state of consciousness is realised and certain sins (weaknesses and transgressions) overcome.[228]

The rest of Revelation, for those who have eyes to see, represents many permutations (in symbology and allegory) of the mystic drama of the true child of God (the true Israelite, initiate or devotee) realising oneness with Christ or Christ-consciousness: the true marriage on Earth of the Soul to the Immortal Christ Spirit; the overcoming of the epithumetic nature and carnal mind by the Christ mind, whereby the fullness of God's grace and love is made manifest here on Earth. One could go on and on about the esoteric meaning of Revelation as it relates to the initiate on the Path of Truth, but sufficient has been said. For those who want to pursue this further via the written word, two excellent books relating to the esoteric meaning of the Bible and other sacred writings are Volumes I and II of *The Hidden Wisdom in the Bible* by Geoffrey

Hodson. Obviously, there are many other outstanding works on the subject that the true initiate, the child of God, the Lover of Truth, will also find illuminating.

(3) The All-pervading Law of Love and a Few Other Immutable Laws of God[229]

In chapter 1 and the beginning of this chapter, we dealt with the fact that all is of Divine Spirit substance; that includes both visible and invisible substances. All life is of substance. "Faith", remember, is said to be "the substance of things hoped for, the evidence of things not seen". "Love" like "faith" is not just a word or an emotion, but is also of substance; it has a particular vibration and colour. It is the highest vibrating substance on planet Earth: the all-pervading, cohesive Spirit of the Universe. The love substance is referred to by some as 'the Ultimate Solvent' that dissolves all evil: it restores purity where there is impurity and balance where there is imbalance. Presently, for those of us that are television viewers, we see advertisements of a host of different fabric cleansers for the removal of different types of stains, be they caused by blood, rust, ink or whatever. In God's esoteric science, the quick vibrating love substance (a product of the Christ Spirit), is the cleanser for all stains (sins/transgressions) that adversely affect our mental, physical and spiritual well-being; it has a quickening effect on the substances of our minds and bodies. Love in action reflects the Soul's attunement and response to the Divine or Christ Spirit within.

For one to get to the root of how the Law of Love or love as a science works, the Law of Love must be understood to be one of God's esoteric, immutable, natural laws that was decreed from the very beginning by the Omniscient Mind of the All-Father as the working basis of all creation. Without such law, no manifestation could occur and nothing we perceive could exist. The purpose of God's laws, including His paramount Law of Love, is to progressively ensure the evolvement and upliftment of all creation; that is, despite the obstacles put up by man (by his ignorance) to thwart their operation. The motive behind those immutable laws must always be understood to be the preservation of life for attaining the ideal expression. With God, the All-Father, justice is always done: balance is always restored and love is always made manifest.

As we have indicated before, in God's perfect Creation all is vibratory and of substance. If we are to understand and live the love science (as Jesus the Christ taught), we must truly imbibe this; this is the bedrock of realising the (Christ) light of love within us and, by extension, in our lives. The low vibrating substances form the more crystallised, static or visible objects: gases, liquids and solids; whereas, other higher vibrations of substance, within a certain range of frequency, are designated as sound or light, as the case may be, and some may say, by extension, what we perceive as colours (which are sensations produced on the eyes by rays of light when resolved by prisms). As regards what we designate as sound, it should be noted that certain very high vibrating sounds vibrate beyond a frequency range that we usually can hear. We are therefore taught of the dog whistle that can be heard by a dog (with its keen sense of hearing), but not by the average person. Likewise, the colours above the colour vibration we designate as violet cannot be seen with the optic senses, but with the help of machines created by man, we perceive the ultraviolet rays and x-ray.

Likewise, it must be imbibed that the vibrations of the mind or thoughts, like radio waves or television signals, travel instantaneously hundreds of miles. It is interesting to note that man, emulating his Creator (the All-Father), creates; hence, he created, amongst many other things, the radio and the television. Remember that that is man, who has not yet realised his ideal, divine expression. Nevertheless, with a radio created by man, we can tune into different radio stations by attuning to the appropriate wavelength and frequency. Similarly, in that every thought is a vibration having a set frequency and wavelength, it is transmitted from the brain like a radio station. Further, the mind and (its 'telecommunications') the brain centre not only operates as a transmitter, but as a receiver par excellence. It is said that the mind is the most important instrument possessed by man (a Spirit-Soul in flesh) and is certainly a crucial instrument in the Law of Creation.

With the foregoing fixed in our hearts and minds, as we live our lives on God's Earth, we must seek to create harmonious, loving environments — starting with ourselves. Obviously, as indicated above, love being of substance, it has its own particular rate and range of vibration, altruistic love being the highest and most dynamic force (substance/vibration) on Earth. When one lives by this high-energy substance of pure, altruistic love, not carnal lust, which is also of substance, but of a vastly different vibration, one encircles himself or herself with the (high frequency) vibration substance of love. This is one's auric shield and highest form of protection. The more one transfers or exudes the love energy to others and things around him, the more one magnetises a never-ending flow of love from the Universal Source.

It may interest some to know that even the teachings of psychology accept that for every idea or thought, there is a corresponding vibration or movement of brain tissue, and to this may be added, an emission, like a transmitter, of the thought vibration. The Bible once again expounds an eternal law (Truth) when one reads: "as a man thinketh in his heart so is he". This represents the sum total of the vibration and frequency of that personality or individual. Hence, just like each radio station has a particular frequency in a wave band and transmits at a certain power, so too does each and every individual who walks this earth.

In light of this, one can therefore better understand the exhortation of Jesus the Christ/Yashua to "love your enemies". Many are puzzled by this precept of "love thy enemies". Others hypocritically mouth it, say they adhere to it and go around hating with gusto. Understanding the Law of Love, however (love being the highest vibrating substance), one is shielded from slower vibrating thoughts of hate directed to him or her, that is, if one lives by the Law or substance of Love.

As an illustration, if A and B hate each other insanely, whatever negative or deleterious thought processes that may be directed from A to B will only be received by B because B, by mutually hating A, is on the same wave-length and by the mental frequency attachment of hate, picks up A's negative thought vibrations. This occurs just as consistently and easily as one tunes in on a radio to a radio station of one's choice, be it 5:95 or 6:10 medium wave band or whatever. That is the law.

We must all remember that when pure love energy is sent forth by a person devoted to living by the Law of Love, it vibrates as a constructive and positive force that repels the slower vibrating thoughts emitted from a person filled with the emotion of anger and hate. In fact, those hateful thoughts are returned to the sender.[230] Hence, always remember to "love thy enemies"; you must pray for them as well. The Holy Scripture indicates: "love is the fulfilling of the Law".

Incidentally, the Holy Bible underscores the power of love by the use of the words "love" and "loved" over three hundred times.[231] If the teaching of Jesus the Christ/Yashua had to be expressed in one word, it would be "love". All wise men, seers, sages, spiritual teachers, prophets and avatars of all cultures have exhorted and emphasised the principle of love. In every major religion of the world the words reflecting 'love in action' are expressed in some permutation of the following words: "Do unto others as you would have them do unto you".[232] Always judge your thoughts and deeds by the query: "Is it from the heart?" Remember, God judges us from the heart; the root-cause of the action is in the heart. The illumined Master Sri Aurobindo indicates that love is "the secret of secrets, the mystery of mysteries", and "(t)here is nothing which is beyond the reach of the God-lover or denied to him".[233] You are therefore advised: "love God with all your heart, soul, mind and strength," and you are assured all the peace, happiness and success you desire. Get your priorities right.

Before moving on to the final subheading of this chapter, to wit, "Sex, the Proverbial Serpent and Spiritual Development", we will deal with two other basic, but important, immutable laws or principles that should be imbibed, if we are to realise the fullness of

God's grace as we tread the path of life. The first is "the Law of Periodicity" and the other is "the Law of Cause and Effect", or "As you sow so shall you reap".

It is taught that God's Natural Law of Periodicity causes a thought or an act to be repeated within a determinate time. The initial intensity with which the thought was projected or the act performed determines the time in which the tendency to repeat itself will manifest (occur). The Law of Periodicity is crucial in the formation of good or bad habits; and therefore, by extension, is important in overcoming bad habits and replacing them with good habits. Here is a simple illustration of the Law of Periodicity, also known as the Law of Periodical Return. If you were to look at an electric light bulb for a few seconds then close your eyes you will notice there is a mental vibration or picture of the light, which is pulsating, rhythmic fashion (appearing and disappearing), growing dimmer with each pulsating appearance, until it fades away entirely.[234]

The above is an example "of the law of periodicity and every thought, ... feeling and ... tendency will" likewise "repeat itself at given periods of time according to the intensity of the initial impulse that gave it birth".[235] Recognising this law, if you observe the exact time your bad habits repeat themselves, you will be prepared to overcome them with greater success. For example, if you think you have a problem and in the privacy of your own room you worry intensely about this 'supposed problem' at six (6) o'clock this evening, rest assured, you can be watching a netball or football match tomorrow evening, and at roughly six (6) o'clock the thought process in relation to that 'supposed problem' will return to you. If you are not aware of this law, you will pick up the thought process and, again, seemingly helplessly repeat it. By the following day and the days after, you have more and more a binding date with that worrisome thought process, which in extreme cases can become an obsession culminating in insanity. Knowing the law, however, you can cut the initial thought process in the bud, replacing the worrisome thought or visualisation of failure, ill-health, sadness, defeat and death with an opposite visualisation and thought process of success, vibrant health, happiness, victory and (abundant) life everlasting.[236]

The other simple but important law that we must deal with is "as you sow so shall you reap", or the Law of "Cause and Effect". Every thought, word and deed to a greater or lesser extent, has its resultant effect. It is like throwing a stone into a pond. From the central point (where the stone entered the water), ripples will go out, causing a reaction on any object floating on the surface. Likewise, you will observe that when the ripples reach the retaining wall of the pond, ripples will also be set in motion, returning to the centre of the pond where the initial vibrating impulse began, where the stone had entered the water. In light of this and accepting that all life is of substance in vibration and that each thought, word or action will bring a natural reaction, I am of the view that we should be all overjoyed that such is God's law and that it is invariable. Because the question may be asked: which farmer would plant a pumpkin seed and expect a watermelon, or plant a mango seed and expect a pear tree? A farmer does not plant one crop and expect another; likewise, in human endeavour plant good seeds in the Mind Spirit Substance Realm with faith and reap God's harvest with certainty. Remember that "faith is the substance of things hoped for, the evidence of things not seen". Hence, we should glorify in the immutable law that whatever we sow into the formative God substances brings back in the physical realm that which was sown in it. If you want only that which is good, then sow only that which is good. Remember always, therefore: "that which is sown is that which comes up". Such is God's law.

(4) Sex, the Proverbial Serpent and Spiritual Development[237]

When relating our minds to the topic of spiritual development, most of us shy away from seriously dealing with 'sex' and the 'proverbial serpent'. But the truth is: sex, the proverbial serpent and spiritual development are all inextricably intertwined. Some people, like the proverbial ostrich, may want to bury their heads in the sand. However, if you are serious about realising Truth you must not run away from any aspect of it that may not appeal to you because it either conflicts with your sex life (your 'macho' or 'sexy' image), or because propagating it may not make you popular.

It should be noticed that most of today's established religions encourage sexual purity; fornication or sex outside of marriage is usually discouraged and frowned upon. Most religions demand, or at least expect, chastity from their religious leaders, holy men and women, pastors, ministers or priests. Hence, even within the framework of today's religious system, the need for sexual purity, and in some instances celibacy, is realised. Whether pastors, religious leaders, priests and people generally are successful in realising this purity is another matter; however, be assured that all that realise this purity in their lives will indeed be blessed. In the Bible it is written: "Blessed are the pure in heart, for they shall see God",[238] and "to the pure all things are possible".[239]

Although sex may be the foremost subject in the hearts and minds of many people, it still remains a 'taboo subject'; you usually have to deal with it carefully (like some fragile article), or not at all, if you don't want to offend some people. The following paragraphs present certain facts about 'sex, the proverbial serpent and spiritual development' that may or may not offend some people but, as some would say: "Truth is Truth", and it should not be an offence.

The act of sex between a man and a woman is a physical expression of the creative life force inherent within them. Some would say sex is the culmination, with orgasm, of physical love-making.[240] As indicated earlier,[241] in many cultures the serpent represents what in esoteric Christianity is referred to as the Christ Fire or Light, the Christ serpentine force or the Flame of Life in the temple of flesh. In Yoga and Eastern philosophy it is referred to as the 'kundalini', represented by a coiled serpent at the base of the spine. It should also be observed that the bony frame of the spine (running from the base of the skull to the tailbone or coccyx) that encases the spinal chord looks very much like a 'bony' serpent.[242]

In the Kabalistic doctrine, which represents the esoteric wisdom of the Hebrews, the tree of life is a symbol of the entire macrocosm, the Universe, and the microcosm, man; in Hindu yoga, the relationship of the Universe and man. To an initiate on the Path of Truth and Self-realisation, the proverbial serpent, entwined around the tree, is represented within man by the human spine and the positive (ida) and negative (pingala) currents of electro-magnetic energy flowing up and down on either side of the spine (more specifically, the central Sushumna coupled with the kundalini). As indicated earlier in this chapter, the same symbolism is demonstrated in Solomon's temple.[243]

Throughout history, the serpent has always represented the duality of wisdom (Perfect knowledge) and sexuality. For example, readers of the Bible should observe references to the two different types of serpents in the story of the children of Israel in the wilderness with their great guide and leader Moses. One was "the fiery serpent" that the children of Israel were supposedly bitten by; that one caused death. Then there was the brass serpent, which God directed Moses to hang from a pole in the centre of the camp site; this one brought health and life to all those that were bitten by the fiery serpent. This duality as regards serpents is also reflected when Moses confronted Pharaoh in Egypt and the good serpents of Moses destroyed the bad or evil serpents of Pharaoh's high priests.

With the foregoing in mind, man, as a miniature creation of God, with the creative force inherent in his divine nature, participates in the creation of life at a physical level. This he presently does by using this creative force or potentiality for physical ends whereby that force flows downward into the generative organs. In this form the creative force is known as sexual energy, which because of our material and carnal emphasis, creates a constant urge for sexual release through sex. From this sexual release children are born (many times out of lustful unions that had nothing to do with procreation or love), and man lives by the sweat of his brow to support his offspring. However, on the other hand, man may sublimate this force by directing this creative, divine energy or force upward to the brain, granting the incarnate Soul in flesh divine attunement, physical regeneration, and wisdom — the Mystic Marriage with his Christ Spirit within.

It should be remembered that Paul of the Bible advised his followers that if they could not be like him, that is, celibate, then they should get married and control their lust with their spouse. In other words, two initiates on the path of life (male and female, who still have carnal desires or lust in them), joined in 'holy matrimony', endeavouring together to realise the Christ Spirit or divinity within themselves. This process can be facilitated by practising sex magic (whereby the married couple make love and have sex without spasm or ejaculation), which causes regeneration, as distinct from normal sex (whereby spasm and ejaculation occurs), which results in generation (and in time, if the chrism or sap of the body is wasted excessively, to degeneration and death). The Christ Spirit (the Bridegroom within the body-temple) is the ultimate grace (gift) of God to each and every one of us — a gift we must all willingly accept if we are to overcome this earth. For those who have eyes to see, let them see: the ceremony of marriage (in a church or a court) between a man and a woman is an exoteric religious ritual (with serious legal implications) representing a deeper spiritual truth: the esoteric marriage that must take place within each one of us. This will be elaborated on further at the conclusion of this chapter.

Accepting, therefore, as reflected above, that the sex force is the said life force of God within us, and that ultimately — as taught by the ancient Masters — without celibacy or sex magic (which is sex without spasm or ejaculation) higher spiritual attainments are quite impossible,[244] we shall now briefly examine the realities of how people relate to sex in today's society.

At this point in man's history, most people will agree that man has reached his decadent best. Sodom and Gomorah were just cities; but today the whole world has, if anything, outstripped the city of Sodom. With our advancements in science and technology, we can pervert ourselves much more efficiently and thoroughly. Selling a chocolate or candy bar on television is usually nothing short of sugar-coated seduction, and most so-called love song videos are 'sex simulations'. Man's abuse of the creative (sexual) force and his sex function has made sex 'deadly': "AIDS" has taken root throughout the world and spread its tentacles like a white plague.

God bless the young people who live in the sewer of our times, because instead of being taught about the value of purity and the truth about celibacy — the power of virtue and the necessity of sound morals — they are being taught about 'safe sex'! What is that? How to put on a condom properly and what condoms are best! Do they tell those young children how to deal with the fact — after a bout of sweat-filled sex — that this so-called 'life-saving' condom worn by the male 'partner' has during coitus, to their dismay, burst (as it does quite often), or that no condom (regardless of brand) is fool-proof to the AIDS virus? We must realise that if we pervert our youth we destroy ourselves. Nothing weakens a people and destroys whole societies, a nation and a world like the abuse and perversion of the sexual or creative force. The creative force within man is a divine force, and must not be abused. In these times, however, carnality thrives and is doing a booming business.

Having said the above, on a more mundane or down-to-earth level, sex can and does play an integral part in the lives of most men and women. In the strict religious sense, this sexual experience should take place during marriage — hence, the statement of Paul referred to above. In the average marriage, as long as the couples are fairly healthy, a fair amount of normal sex is indulged in. This is not only accepted by most people as legitimate indulgence, but is expected behaviour — a matrimonial right, so to speak, commencing with the obligation to consummate the marriage. Despite our passion for sex and our need to be macho (in the case of men) or sexy (in the case of women), we must observe that even the common dog, as well as most other animals, indulges in sex only when procreation is possible. Hence, it is clear that either the sex force and fluids should be used for generation or for regeneration, whereby the seed is retained and the Golden Child or Christ Spirit is consciously realised in the body-temple.

However, before we have reached the level of understanding, control and illumination, whereby one does not need or desire to have sex, sex as a physical and pleasurable act can be positive between two people in love. It is said that those who have not purified their blood[245] and their thoughts[246] will find it difficult, if not impossible, to practice celibacy or sex magic. They may burn up mentally with carnal desires racing through their minds; their nervous system may deteriorate from the sexual tension (including spasm and ejaculation) and anxiety. Hence, for those Souls (which include most of us) the occasional release of sexual tension (including spasm and ejaculation) may be necessary and pleasurable.

The truth is, most people cannot at this juncture relate to celibacy or sex magic; that is just too much to ask of them. Despite this, normal sex is usually still a problem for them and represents an area of tension and frustration in their lives. Many men frustrate women and vice versa by their total lack of understanding and sensitivity to each other. Both parties should have foremost in their minds the feeling of love, pleasure, harmony and completeness that they desire for their companion and lover. Their bodies should be clean and healthy so that both parties can enjoy each other to the fullest; as some would say, all parts of one's body are capable of high sexual arousal and pleasure, if dealt with with love and sensitivity.

Men who want to be good lovers should always remember that generally women take longer than men to reach their climax, so women need to be nurtured and aroused with embraces, kisses and foreplay. All men who genuinely desire to please their mates should learn to breathe deeply, rhythmically and completely, as taught earlier in this chapter.‡ Having mastered the complete breath, during the act of sex a man must breathe rhythmically and slowly through his nose (not through the mouth as many do as they pant to uncontrolled orgasm). If he consciously breathes rhythmically through his nostrils, as advised, his ability to 'ride and stay in the bucking saddle of love' will increase dramatically. This improvement will not only be to his satisfaction but to the complete satisfaction and undying gratification of his mate.[247]

Having said the above, we must not digress too far from the underlying reality that every orgasm dissipates tremendous vital energy and life force. The French traditionally refer quite rightly to "orgasm" as "petit mort"; this reflects a profound esoteric truth. Some authorities indicate, however, that when a man and a woman who eat nutritious, wholesome food occasionally engage in sexual intercourse, this does not destroy them, but on the contrary, may keep them harmonious and together, although it would be folly to believe that such indulgence does not also extract its toll. On the other hand, people who are undernourished that indulge in excessive sexual activity find themselves considerably weakened in mind and body. That they are aware of it or not, their mental and physical capacity declines and ill health and death follows. Many a materialist cynic would say that disease and death are certain regardless, so let us have sex wantonly, drink and make merry because tomorrow you die anyway. That is the guidance and ensnarement of Sodom.[248]

The above guidance of Sodom, it must be emphasised, is contrary to what has been taught and demonstrated by Jesus the Christ and the great Spiritual Masters. Further, in harmony with Christ's teachings on overcoming death, some scientific authorities of today indicate that there is no real reason for the physical body of a human being to die, in that as long as the blood is kept healthy the body continuously renews itself. Those authorities base their conclusions on a material science (biochemical standpoint) that in no way takes cognisance of the underlying spiritual laws as well as the other more subtle bodies of man — such as the Vital or Etheric (electro-magnetic) body and the Astral or Desire body — that interpenetrate and influence greatly the health of the dense (biochemical), physical body.

_____

‡ See text immediately following n. 62.

Although not generally taught and emphasised by the exoteric religious teachings of today, esoteric wisdom throughout the ages teaches that the sublimation and transmutation of the life (sex) force brings about the regeneration of the body and the mental faculties, thereby allowing the incarnate Spirit-Soul to eventually manifest as God planned it. This regeneration can be realised as indicated before through celibacy or by a married couple practising sex magic, because both methods transmute the sex force by assimilating it within the temple without spilling or wasting the holy chrism or seed. The sex force and sap of the physical body should be used either for generation or for regeneration.

At a basic biochemical or physical level, esoteric law teaches that the "golden oil"[249] or "oil"[250] within the body-temple — also known as Chrism or the Christ substance in man — flows from the head (the heavenly sphere in man), more specifically, from the thalamus (the interior region of the brain where the sensory nerves begin) down the spine to the solar plexus (esoterically called "Bethlehem" or "the house of bread"). Therefore, to the initiate cum Master, Christ or Chrism comes down from heaven (the head) to be born in Bethlehem (the solar plexus).[251] Hence, when one reads that "Our Lord (golden oil, Chrism) was crucified in Egypt" (the lower body or generative organs), this refers to the consumption of the golden oil or life force in sexual activity.[252] The secret of life, which most people do not want to hear, is that when man subdues or crucifies his lower self and realises the virtue of sex magic or celibacy for a seven-year period, the holy Chrism or golden oil no longer flows downwards into the reproductive organs (Egypt) but flows back up from the solar plexus to the brain, where it drips back into the optic thalamus, thereby activating the pituitary and pineal glands, which opens the Inner or Central Eye of the temple of God.[253] When that spiritual eye is opened, "the sun shall be no more thy light by day; neither for brightness shall the moon give light unto thee: but the Lord shall be unto thee an everlasting light and thy God thy glory".[254]

At that juncture the three-fold body (the Desire, Etheric and Physical) will be in perfect harmony with the three-fold Soul (the Emotional, Intellectual and Conscious), both of which will be in total harmony and submission to the three-fold Christ Spirit (the Human, Life and Divine). Esoterically, the loving, willing submission of the Bride (the three-fold Soul) to the Bridegroom (the three-fold Christ Spirit) is the Mystic Marriage that must take place here on Earth in the temple of flesh. When this occurs, the three-fold body (the temple) is transmuted from mortality to immortality. From that moment onwards, that son or daughter of God has overcome this Earth, having graduated with excellence. Death thereafter loses its sting and that Spirit-Soul may materialise himself or herself on Earth at will without passing through the womb of a woman. This feat is achieved by these illumined Spirit-Souls' ability to magnetise the molecular structure necessary to be seen and touched; these sons and daughters are then said to be in this world but not of this world. Those sons and daughters of God (having fully realised with all the fullness of their consciousness that they are children of the All-Father) shall forevermore have access to all the other Rooms, Realms or Mansions of the All-Father's House or Creation.

Conclusion

In conclusion, with the above reality of your true potential permeating your being, the following should be considered as you live the Will and the Way:

"... the kingdom of God is within you".[255]

"Know ye not that ye are the temple of God, and that the Spirit of God dwelleth in you? If any man defile the temple of God, him shall God destroy; for the temple of God is holy, which temple ye are".[256]

"It is reported commonly that there is fornication among you...."[257]

"Flee fornication ... he that committeth fornication sinneth against his own body. What? know ye not that your body is the temple of the Holy Ghost which is in you, which ye have of God...?"[258]

"Know ye not that the unrighteous shall not inherit the kingdom of God? Be not deceived: neither fornicators, nor idolaters, nor adulterers, nor effeminate, nor abusers of themselves with mankind. Nor thieves, nor covetous, nor drunkards, nor revilers, nor extortioners, shall inherit the kingdom of God".[259]

"For when ye were servants of sin, ... what fruit had ye then in those things whereof ye are now ashamed? For the end of those things is death. But now being made free from sin, and become servants to God, ye have your fruit unto holiness, and the end everlasting life".[260]

"For if ye live after the flesh, ye shall die: but if ye through the Spirit do mortify the deeds of the body, ye shall live".[261]

"Have I any pleasure at all that the wicked should die? saith the Lord God: and not that he should return from his ways, and live?"[262]

"Cast away from you all your transgressions, whereby ye have transgressed; and make you a new heart and a new spirit: for why will ye die...?"[263]

"For I have no pleasure in the death of him that dieth, saith the Lord God: wherefore turn yourselves, and live ye".[264]

"... As I live, saith the lord, I have no pleasure in the death of the wicked; but that the wicked turn from his way and live: turn ye ... from your evil ways; for why will ye die...?"[265]

"Your fathers did eat manna in the wilderness, and are dead. This is the bread which cometh down from heaven: that a man may eat thereof, and not die. I am the living bread which came down from heaven; if any man eat of this bread, he shall live for ever...."[266]

"And as Moses lifted up the serpent in the wilderness, even so must the Son of man be lifted up: That whosoever believeth in him shall not perish, but have eternal life".[267]

"Verily, verily, I say unto you, If a man keep my saying, he shall never see death".[268]

"For as many as are led by the Spirit of God, they are the sons (and daughters) of God".[269]

Finally, always remember: Love is the Spirit of God in action. Live love by using your talents to serve others. Always do what you perceive in your heart to be the right and loving thing to do in any given situation. Do this with detachment and you are assured an Eternal Blessing of Universal Love, power, peace and success. And so it is.

CHAPTER 3

BEYOND THE VEIL OF HISTORY

To the initiate on the Path of Truth: The veil cannot be lifted unless you approach with clean hands and a pure, contrite heart. "And behold, the veil of the temple was rent in twain from the top to the bottom...." Matt. 27:51.

<u>Introduction</u>

The present is just an instant, but the past is a vast eternity, much more so than most of us closeted mortals believe, or would like to believe. The spirit of Truth is most potent upon the earth, and the wax of ignorance that impedes our vision of history melts away with the heat of historical reality. All we are actively conscious of presently can be said to be already in the past and therefore part of history.

That a child learns that it is unwise to touch a boiling kettle by the excruciating pain received by the initial or subsequent experience is exemplified, multiplied and amplified by the experiences of life's struggles. The experiences gradually become more subtle and complex; hence, our illusions and arrogance, until the pain of the experience transcends the pleasure to be derived.

Indeed, like the child mentioned above, we learn from our past, from our experience. Experience is a phenomenal teacher, the true source of education. Wise action may be said therefore to be based on the nuggets of truth that have been granted to us by our struggles and experiences in life.

Each experience in our lives may seem distinct and complete in itself, but each experience should be seen as a cohesive continuity, as a link in a chain. And like a chain, it is important that the connection and continuity of the links be maintained. That we are aware of it or not, the chain of events, and hence the experiences of life, are all linked by the underlying esoteric Law of 'Cause and Effect'. It is therefore important for man to be consciously aware of and learn from his past experiences or history, that is, if he is to make the most of his present and future experiences and realise his full potential.

History has been referred to as the memory of human group experience. To the extent that it is forgotten, ignored or hidden, for whatever reason, we lose some of our humanity and culture. Without history, we have no knowledge of who we are or how we came to be. We become like people who have lost their memory, blindly groping in the dark to find their identity.

History is a source of great power generated by the inspired, past aspirations and accomplishments of our forefathers who struggled to realise peace, happiness and success on Earth.

History is a gift to all of us who are yearning to find self, yearning to know self, and searching for self-identity and Self-realisation. All genuine soul-searchers and initiates on the Path of Truth need to know their history. It has been said that a people's realisation of God can be equated to the evolvement and deification of their culture. History allows those of us who take cognisance of it to see, in retrospect, right and wrong, wisdom and error. It gives us the necessary understanding to desire to improve ourselves so as to realise the fullness of God's grace, which (ultimately) is divinity.

History is the record of experience, and a people must know their history if they are to begin to understand themselves and the world of which they are humble inhabitants. Also, by knowing our history we may live within the protective shield of hard-earned experience and wisdom.

From the book, *Destruction of Black Civilization*, by Chancellor Williams, an extract of a Sumer legend reads as follows: "What became of the black people of Sumer?" the traveller asked the old man. "For ancient records show that the people of Sumer were black. What happened to them?" "Ah!" the old man sighed, "they lost their history, so they died".

The Materialisation of the Heavens and the Earth

In our search, therefore, beyond the veil of history, we start at the very beginning when God, exercising His attributes of Will, Wisdom and Activity, created the Heavens and the Earth. "... (T)he earth was without form, and void".[1]

God, who is Alpha and Omega, Supreme and Divine, the Omniscient Force and Emanator of all forces, put forth His consciousness and vibrational potentiality into the vast essence of His Being and by the modality of the Logos, the vibration of the Word, created as the heat of fire, the moisture of water and the seed of all existence the firmament in the midst of the waters. Hence, perceivers of Truth, the spoken word is but a vibration. All being is vibratory and the whole world of form is but spirit substance in vibration at certain established rates; the slower the vibration, the more crystallised the manifestation. This esoteric understanding of life, which is of paramount importance to the initiate on the Path of Truth, has been thoroughly dealt with in chapter 2.

So we read: "In the beginning was the Word, and the Word was with God and the Word was God";[2] "And God made the firmament, and divided the waters which were under the firmament from the waters which were above the firmament.... And God called the firmament Heaven.... And God said, Let the waters under the heaven be gathered together unto one place, and let the dry land appear.... And God called the dry land Earth; and the gathering together of the waters called he Seas: and God saw that it was good".[3]

The Garden of Eden

It should be noted that in a practical sense, in those remote days of antiquity the whole earth was one plot of land, the plantation of God, because the ocean had not yet separated the landmass into the continents as we know them presently.[4] The continents of America (North and South), Europe and Africa were all fitted together in conjunction with a huge landmass referred to by the ancients as the land of Mu.

The land of Mu was later named by scientists the land of Lemuria. Initially, the land of Lemuria occupied a large portion of today's Pacific Ocean and lapped over into Asia and Africa.[5] A portion of this landmass, which was one with Northeast Africa, was the only habitable land sufficiently above water to have any considerable degree of vegetation. Hence, we learn that the Absolute Omniscient Light, Creator of the Universe, created a resplendent garden called Eden: a heavenly park of luxuriant green and gushing streams reminiscent of the beautiful Caribbean island, Dominica, but far more beautiful and breathtakingly vast in comparison. In all its pristine virgin purity, Mother Nature, whom we must love and harmonise with, was then manifest in one harmony with the Spirit of the Heavenly Father.

Thus, in the Holy Bible we read: "And a river went out of Eden to water the garden; and from thence it was parted, and became into four heads. The name of the first is Pishon: that is it which compasseth the whole land of Havilah, where there is gold.... And the name of the second river is Gishon: the same is it that compasseth the whole land of Ethiopia. And the name of the third river is Tigris: that is it which goeth toward the east of Assyria. And the fourth river is Euphrates".[6] It should be noted that Gen. 10:7 tells us quite clearly that "Havilah" was a son of Kush (also spelt Cush); and the ancient people of Kush (the Kushites) have always been the African people of Northeast Africa. Incidentally, the land of Kush was subsequently referred to by the Greeks as "Aethiops" and later "Aethiopia" or "Ethiopia".[7] Hence, the Bible clearly reflects that the first two rivers of the Garden of Eden began in the heart of Northeast Africa[8] and extended to the boundaries of "the fertile crescent" where the two other ancient rivers flowed. The fertile crescent area later became known as Mesopotamia.[9]

In keeping with the above, we read in the book *Ancient Egypt: The Light of the World*, a translation from the Egyptian scriptures by Gerald Massey: "The Egyptian record when read, will tell us plainly that the human birthplace was a land of the Papyrus reed at the horn of the Earth, that is the Equator, from whence the sacred river ran, the Valley of the Nile, with plenty. The Gulf of Aden at the east coast of Africa is also a traditional name somewhat similar to Eden, the name of Adam's garden". To this may be added, the entire area that is (in recent history) referred to as the Middle East,[10] which traditionally was considered part of Northeast Africa.

Dr. A. Herman, a German scientist is quoted by Colonel A. Brighane in his volume, *The Shadow of Atlantis*, page 206, as having come to the conclusion that river Gishon was nothing else than the Nile and that the site of Eden should be sought in Abyssinia, Ethiopia or Aethiopia.

In the book *The African Origin of Civilization: Myth or Reality*, by Cheikh Anta Diop, we read at page 266 that: "the most distinguished pre-historians and anthropologists nowadays — Abbe Breuil, Professor Arambourg, Dr. Leakey" and others — "consider Africa the cradle of humanity".

Original Man: First Adam

Having produced immutable Natural Laws, the Heavens and the Earth and the Garden of Eden, the Lord God, Father of the Universe, created man. "God created man in his own image, in the image of God created he him; male and female created he them".[11] As biblical history relates, the first man Adam and woman Eve were created out of the elements of our Earthly Mother and the cohesive Spirit of the Heavenly Father. The Eternal Spirit of the Heavenly Father coupled with the internal elements of the Earthly Mother, and brought forth living breathing beings: "And the Lord God formed man of the dust of the ground and breathed into his nostrils the breath of life; and man became a living soul".[12] "And the Lord God took the man, and put him into the garden of Eden to dress and keep it".[13]

Dr. Churchward, a famous English anthropologist, agrees with Gerald Massey's findings referred to earlier, as to the origin of the first race of man when he writes: "From studies I have made during many years, I am fully convinced that ... the human race did not originate in ... any other part of the world but in Africa".

Over the years, the flame of Truth has been further enhanced by the findings of the son of an English missionary, Professor Louis Leakey. This world-renowned archaeologist endorsed that Africa is the Cradle of Mankind. Professor Leakey "and Dr. Donald Johnson of Case Western Reserve University in Cleveland and Curator of Physical Anthropology at the Cleveland Museum of Natural History, held an electrifying press conference at the National Geographic Society to disclose the discoveries of 3-million-year-old human hands and a million-and-a-half year-old human skull in the fossil rich sediments of Eastern Africa".[14]

In *Fossil Men*, by Marcellin Boule and Henri Vallois, translated into English by Michael Bullock, archaeological findings were compared, considered and aptly summarised, when we read: "On the strength of evidence, we must recognise in all objectivity, that the first Homo Sapiens were 'Negroid' and that the other races, white and yellow, appeared later ... the human remains found up to now in East Africa, do not differ from the present inhabitants of that country or neighbouring countries".[15] Today's Masai is considered as one of the most authentic representative types.[16]

It is noteworthy that in 1988 scientists of another discipline, namely geneticists, claim to have found humanity's common ancestor: a woman who lived thousands of years ago and left resilient genes that are carried by all humanity.

"The scientists' Eve ... was likely a dark-haired, black-skinned woman". She was very fruitful, "if that is measured by success in propagating a certain set of genes. Hers seems to be in all humans living today: 5 billion blood relatives".[17]

"Versions of the Adam and Eve story ... have been told in cultures from the Mediterranean to the Pacific to the Americas". All the stories are based on the same assumption as the scientists: "that at some point we all share an ancestor ... possibly one from the time when modern humans arose".[18]

These new breed anthropologists trained in molecular biology, "looked at an assortment of genes and picked up a trail of DNA that led them to a single woman from whom we are all descended. Most evidence so far indicates that Eve lived in Sub-Saharan Africa".[19] "The evolution from archaic to modern homo sapiens seems to have occurred in only one place, Eve's family". As time elapsed, "a group of her progeny left their homeland endowed apparently with some special advantage over every tribe of early humans they encountered. As they fanned out, Eve's descendants replaced the locals, eventually settling the entire world".[20]

Some archaeologists referred to by some as "stones and bones" anthropologists accept this interpretation of the genetic evidence. However, others think, although they agree that the first Homo sapiens were born in Africa, that our common ancestors lived much "further in the past at least a million years ago, because that was when humans first left Africa and began spreading out over the world, presumably evolving separately into the modern races".[21]

Stephen Gould, Harvard palaeontologist and essayist, is quoted in the *Newsweek* article "The Search for Adam and Eve", as follows: "This makes us realise that all human beings, despite differences in external appearance, are really members of a single entity.... There is a kind of biological brotherhood that's much more profound than we ever realized".[22]

This brotherhood of scientists is confident that the "DNA Tree began in Africa (Eden), and then at some point a group of Africans (People of Eden) emigrated, splitting off to form a second branch of DNA and carrying it to the rest of the world".[23] It should be noted that in harmony with W. S. Cerve in his book *Lemuria*, which is referred to later,[24] it is stated in the *Newsweek* article aforementioned that "skin colouring, for instance, is a minor adaptation to climate.... It takes only a few thousand years of evolution for skin colour to change".[25]

In the book, *Redemption of Africa and Black Religion*, by Saint Claire Drake, page 57, we read of Edward Wilmott Blyden, a brilliant Black scholar who came to the forefront in the 1870's and 80's. He indicates from his research into Ethiopia's glorious past that in the earliest traditions of nearly all the more civilised nations of antiquity, the name of this distant people, the Ethiopians, is found. The annuls of the Egyptian priests were full of them; so too the nations of inner Asia on the Euphrates and Tigris.... When the Greeks scarcely knew Italy and Sicily by name, the Ethiopian was celebrated in verses of their poets as "the most just of men, the favorites of the gods".

That the ancients thought of the Ethiopians as having superior virtue is further elucidated on page 58 of Drake's *Redemption of Africa and Black Religion* by a quotation from Homer which reads: "The sire of gods and ... the ethereal train, on the warm limits of the furthest main, nor mix mortals nor disdain to grace, the feast of Ethiopia's blameless race".

Blyden felt that the conclusion from his researches showed that the ancients seemed to regard the fear and love of God as the peculiar gift of the darker races, stating that in the version of the Chaldean Genesis as given by George Smith, the following passage occurs: "The word of the Lord will never fail in the mouth of the dark races whom He has made".

From the book *Crucial Insights into African History*, on page 79, we read an enlightening quotation of Aeschylos the Greek dramatist, who makes the point clear when in *Prometheus Bound* he writes the following injunction: "After thou shall come to a far land, a dark-skinned race that dwells beside the fountains of the sun, whence flows the river Aethiops: follow its banks until thou comest to the steep down slope where from the bibline mountains Nilus Old pours the sweet waters of His holy stream".[26]

Herodotus, the Greek historian, in his book *The Histories* wrote: "The Colchians, Ethiopians and Egyptians have thick lips, broad noses, woolly hair and they are burnt of skin".[27] Hence, the verse, "Can the Ethiopian change his skin or the leopard its spots?" in Jer. 13:23; remembering that none other than Yashua or Jesus the Christ said, "the children of Israel are like Ethiopians among the people...."[28]

The Northeast Africans are again referred to in Isaiah 18 when we read: "Ethiopia, ah land of whirring wings, which is beyond the rivers of Ethiopia, which sends ambassadors by the Nile in vessels of papyrus upon the waters ... a nation tall and smooth, to a people feared near and far, a nation mighty and conquering whose land the rivers divide".

That the human race must have been born in the upper Nile area of Ethiopia,[29] where the two causes of life, heat and humidity, are ever present and where, before ordinary calculations of history, a social organisation appears fully structured with its religion, laws and institutions, is further authenticated in La Cherubine's *Nubi Paris: Collection L'Universe* (1847), pages 2-3.

In *The African Origin of Civilization*, at pages 281-282, the following passage from Diodirus of Sicily is quoted: "The Ethiopians call themselves the first of all men and cite proofs they consider evident. It is generally agreed, that born in a country and not having come from elsewhere, they must be judged indigenous. It is likely that located directly under the course of the sun, they sprang from the earth before other men. For if the heat of the sun combining with the humidity of the soil produces life, those sites nearest the equator, must have produced living beings earlier than any others".[30] Hence, Ethiopia (that is, the whole of Northeast Africa, in that Northeast Africa was referred to by some as "Ethiopia" in times past) and today's Middle East was, in the beginning, the most accommodating area of the plantation of God to cradle original humanity; original humanity, it must be remembered, that was created in the image and likeness of God.[31]

Professor Jerome Dowd, in *Negro Races*, Volume 3 at page 288, writes as follows: "The connection between palaeolithic man and the Negro is very apparent. The African Negro seems to be the survival of the first inhabitants of the earth. The palaeolithic man who remains in Africa may have there developed a dark skin and woolly hair, while those who had migrated North and East may have developed in transit the Caucasian and Mongolian".

With the foregoing in mind, before dealing with the land of Lemuria, it should be mentioned that there is also what can be referred to as an accommodating school of thought that propagates the idea that there were many Adams, so to speak; one for every race. For example: a black Adam and his family of people with pigmentation to deal with the hot equatorial sun in Africa; a red Adam and his people to harmonise with the predominantly red soil of Atlantis; a brown Adam and his people to harmonise with the windswept, undulating land of Lemuria in the Pacific; a yellow Adam and his people to harmonise with the yellowish soil of the Orient; and a white Adam and his people to harmonise with the environment of Europe, where winter is prevalent and little pigmentation is necessary.[32]

Lemuria or the Land of Mu

As indicated before, what was referred to as the land of Mu lapped over and was part of the continents of Asia and Africa. At this juncture the whole of Europe, as well as North and South America, were either submerged or swampland and therefore totally uninhabitable. Certain parts of the present continents of Asia and Africa (outside of the Garden of Eden area) were also purported to be, to some extent, swamp lands. Hence, it is posited by some authorities that this ancient continent of Mu, which is now called

Lemuria, could share the honour with Northeast Africa and Asia Minor (the Garden of Eden) as the cradle of the human race.

Even if the above honour is bestowed on Lemuria, it must be realised that Lemuria was populated from the original people of the Garden of Eden, that is, the indigenous people of Northeast Africa and Asia Minor, who lived in the area between the river Nile (Gishon) and the Tigris and Euphrates rivers. In all ancient records and among all cultures and tribes of people, it should be noted that there is a trace of the same traditional story of the creation of man in the Garden of Eden just like the Genesis story of the Bible. This is so because all the traditional creation stories, including those of the ancient Babylonians, Assyrians, Chaldeans and Hebrews, are all based on the most ancient, original: the creation story of the Northeast Africans. For a masterful presentation on this, one should read Gerald Massey's *Ancient Egypt: The Light of the World*, Volume 1-B, pages 398-469.

For one hundred thousand years or more, the ancient continent of Lemuria (which was originally one with Northeast Africa, Asia, the Pacific Islands and Australia) rocked the early born of many tribes that descended from the earliest humans. It should be noted, however, that Northeast Africa and Asia Minor at the outset were the driest and most habitable portion of this vast continent or estate of God called Lemuria. Thus, the old biblical story representing the ancient traditions of the history of man is correct when it indicates that God created man in the Garden of A/Eden after having created the other life forms or creatures over whom he was to have dominion. This in no way negates the divine evolutionary process of God's magnificent Creation; an ordained process from the inception of Creation.

Man developed to great heights over a period of millions of years on the now separated continent of Lemuria, as over time great seismological magnetic waves, moving in an east to west circuit, had brought about vast changes on the surface and below the surface of the land and waters of this earth, leaving the continent of Mu, Lemuria, a smaller continent located entirely in the Pacific Ocean. The landmass called Lemuria was now therefore a separated continent from Africa and Asia. Despite this, however, the still existing birthplace of man, Africa and Asia Minor, which was then inhabited by Black people, still cradled in its loving arms the first children of divine heritage, along with the people of the now separated land of Mu or Lemuria.

These children of divine heritage, at this time in history, were well aware of and naturally subscribed to the law of opposites and were in harmony with the creative force of the Absolute One, the All-Father. Those Divine Spirit-Souls, freshly incarnated in temples of human flesh, lived in one harmony with God's word. They were aware that there was one dependable source of life, love and wisdom, that is, the All-Father and Creator of all that there is. Therefore, living in harmony and conscious recognition of God's natural laws came naturally to our ancient forebears. The Dense or physical body (the flesh, blood and bones body) was new to original man, hence his attunement to God's spiritual and natural laws came easier. He was not yet ensnared by the flesh.

Our forebears accepted God as the grantor of all knowledge and grace; hence, knowledge "was looked upon reverentially instead of as a commercial asset. That knowledge should be applied in a practical way seemed natural to them, for otherwise there would be no purpose in the revelation of knowledge".[33]

We read, therefore, in a revealing book entitled *The World Before* by Ruth Montgomery, at page 36, that "early souls in human flesh were highly advanced beings capable of direct communication with those not yet fitted with the physical raiment of material earthly existence, and were also born with the natural awareness of God and man, the equality of all beings in the eyes of God and the necessity each for the other to comprise a total whole".[34]

As regards the land of Mu, W. S. Cerve indicates in the book *Lemuria* that it was mainly of a tropical nature; and living things of the vegetable kingdom as well as the animal kingdom lower than man, in intellect and spiritual evolvement, grew to huge proportions. In various islands of the Pacific, specimens that have been discovered embedded into the soil and preserved through centuries indicate that even small insects grew to an enormous size; that which we call the ant today was at least two inches in length.[35] The largest among the animals belonged to the class of the dinosauria, which were undoubtedly the greatest destroyers of both animal and vegetable life.[36]

It is interesting, however, to read in *The World Before*, at page 197, that there were few gargantuan creatures in Africa, and further that Africa was not overrun by dinosaurs. The animals there were said to have been restrained and not overproducing as were the dinosaurs and mammoths in Lemuria.

Early man, as indicated earlier, had an excellent understanding of natural laws and their conception of God, "was of a universal principle both positive and negative, male and female, creative and loving in every sense. They looked upon all the processes of nature as constructive even when temporarily destructive and considered these as established laws of evolution, having been created by a loving God in the beginning of time. Their interpretation of God as analogous to the human individual was much like comparing God with a great Master as well as parent of all living beings".[37]

Man of the Adamic era was therefore spiritual to the point that he was said to still walk with God receiving direct instructions from the Divine Source. These are the same original beings of the Garden of Eden, of which Alexander Winchell in his book *Preadamites*, page 158, says: "(t)here is indeed a legend in existence which has obtained a widespread currency according to which first the man was black or dark in complexion. There is even said to be a tablet in the British Museum brought by the late George Smith on which is an inscription which lends strange continence to the legend of the Black Adam".[38] The bulk of authorities who write of the early men of Mu or Lemuria refer to them as a people of dark or brown complexion. Braunton, in *History of Ancient People*, at page 31 indicates: "According to progressive theory the Earth may have been first peopled by men black in colour. If so the blacks reached their cultural climax in the ancient times. However, how much ... India and Southern Europe owe to them may never be known".[39]

At this juncture, it may be worthwhile to note an observation made by Chancellor Williams in his book *Destruction of Black Civilization*, at page 35. He writes: "An important factor that should be well known is that all unmixed Africans are not jet black for while the great majority are black-skinned, countless thousands who lived for centuries in cool areas have lighter complexion — and no Caucasian blood at all". As may be observed, through time the people and descendants of the African motherland have always been categorised by variations of the hues and shades one from another. That they are called black, brown, red or tanned is of no significance in that they are the self-same people, whom throughout history have been referred to as those of the Black race, 'Negroes' or people of 'Negroid stock'. That the sons of that huge landmass called Lemuria, which was once one with Africa and Asia Minor, were referred to as brown as distinct from their brothers in Africa who were and are still referred to as black, needs not mystify any one of us today, because as we know, within one colloquially termed "Negro family," we find children called black, brown and red.[40]

And as before observed, the physical characteristics and complexion of a people change through time depending on the climatic and environmental conditions. Hence, the Lemurian developed, over a period of time, what may be termed a brownish hue as distinct from the slightly darker inhabitants of the African motherland; this occurred because the separated continent of Lemuria was a vast land with some portions of it being semi-tropical in the windswept Pacific Area. "Environment", therefore, "and the consequential effects of it, will change the nature, appearance, habits and customs of any race," writes W. S. Cerve in *Lemuria*, "... and it is perfectly possible for all of the races of man to have had one common origin and to have been identical in countenance, customs and habits until the members of this one original race became scattered in various parts of the world and developed future generations having such modifications as the effect of environment would produce".[41]

The Lemurian is described with what any Caucasian (white) would consider a pronounced African or Negroid characteristic. We read: "The nostrils were larger and the nose was broader and more flattened on the face than we find among the people of the Western world of the present period".[42] Also, it is stated that although most of the Lemurians were exceedingly tall by today's standards, six to seven feet tall with long prominent foreheads, there were others in the early times that were tinnier than midgets, all loving to sing and dance to rhythms.[43] The above idiosyncrasies are still easily traceable to the Africans commonly referred to as Watutsis and Pygmies, respectively.

The Lemurian's hair, which grew far back on the head, "grew very long and was often braided or arranged in very fancy forms across the shoulders or down the back",[44] which is not unlike all the ancient inhabitants of Ethiopia and the Nile Valley who are seen in all temple drawings, carvings and statues with braided hair down their backs. Initially, the Lemurians' 'cyclops-type' third eye (the centre between the eyebrows) was said to have been highly developed, and mental telepathy was the norm.[45] Later in Lemurian history, however, they were said to have sent long distance messages by drums to whole communities at a time, as is traditionally practised in some parts of Africa. The Lemurians are said to have been primarily vegetarians and generally considered a very healthy people.[46] From time immemorial herbs were used in Lemuria for healing and maintaining health; but spiritual healing via prayer, meditation, incantations and the laying of hands was commonplace.[47]

From research and findings of anthropologists, it is submitted that those early people of the Adamic era developed a very high culture, with a great sense of community spirit. It is stated "that the Lemurians issued no coins and had no such commodity or device as money. No one received any form of remuneration for his effort except the privilege of sharing in all the community interest".[48] The Lemurians were not considered very inventive people, "but the superlative development of a philosophy for living and their dedication to divine laws" made them leaders in goodness and thought.[49]

Fall of Man

In those remote times, some portions of the earth, especially the land of Mu, were constantly in a steaming condition due to large areas of boiling lava. There were cataclysms and volcanic eruptions, hence through thousands of years of struggle and experience, early man came to realise attachment and loss, pain and suffering. Eventually, from experiencing such loss and pain, many Lemurians understood that attachment to earthly material was folly and at its best transitory. Material possessions were therefore considered unreliable and the unreal part of life.[50]

Those early beings "were not only firm believers in the doctrine of reincarnation, but they had ample time and the faculty with which to prove that reincarnation was a fact, and that there were those living among them who had lived before on the same continent and in intimate contact with them...."[51]

Knowing of reincarnation, they viewed what we commonly called "death" as a mere transition from the three dimensional plane whereby the Spirit-Soul Essence finally departs from the body by the severance of the silver cord, as explained in chapter 2.[52] Also, as explained in chapter 2, they knew that the physical body is of the earth kingdom; hence, if it is not spiritualised by the Christ Spirit, it is returned to the elements of Mother Earth from whence it came, and the Spirit-Soul moves on to the heavenly sphere, the other mansions of the Father's house. There the Spirit-Soul dwells until rebirth in another earth life. The Spirit-Soul then makes another effort at overcoming the Earth schoolroom by the realisation of the Christ within. The foregoing was common knowledge in this era of our forebears.

Death or transition to the heavenly spheres was not shrouded with fear and mystery but was well understood. "Each knew his place, in the scheme of things, and for that reason, there was no violence and no revolt. Parents understood that these little ones were souls, whole as themselves, who had chosen them as parents to learn the lessons of the flesh and they were therefore regarded as peers".[53]

Through the effluxion of time, however, those beings of whom it is said were as unconscious of this physical world as we are in our sleep, became deeply and smugly immersed in the garments of flesh. In time the wearer of the flesh, blood and bones body was less capable of distinguishing himself from the garment; much like man of today.

The Lemurians, who lived lives filled with impending danger from unexpected volcanic eruptions, earthquakes, tidal waves and attacks from hordes of wild creatures, were a people severely tested.[54] Some, in desperation, had to live under trying conditions of swamplands and boiling lava, and they gradually generated a negative current of thought doubting the wisdom of the Divine Sculptor, Originator, and Creator.

Their faith was sorely shaken and gradually their fine attunement to divine plan was dulled. Man wanted to be a free moral agent. Hence, he was given his full freedom; free will to choose his own course. God did not compel man to do or not to do this or that, but indicated to him that blessings would be his if he acted in love and harmony with the divine plan, and of necessity, as a natural requisite of Divine Justice and balance, as a rule, contrary actions to divine law would magnetise what some would term punishment, divine rectification, or retributive rehabilitation.

Man's descent into the flesh was now complete. Being totally immersed in the bodily frame he explored in his own manner, and as a result lost track of his original identity and divinity. He became more strongly controlled by the senses, as the material thoughts and desires of generations beclouded the lustre and allurement of his spiritual origin. Man steadily became more accustomed to nurturing negative thoughts of fear, self-doubt, selfish desires, hatred and foreboding evil. From this followed warped desires and actions and a general falling away from Divine will. Thus, the arrival of what is referred to as evil, personified by Lucifer. Through time, however, even this is to realise an honourable purpose: that of strengthening man's will for good; not just a passive acceptance of good but causing him through life's struggles to experience a higher state of consciousness, culminating in a conscious at-onement with and wilful submission to God's will, power, activity and purpose.

At this time, however, in the Adamic era or Lemurian epoch, the battle of the Indwelling Spirit-Soul against the ever increasing earthly prompting of mortal flesh became a living reality. Man, having demanded free will, and being able to arrive at decisions after reasoning, decided his own path, and in consequence, some fell by the wayside. They, it may be added, were ably assisted by this negative force epitomised as Lucifer of whom the prophet Isaiah speaks when he says: "How art thou fallen from heaven O Lucifer, Son of the Morning. How art thou cut down to the ground which didst weaken the nations. For thou hast said in thy heart: I will ascend into heaven, I will exalt my throne above the stars of God, I will sit also upon the mount of the congregation in the sides of the North, I will ascend above the heights of the clouds, I will be like the Most High, yet thou shall be brought down to hell, to the side of the pit".[55]

Hence, we read in the Bible of the temptations of Eve and the concomitant fall of man, orchestrated by the evil force, Lucifer. In the allegorical form of the serpent, Lucifer deceives Eve into eating the forbidden fruit from the tree of knowledge of good and evil. In Gen. 14:9, we read of the universally known tree of life in the midst of the garden. And at Gen. 3:2-6, we read: "And the woman said to the serpent, we may eat of the fruit trees of the garden, but God said: You shall not eat of the food of the tree which is in the midst of the garden, neither shall you touch it, less you die. But the serpent said to the woman: You will not die, for God knows that when you eat of it, your eyes will be opened and you will be like God, knowing good and evil". It is noteworthy that the symbol of the tree and the serpent, which has been thoroughly dealt with in chapter 2, is used in just about all the legendary works of antiquity and wisdom throughout the world.

As pointed out before, the serpent represents the duality of wisdom (perfect knowledge) and sexuality. Man, therefore, being a miniature creation of God, with the creative force inherent in his divine nature, helps to create. This he does by utilising this creative force or potentiality for either physical ends, whereby that force flows downwards into the generative organs (for sexual purposes); or, on the other hand, may direct this creative force into the realisation of Truth whereby this divine energy goes upward to the brain granting the incarnate Soul in flesh, divine attunement and spiritual illumination — the Mystic Marriage with his Christ within, which has been thoroughly dealt with in chapter 2.

The decline of the Adamic period or the Garden of Eden era (when all was beautiful and harmonious) is personified by the original embodied Soul Adam and then Adam and Eve in the Garden of Eden. At first they lived lives of perfect health and happiness, in harmony with God's will (God's laws), but subsequently being ensnared by Lucifer, represented by the serpent, they fell away from the Will and the Way of God. And as indicated above, the tree of life is a symbol of the spinal cord and the brain. "The snake was merely a symbol for the kundalini (the creative power which lies coiled like a serpent at the base of the spine until awakened), and the forbidden fruit was the opening of the seven chakras (the psychic centres, their physical counterparts being the ductless endocrine glands) too suddenly, with emphasis on the gonads (the earthly centre) rather than on the pineal gland (the Holy Spirit centre) and the pituitary gland (the master gland or god force). This kundalini or creative force makes man divine whereby great power is released within him. The misuse of the resultant power does not lead to divinity, but of necessity leads to the degradation of the recipient".[56]

Man, then, was still capable of awakening the kundalini, serpentine, or Christ force within him and his psychic centres, but his carnal mind was now in control; thus, he abused his life force. As mentioned above, the trunk of the tree in the microcosmic sense or within man is represented by the spinal column, spinal cord and brain. The spreading branches are the afferent and efferent nerves in the body, the flowers are represented by the force centres or chakras in the Etheric and super-physical bodies, together with their associated nerve centres and glands in the physical body".[57] The "fruits" of the tree in man "consist of the natural (attributes or) products of the evolutionary process" and in nature "represent the varied life-imbued forms which she, with such prodigality, ever continues to produce".[58]

Man's existence, therefore, during the Adamic era of the Garden of Eden may be likened to the innocence and faithful obedience of an individual's childhood where the parents' guiding light is the order of the day. Whereas, man's estrangement from this orderly state of affairs by his wanting to be a free moral agent may be likened to the period of puberty and adolescence when the vast changes in the physical make-up take place, the Desire body is fully formed, mistakes are abundant and many a painful lesson learnt.

As before alluded to, the descent of the Spirit-Soul into the fleshy embodiment was now complete. Man, having lost sight of his higher spiritual consciousness, naively overemphasised his physical sexuality by wrong concentration of mind, which resulted in an excessive concentration of divine energy in the generative organs.

In the book, *The Hidden Wisdom of the Holy Bible* by Geoffrey Hodson, page 152, it is succinctly put as follows: "Between the innocence of Eden and full redemption or ascension into adeptship, man passes through a period of bondage in captivity, subservience to materialism, selfishness and sensuality...."

It cannot be over-emphasised at this juncture that the Creator is the Epitome of justice and He works through universal laws, which are imbued with perfect justice. Anything short of this would lead to an erratic universe. Therefore, the prerogative of justice is the impartial implementation of those laws coupled with grace, understanding and love. Hence, a rejection of God's ordained laws of life of necessity creates a reaction so as to right the wrong or momentary imbalance, which we in our material limited perspective would refer to as punishment. The impersonal Universal Law of Justice (karma), or "as you sow so shall ye reap", should not therefore be understood as condemnation, retribution or punishment, but as the manifestation of Divine Love, creating harmony where there is disharmony, and the gaining of redemption from past folly — substituting wisdom for ignorance. It provides man with a means of subsequent joy and blessing for his past sufferings and failures. Hence, Divine Justice can be seen as one of the attributes of the Absolute One, which indicates, unreservedly, the patience and loving kindness shown by God to struggling humanity.

Mankind in those days was indeed struggling. Not only was he experiencing inner turmoil at the emotional and spiritual level, but his immediate material environment also manifested awesome upheavals and cataclysms. It must be remembered that, unlike the now separated African continent, steamy conditions always existed on the Lemurian continent, with large turbulent areas of boiling lava.[59] This created great disillusionment in the Lemurians. Sickness, pain and death seemed to be the now ever-present bitter fruits of their harvest.

The continent Lemuria itself was continuing to sink. The western portions of Lemuria were sinking quite rapidly, forming the new continent of Australia, the islands around it and the Pacific Islands. The present-day continents of North and South America were, however, now rising rapidly and becoming covered with heavy vegetation.

W. S. Cerve, in *Lemuria*, indicates that today's North and South America began to drift and separate itself from the rest of Europe and Africa,[60] which, incidentally, is on all fours with Alfred Wegener's Continental Drift Theory. Cerve continues: "(t)o those who may wonder whether or not it is possible for a continent to drift let me say that there are many and sufficient proofs in the sciences of archaeology and geology to show that this is possible; not all land on the surface of the earth is a part of the submarine floor or body of the earth. Even when continents are attached to the body of the earth, these continents can be moved and have moved through the changes in the surface of the earth caused by earthquakes and cataclysms of various kinds".[61]

Cerve also posits that on studying the earth as a sphere, there must be internal regions of space filled with intense heat and gases or what is referred to in the book *The World Before* as 'gas pockets'. In consequence, during cataclysms of the past, land that has been engulfed by these vast internal spaces of the earth has disappeared and may not therefore always be discoverable through deep-sea exploration. "In keeping with the magnetic pulsations and earthquakes moving in a westerly direction around the earth, the continent that became North and South America moved westerly in a gradual manner separating itself entirely from Europe, Africa, and Greenland".[62] This created a vast, unstable area between these continents, more specifically in the area that became known much later in history as the Atlantic Ocean. Some authorities indicate that the final tumultuous destruction of Lemuria as a continent took place around 48,000 B.C;[63] other authorities cite the event much earlier, more like 100,000 to 80,000 B.C.

Besides the ancient lands of Northeast Africa and Asia Minor, which were once fused with Lemuria, Lemuria can be best experienced in Australia, Polynesia, Hawaii and Tahiti, although its philosophy, culture and religion may to some extent be experienced in India.[64] It is also interesting to note that it is written that, after the first great catastrophe that destroyed most of the vast continent of Lemuria, the smaller continent that remained in the centre of the Pacific developed trade and other linkages with the new South American continent, especially the northern part of it. Today's North America was said still to have been swampland.[65]

Atlantis

"At the same time, we find that a new continent was beginning to rise in (today's) Atlantic ... contacting and uniting North America with the shore of Europe and Africa".[66] Some authorities are of the view that this continent began as a land bridge connecting the so-called 'New World' to the 'Old World,' later becoming a "large continent — which was finally broken up into a series of separated islands".[67]

This continent, which was known as Atlantis,[68] arose above the surface of the water between seventy-five and fifty thousand years ago.[69] The continent initially occupied a vast area in the Atlantic, the peaks of its mountainous western shores being today's Caribbean chain of islands. Many of those islands are washed by both the Caribbean Sea and Atlantic Ocean. Those mountain peaks of the submerged continent run from Florida through the Caribbean chain of islands to South America.

Today's North and South American continents are said to have risen considerably with the rising of Atlantis.[70] In North and South America new rugged mountains, highlands, lakes and rivers were formed; one was formed in South America.[71] The Caribbean chain of islands and a fair portion of what is immersed under the Caribbean Sea in the Gulf of Mexico was initially shown to have been connected to the Atlantean continent.[72]

In *The World Before* we read: "Atlantis stretched from the East rim of the Americas, including the coastal parts of Georgia, the Carolinas, Virginia, the West Indies (Caribbean), and Brazil, across what is now ocean ... nearly to the west coast of Africa".[73] It is noteworthy that today it is well accepted that "the Atlantic is one of the least stable parts of the world's crust and is subject to upheavals along the whole submarine Northern Mid-Ridge, which extends along the sea bottom from Northern Brazil to Iceland, and where upheavals can still cause raising or lowering of land mass".[74]

On the rising of Atlantis, the leading civilisations or high cultures were cradled in Lemuria, Africa (Alkebulan), and Asia Minor — today's Middle East. Initially the early settlers came from those places of civilisation; later white inhabitants also formed part of the Atlantean Empire coming from the area of the Caucasus mountains.[75] At a later stage in history, as will be elaborated on below, there was a tremendous influx of people from Asia and the Far East via the Bering Strait (which was then one with North America) and from there to the remnants of Atlantis in the Caribbean area as well as Central and South America.[76]

Although there were Atlanteans who would be called black, white, or yellow people, over time, the Atlanteans were described as reddish-brown in colour; generally, through the ages Atlantis became known as the continent of "the red people". They were also generally described as people with black, piercing eyes and black, thick, shiny hair, very much like the Indians of North and South America, the Carib (Kalinago) Indians of the Caribbean and the Arabs of Northeast Africa and today's Middle East.

Many authorities indicate that the atmosphere of the early Atlantean continent was considerably different from ours today. In the early days, the atmosphere was foggy and heavy. This was due to the meeting in Atlantis of two currents of air, that is, the fiery currents of air that swept northward from the still turbulent, fiery volcanoes from the South and the cold air that wafted down from the Northern polar region.[77] The early Atlantean is said to have depended more on inner perception than external perception, such as their eyesight. Initially their higher vehicles or bodies, such as their Etheric body, were not yet a perfect fit with the dense, physical body. "The spirit was not quite an indwelling spirit(.)"[78] The subtle Etheric and Astral Worlds were perceived by early Atlanteans. As time elapsed, however, the atmosphere of Atlantis cleared up and the higher vehicles of Atlanteans became completely fused with their dense, physical bodies; thereafter, the perception of those subtle worlds became less common. The brain developed further and the faculties of the mind, the intellect and reasoning came to the fore; unfortunately, at that juncture of human development, this was at the expense of spiritual sensitivity and vision in many Atlanteans.[79]

When Atlantis was at its zenith, it was considered a land of milk and honey, a veritable paradise.[80] Some authorities refer to the time of Atlantis as the last golden era of man. The great being referred to as King Atlas, who many think of as mythical, is said to have existed and was like the Adam of Atlantis, the founding father and ruler of

Atlantis.[81]   The initial language of King Atlas and his descendants was one of symbolism coupled with thought transference. He is said to have been capable of not only projecting his thought-forms but also materialising his thought-forms.[82] The kings and rulers through the early ages of Atlantis were seen as divine kings and rulers by the grace of God, so to speak. In time, however, in the later stages, even the rulers became not only very 'human' but intoxicated with power and decadent.

The Atlanteans, for a long time, or during what is referred to as 'the Atlantean era', were looked up to as the most advanced in the world in science, technology, education and material development; although many authorities would, with good cause, suggest that the continent of Atlantis, even at its zenith, never transcended Africa (Alkebulan) and Lemuria in religion, philosophy and high culture (civilisation).[83]

In the latter stages of Atlantean history and civilisation, in keeping with what was said above, the mind, its physical counterpart — the brain — and by extension the intellect and reasoning, developed rapidly at the expense of spiritual sensitivity and attunement. The result of this transition of emphasis was materialism and selfishness. Gradually, even their rulers and kings, as above mentioned, became intoxicated with their power and influence world-wide. They worshipped themselves and their material science. Their understanding and utilisation of electrical and other forces of nature were outstanding, but eventually disastrous. They were said to have mastered the art of harnessing electro-magnetic energy by the use of solar (sun) energy via geometrically cut crystals. In the hands of heartless materialists, such power always spells disaster. Any human being with a highly developed intellect without the balance of a loving heart, in today's world of Sodom, is usually a selfish, egotistical warp: sometimes a devil incarnate.

Atlanteans, in the later stages of their history, were generally categorised as either the scientific, ruling class, referred to as "the Sons and Daughters of Belial", or the peace-loving, natural living, humble class, referred to as "the Children of the Law of One" or "the Sons and Daughters of Light". The ways of the Children of the Law of One were seen as antiquated, unscientific and quaint; for that matter, their natural, God-centred, simple lifestyle was ridiculed and frowned upon. They were the Noah element of Atlantean society.

Before the beginning of the end of the Atlantean Empire (which was the first cataclysm that rocked Atlantis), the Atlanteans had perfected a huge, geometrically cut crystal referred to at different times as the "Terrible", "Bestial" or "Great" Crystal.[84] This "Terrible Crystal", as it was called by Ezekiel of the Bible, was supposedly housed in the scientific headquarters of the continent. The scientific headquarters was said to have been located in the area of today's Bermuda Triangle, formerly called the Sargasso Sea.[85]

The Terrible Crystal was said to have been in the control of the sons of Belial, the demi-gods of the day. They arrogantly harnessed tremendous energy from the sun, which in time (by dint of warped hearts and minds) they used for destructive purposes — causing volcanic eruptions, earth tremors, earthquakes and cataclysms wherever they so desired; at least so they thought, as will be explained below. The harnessing of electro-magnetic energy (by the use of solar energy and crystals) was akin to what nuclear energy represents in today's world, but it was a far cleaner and more potent energy or power source than nuclear energy. It should be noted — by those who have eyes to see and ears to hear — that Ezekiel, the priest and son of Buzi, spoke of "the colour of the Terrible Crystal".[86] He clearly referred to "the Terrible Crystal" in a manner that reflected that the people he addressed were not only aware of this "Terrible Crystal", but the colour of it as well.

As indicated above, the Atlantean demi-god rulers used electro-magnetic power generated by the Terrible Crystal to cause cataclysmic destruction wherever they desired until, eventually, their misdeeds caught up with them. Some authorities indicate that when the Atlanteans directed electro-magnetic energy like a laser beam through the earth's crust in an effort to destroy the ancient Empire of Kush, they disturbed the gaseous pockets and weaknesses beneath their own continent. Other authorities indicate that the Atlantean attack was not directed at Kush but at the ancient Chinese Empire. Be that as it may, the result was the first big cataclysm that not only rocked Atlantis, but also sank vast parts of the ancient continent.

The scientific headquarters with its bestial contents, the Terrible Crystal, sank beneath the ocean, where it is said to remain buried to this day — off two small Bahamian islands, namely, Andros and Bimini. After the first cataclysm, which is said to have occurred around 20,000 B.C., the remnants of Atlantis were comprised of many small islands and two very large islands that became known as Poseidia and Og. Thereafter, the area of the Atlantic Ocean was less stable than before. Eventually the last big upheaval took place around 12,000 B.C. The islands of the Atlantic Ocean and Caribbean Sea remain as remnants of this ancient continent.

By and large the most direct bloodline descendants are said to be the Indians of North, Central and South America, the Arawaks (now largely deceased), and the few surviving Caribs (Kalinago people) who, like the Indians of North, Central[87] and South America, managed to survive by the grace of God the onslaught of the Europeans much later in history.[88] Before moving on, it should be noted that later in history the Atlantean descendants in North, Central and South America as well as in the Caribbean interbred heavily with Asians. This occurred around "12,000 years ago, the end of the last Ice Age, (when) small bands of Asian nomads began to cross the dry land bridge that spanned what is now the Bering Strait, between Siberia and Alaska. The migrations continued intermittently, and when melting ice flooded the land bridge, they stopped".[89]

On the sinking of Atlantis, there was also said to be some inter-breeding with their original forebears, the Africans, especially from Northwest and Northeast Africa, the Asians of Asia Minor, as well as the early inhabitants of today's British Isles. It is indicated by some authorities that the more advanced Atlantean Souls journeyed to Northeast Africa, more specifically, Egypt.[90]

Unfortunately, some of those authorities try to give most of the credit for the great Egyptian civilisation to Atlantean influence, which is totally misleading and sometimes undeniably racist. It must never be forgotten that although the Atlantean presence in Egypt and Asia Minor must have had some influence, the Northeast African civilisation (high culture) antedates that of the Atlantean and I daresay even the Lemurian civilisation. The history of the Northeast African is the essence of antiquity; it represents the Adamic or Edenic era of human existence.

Today, the influence of ancient Atlantis can be seen in many books, articles and stories that speak of the strange occurrences in today's Bermuda Triangle; and in the distant past, of strange, if not eerie experiences in the area of the Sargasso Sea. Incidentally, the Sargasso Sea occupied the same area as today's Bermuda Triangle. The ancient Sargasso Sea has always been described and portrayed as a murky area shrouded in cloud; an area where the sea was always full of floating sea weed with thick vegetation (quite visible) just beneath the surface of the water; an area where sailors, who were brave enough to ply its waters, experienced an overbearing, stagnant heat and an unforgettable stillness.

The above description of the area of the Sargasso Sea is in keeping with the tremendous atmospheric and geophysical changes that would be expected from the horrendous volcanic eruptions and other seismic activity that was experienced in the area of ancient Atlantis.

After the devastation of Atlantis, the area of the Atlantic and today's Caribbean took, of necessity, a long time to settle down and 'heal' itself, so to speak. There would have been a vast amount of volcanic ash in the area accompanied by dark, dense volcanic clouds; weather patterns would also have changed dramatically. Oozes of molten lava would have been experienced in unstable areas; this would have been accompanied by gaseous fumes and mist. Dense vegetation having recently been plunged beneath the ocean would also have floated eerily, just beneath the surface of the water. It is submitted that the smog sometimes experienced in the area of the Sargasso Sea was also partly the result of the cold currents from the North coming in contact with the new, warm Gulf Stream flowing northward from the South. This new, warm Gulf Stream, now unobstructed by any landmass, flowed rapidly northward, causing tremendous melting throughout the Northern area, including the area we refer to as the Bering Strait.

Africa or Eden and Its Contribution to Civilisation

Having dealt with the birth and development of humanity — that is, from the Adamic era in Africa and Asia Minor, then in Lemuria and Atlantis — we will now examine Africa and its contribution to civilisation. Such an examination must of necessity observe the progress of African people, who are the direct blood descendants of the Adam and Eve family. This historical fact really needs no further elaboration as the evidence of this has been thoroughly presented earlier in this chapter. However, despite the mountain of evidence, some detractors may still glibly say that the writings of the ancient historians (now endorsed by the scientific findings of archaeologists, anthropologists and geneticists) are all wrong. May those bigoted souls be blessed and refined by the spirit of Truth.

Before doing a brief examination of Africa and its contribution to civilisation, it would be remiss of me not to call to mind the Omniscient, All-Father's undying love for Eden/Aden, the African Motherland, the birthplace of humanity. This love is clearly reflected by the enduring nature of the African continent; some may even say everlasting nature, which is a blessing indeed. Because, whilst we speak of Lemuria through the haze of antiquity, and nowadays, of the possible re-emergence of Atlantis, the continent of Africa has endured through the ages, and indeed, so has its progeny.

Around the time of the initial destruction of vast parts of Atlantis (around 20,000 B.C.) and right through to the time of its final sinking (around 12,000-10,000 B.C), there thrived in Northeast Africa a great empire known as the Empire of Kush or Cush, which, as indicated above, was later referred to by the Greeks and Europeans generally as Aethiopia or Ethiopia.

This Empire of Kush was said to have been ruled around 19,000 B.C. by a great Kushite king called Minos or Min. Unfortunately, this Kushite king called Min has been merged by some European authors with another great Kushite king named Menes, who overran, much later in history, what became known as Lower Egypt (today's Egypt). Menes overran Lower Egypt in 3100 B.C., and therefore lived roughly sixteen thousand years after King Min. This blending of the two Kushite personalities into one by Western histography was clearly done to lessen the antiquity of Egyptian civilisation (so as to give the impression that Egyptian civilisation suddenly dropped from the sky),[91] as well as to attempt to erase the undeniable blood and cultural ties between Egypt and Kush (Ethiopia). However, the kinship of Egypt, Nubia (Sudan) and Kush (Ethiopia) is undeniable, and this family tie is reflected in the biblical fact that Mesraim and Kush are both sons of Ham.[92]

It is submitted that the de-africanisation of Egypt and Ethiopia[93] has become almost an obsession of some modern, Western writers, who are unfortunately tainted with the schism or cancer of today's world: white racism.[94] This racism did not exist when many of the ancient historians and scholars wrote of the ancient African people. These Africans were known to have developed colonies and empires both in Northeast Africa and Asia Minor; and for that matter, from the inception of humanity, the progeny of Africa spread all over the habitable land of ancient Lemuria, where they developed separately in a different environment. Later in history, they spread their civilisation (high culture) to Greece and other parts of Europe.

For a masterful critique on Western histography of ancient Kush and Egypt, one should read chapter 6 of the book entitled *Crucial Insights into African History*, written by Professor George O. Cox. The entire book is most enlightening and worth reading.

This great empire, called Kush by the Hebrews and Ethiopia by the Greeks, thrived under King Min. Historical records reflect that it was Kushite/Ethiopian colonists of King Min who were sent north to drain the swamplands after diverting the course of the great Nile River. It was the said Kushite/Ethiopian colonists of King Min who built and inhabited the original city of Memphis. But before the establishment of Memphis, the Kushite "governmental headquarters" was Thebes or Egypt, as it was then called, located higher up the Nile Valley. That is why Herodotus, the ancient Greek historian, indicates in his writings that in ancient times, the name of Egypt was used to refer to what became known as Thebes.[95] What we refer to as Egypt today is the Delta area of the Nile or what was referred to as Lower Egypt.

The direct link between Egypt and Ethiopia/Kush is substantiated by classical literature. The ancient historian and geographer called Diodorus of Sicily wrote that the original Egyptians were Ethiopian colonists.[96] Further, as indicated before, early European scholars like the geographer Strabo referred not only to Northeast Africans, but also to all Africans, as Ethiopians.[97] As pointed out by Professor Cox, the genealogies that are usually given of the so-called dynastic rulers of Egypt (that is, lower Egypt) do not take into account the Egyptian, Ethiopian or Kushite rulers predating the settlement of lower Egypt (today's Egypt or Egypt of the Delta).[98]

It must always be remembered that when Menes, as distinct from Min, conquered Lower Egypt, "Egypt had already established its independence from Kush"/Ethiopia, its former colonisers.[99] And as pointed out by Professor Cox, "since Kush/Ethiopia on several occasions overran, conquered and ruled over Egypt, this means that Kush, which on such occasions of her conquest of Egypt, came to rule over Egypt and the Egyptian Empire in Asia and Europe, was the ruler of the largest world empire, second only to that of the (British Empire)",[100] which was developed much later in human history.

Wherever the Kushites/Ethiopians went they brought with them their culture, "including religion, extraordinary engineering abilities, history, literature, art, the sciences of astrology, astronomy, government, agriculture and several other cultural achievements".[101] It is interesting to note that the name of one of its first colonies, Egypt, is linked to the word "Hikuptah", which is said to mean "'Mansions of the soul of Ptah', a Kushite Pharaoh, who ruled from the city of Thebes, which was the first place to be called Egypt. (And) from the name Hikuptah came the Greek word Aigyptos from which we have the modern name, Egypt".[102]

With the above in mind and remembering that the initial place known as Egypt, later to be known as "Thebes" and "Upper-Egypt", was in fact located in Kush/Ethiopia, the ethnic and cultural roots of Egypt are undeniable. Any unnatural severance can therefore be seen for what it is: a sham, if not a racist attempt to distort history and to negate the reality that Egyptian wisdom, theology and civilisation were African. And as the people of Kushite/Ethiopian origin gradually developed the Nile Valley, right down to Memphis or Lower Egypt (modern-day Egypt at the mouth of the Nile River), this vibrant African culture and civilisation spread (through the doorway of Egypt) to the rest of the world.

In this vein, the pursuits and accomplishments of the Pharaoh Sesostris throughout Asia and Europe must be noted. This is a well-recorded fact of history. The European father of history, Herodotus, indicates amongst other things, that during Sesostris' conquest of Asia and most of Europe, he erected pillars on which were inscribed his name, country and words to the effect that by the might of his armed forces, he had been victorious. He also added on a few of those pillars a small symbol which reflected that his opponents had not fought like men. His victorious march through Asia is said to have continued until his conquest in Europe of the Scythians and Thracians.[103]

Although the link between the Ethiopians/Kushites, Egyptians and Colchians has already been mentioned above, it should be noted that it is during his discussion of the exploits of Sesostris in Asia and Europe that Herodotus established the strong ethnic link between the above-mentioned people. This deduction was made because he observed that the Colchians were black-skinned and woolly-haired. Ironically, he went on to reflect that these African or ethnic traits were seemingly commonplace in other nations of the region. He goes on to further strengthen his argument for linking the Ethiopians/Kushites, Egyptians and Colchians by indicating that they are the only races from ancient times that practised circumcision.[104] The Phoenicians and Syrians of Palestine are also said to admit that they learnt this practice from the Egyptians.[105] Hence, it can clearly be seen that the well-publicised practice of circumcision by the Jews originated in Northeast Africa.

Before saying a little more about the Empire of Kush and African civilisation generally, it should be mentioned that the Minoan civilisation on the island of Crete was yet another civilisation of African origin, more specifically, of Kush and Egypt. Professor Cox, in *Crucial Insights Into African History*, quotes the British prehistorian V. Gordon Childe who, when writing of the island of Crete, indicated that "(t)he 'neolithic' phase was ended by a quickening impulse from the Nile, which permeated the rude island culture and transformed it into the Minoan civilisation".[106] Incidentally, it should be noted here as well that the name of the "Hindu Cush" mountains in Asia originated from the exploits of a Cushite/Kushite king, who with his armies extended the Cushite/Kushite Empire to the Hindu Cush mountains. The name of the mountains in Asia records this undeniable, historical fact.[107]

As reflected above, the Empire of Kush extended at times outside of Africa to include Asia and a great deal of Europe. Babylonia and Palestine were said to have not only formed part of the Empire of Kush, but were peopled and ruled by Kushites.[108] Kush is said to have been a theocratic state, with its rulers traditionally being chosen from the priesthood. The priests were usually the most educated in the Empire; hence, the emperors were chosen from amongst them on the basis of wisdom and physical fitness. This criteria for choosing leaders was later used in Egypt and is still the practice in some parts of Africa.[109]

As we continue our brief examination of the African contribution to world civilisation, it must be understood that what is being given here will be mere 'tit-bits', because over the years millions of words and hundreds of books have been produced on the African contribution to civilisation by world-renowned authorities. I therefore write with great humility on the topic as we continue our examination of the African contribution to civilisation. We will now look at the African contribution to the religions of the world; religions that have undeniably influenced civilisation as we know it.

Count C. F. Volney boldly proclaims in his book, *Ruins of Empires*: "All religions originated in Africa". This is supported by Professor Breasted and many other authorities.[110] In the publisher's preface of the said book, one reads: "we are in reality indebted to the ancient Ethiopians ... for the various religious systems now so highly revered by the different branches of both the Semitic and Aryan races...."[111]

We will now deal with the Gods of antiquity. The cornerstone of all religion is the God concept. Hence, we will turn our attention to the ancient Gods of various cultures and people who have admittedly developed some degree of civilisation or high culture. Incidentally, it is written that the ancient people of the world traditionally viewed the sacred image of divine as Black and that the holy race of the Gods was African. The following Gods of antiquity were all Black: Zeus and Apollo of Greece; Osiris of Egypt; Isis and Horus of Rome, who are also part of Egyptian mythology, theology and history; Fuhi of China; Zaha of Japan; Quetzalcoatl of Mexico; Krishna and Buddha of India; as well as the Black Omlec Gods of ancient America. Incidentally, the Omlec Indians of Mexico constructed giant stone heads to honour the Africans who visited the American continent between 1000-700 B.C.[112] The historian and author J. A. Rogers not only indicates inter alia that "the earliest Gods ... on all the continents were black", but that all the Messiahs as well were black.[113]

Undeniably, the spiritual leader or Messiah represents the dynamic centrifugal force at the centre of every religion. Hence, to endorse what was said above, I quote Gerald Massey in *A Book of the Beginnings* (Volume 1): "It is certain that the Black Buddha of

India was imaged in the Negroid type ..., the features and hair of Buddha belong to the black race and Nashi is the Negro name".[114] We are informed by Indus Khamit-Kush in his book, *What They Never Told You in History Class*, that Heinrich Zimmer pointed out in his book, *Philosophies of India*: "the Buddha belonged to a culture that inhabited the Indus Valley known as the Harappa. These people were of the black race. It was within the rigid philosophical and scientific cultural structure of these people that gave birth to yoga, the Ayur-veda (Eastern system of medicine), and a comprehensive understanding of the functionality of the Universe and how it relates to man".[115] T. A. Buckley and Professor T. Inman in their books, *Cities of the Ancient World* and *Ancient (Pagan) and Modern Symbolism*, contain inter alia the following statement: "From the woolly texture of the hair, I am inclined to assign to the Buddha of India, the Fuhi of China, ... the Zaha of the Japanese and Quetzalcoatl of the Mexicans, the same ... African, or rather Nubian, origin". Interestingly, in the Cambridge Encyclopaedia we read: "Quetzalcoatl was recognised as the Messiah by the seers...; his complexion was black; his hair was woolly, he performed many miracles".[116]

In ancient drawings and statues the woolly hair of Negro people was always reflected by the peppercorn hairstyle, and J. A. Rogers in his book, *100 Amazing Facts about the Negro*, indicates that "the pepper corn hair was a sign of divinity".[117] The early images of the Massu, Christ Jesus or Yashua, were all black. The earliest images of Christ (for example, on an ancient coin of the time of Justinian II) depict him with the same peppercorn hairstyle typically reflecting divinity and the woolly hair of a Negro. For a picture of such a coin, one should see page 47 of the book *African Origins of the Major Western Religions* by Professor Ben-Jochannan and three other authorities. This book, incidentally, is an excellent presentation on the subject.[118]

It must be remembered that even the Bible reflects an image of the Almighty with "hair like lamb's wool" (Rev. 1:14) and "feet like burnt brass" (Rev. 1:15). Josephus, the Jewish historian, and numerous authorities all describe Christ as dark or black-skinned and woolly-haired. In Revelation we read: "... a throne stood in heaven with one seated on that throne! And he that sat there appeared like jasper and carnelian". Both of these rare stones are dark. In all early Christian art, pictures and portraits, Jesus the Christ is consistently represented as a Black man.[119]

Before moving on from Messiahs and leaders of religions, it is of interest to note that Moses of the Old Testament was also an African from the Haribu tribe of Northeast Africa, also referred to as Hebrews. It must be remembered that, according to the Bible story, he was placed in a basket and floated down the Nile where he was saved and raised as a Prince in Egypt, and he looked so much like his black brothers in Egypt that the Bible indicates that he passed off as an Egyptian; no one could tell him apart.[120]

It must also be imbibed that Mohammed, the Prophet of Islam, was Black. In fact, a contemporary of his describes him as dark with fuzzy hair. His mother was African and his grandfather, Abd El-Muttalib, is spoken of as being very dark. Al-Jahiz, in his *The Book of the Glory of the Black Race*, asserts that Abd El-Muttalib, grandfather of the prophet Mohammed, was "black as the night and magnificent".[121] Another historical fact that should be known is that, for centuries, the Blessed Virgin Mary and Infant Saviour were always represented as black until around the Renaissance period; since that time a Florentine (white) maiden and white child have been portrayed.[122] Professor Ben-Jochannan indicates in lectures and in his book *Black Man of the Nile* that Michelangelo was asked by Pope Julius in 1509 to paint his visualisation of the holy family, and he painted his uncle and his uncle's wife and child. From then, we of African heritage in the Caribbean and the Americas have been 'blessed' by a 'whitened' Mary, Jesus and Joseph.

Despite the above, the Black Madonna can still be seen throughout Europe. For example, in Spain she is referred to as the Queen of the Pyrenees and in Russia and Poland, she is referred to as the Virgin of Kazan.[123] Pope John Paul II, a native of Poland, can even be seen in the *Jet* magazine of February 15, 1982 standing and praying before the Black Madonna during a ceremony at Jasna Gora Monastery in

Poland. If you go back in time you may remember when the said pope was unfortunately wounded.[124] He is shown in the *Newsweek* magazine that reported the incident lying wounded on the ground completely encircled by statuettes of the Black Madonna.

There are many other icons, practices, moral laws and theological precepts of the major religions of the world that can be traced to the indigenous Africans of the Nile Valley. Even the Ten Commandments of Moses can be traced to "The Negative Confessions", which were written and existed in Africa for over a thousand years before Moses.[125] Incidentally, for those of us who may not know this, the Founding Fathers of Christianity were black, namely: Tertulian, first of the church writers who made Latin the language of Christianity; Cyprian, well known as a Bishop and martyr; and St. Augustine, one of the most famous "Fathers of the Church". Hopefully, many of us know this, as many of us profess to be Christians.[126]

The Khamitic (Egyptian or African) influence on Judaism, Christianity, and Islam is well reflected in Professor Ben-Jochannan's *Black Man of the Nile*, as well as his *African Origins of Major Western Religions*, referred to before. Incidentally, the author is of the view that the outstanding scholarly work of George G. M. James — to wit, *Stolen Legacy* — should be required reading for all Africans in Diaspora. This book inter alia indicates that the term Greek philosophy is a misnomer. The Egyptians of Africa from antiquity had developed a complex religious system, called the Mysteries, which was also the first system of salvation.[127]

This African system of Egypt regarded the human body as a prison house of the Soul, which could be liberated from the ensnarement of the body, through the disciplines of the arts and sciences, and advanced from mere mortal to immortal. This was the notion of "summum bonum", or greatest good, to which all men must aspire; the basis of all moral and ethical codes. The Egyptian Mystery System's teaching was graded and given orally to all members. The Egyptians developed secret ways of writing and teaching in symbolism and forbade their initiates from writing what they had learnt. A life of devotional service and virtue was a condition required by the Egyptian Mystery Schools.[128]

After thousands of years of prohibition against the Greeks, they were allowed to enter Egypt to be educated, generally, as well as in the secret mysteries of Egypt. First through the Persian invasion, then through the invasion of Alexander the Great — that is, from the sixth century to the death of Aristotle in 322 B.C. — the Greeks made the best of their chance to learn all they could about Egyptian culture. Many Greeks received their instructions directly from Egyptian priests, but after the invasion by Alexander the Great, as he was called, the royal temples and libraries were plundered and pillaged, and Aristotle's school converted the Egyptian library of Alexandria into a research centre. It is not surprising that many authorities doubt the authenticity of the amount of books ascribed to Aristotle — in that no man could write so many books in one lifetime. Possibly, if the Greeks had photocopying machines in those days they may have done a much better job of copying the material.

From here, it is easy to see how the Motherland, Africa, gave its history, experience and culture to the Western world through the doorway of Greece. Incidentally, the Greeks are accepted to be the first civilised men of Europe, and they were educated by the Egyptians of Northeast Africa; all the great Greek philosophers and thinkers, such as Pythagoras, Socrates, and Plato, were taught in Egypt. In a nutshell, what became known as Greek philosophy was merely the offspring of the Egyptian Mystery System. The Egyptian teachings of salvation, which are the earliest known to man, became the very purpose of Greek philosophy. The Egyptian or Northeast African Mystery System teachings of salvation, from antiquity, had as its main object the salvation and ultimate deification of man by liberating the Soul of man from the fetters of the body.[129]

As Greece suckled itself on Mother Africa, it became civilised and, in time, powerful. In time all links between Africa and Greece (and by extension the rest of the white world) were severed. Western or European civilisation needed to whiten its past, to whiten its history.

With the above in mind, the edicts of Emperor Theodosius in the fourth century A.D. and Emperor Justinian in the sixth century A.D. abolished not only the Mystery Schools of Northeast Africa but also its philosophical schools located in Greece and elsewhere. As a result of this, intellectual darkness spread all over Europe and the Graeco-Roman world for ten centuries. That era is generally referred to as the 'Dark Ages'.[130]

It is interesting to note that during the Persian, Greek and Roman invasions, large numbers of Egyptians trained in the Egyptian Mysteries fled not only into the desert mountain regions, but also to adjacent lands in North Africa and Arabia, where they lived and secretly developed the teachings which belonged to their Mystery System. As such, the people of North Africa, who were neighbours of the Egyptians, became the custodians of Egyptian culture, which they spread to Asia Minor and Europe as well as other parts of Africa, especially the west coast.

Before making a few statements about the exploits of the Moors in Spain, another important linkage between the Africans of North and Northeast Africa and those along the west coast should be noted. Many authorities write that from antiquity there were Black African Jews (Hebrews — those of the Haribu tribe) of Egypt and Ethiopia (Cush);[131] and it is generally accepted by those Black Jews of Northeast Africa that King Solomon and the Queen of Sheba, or Makeda, had a son called Menelik. After Menelik's education in Jerusalem, he is said to have returned to Ethiopia, where he established the first Jewish colony around the tenth century B.C.[132] Hence, from this early beginning, records reflect that Ethiopia or Abyssinia (the Arabic name for Ethiopia or Cush) was of Jewish persuasion before it adopted Christianity or Islam. This is well elucidated in the books, *Hebrewism of West Africa* and *From Babylon to Timbuktu: A History of the Ancient Black Races Including the Black Hebrews*, by Joseph Williams and Rudolph R. Windsor, respectively. These books also trace the times of and reasons for the migration of Black Jews (Hebrews) from East Africa to West Africa.

As regards this African 'East/West' interlinkage, suffice it to say that the Hebrew (Haribu) culture and religion of Northeast Africa — and by extension the Wisdom Teachings or Mysteries of Egypt — greatly influenced the religious beliefs and lives of Africans throughout the west coast of Africa. It is not uncommon, therefore, not only to read of Black African Jews or Hebrews of Egypt and Ethiopia,[133] but of West African Jews, or to be more specific: the Black Jews of Dahomey;[134] or of the Yoruba Jews of Nigeria;[135] or of the Bavumbu Jews of Angola;[136] or of the Ashanti Jews of the Gold Coast (Ghana); or, for that matter, of the great Black Jewish Empire of Ghana.[137] Subsequently, the African East/West interlinkage also brought to the west coast of Africa tremendous Islamic influence from the religion of Islam.

In the eighth century A.D., the Moors, natives of Mauritania in North Africa, invaded Spain and took with them the Egyptian culture that they had preserved. Knowledge in the old days was centralised, i.e., it belonged to a common parent and system, namely, the Wisdom Teachings or Mysteries of Egypt. It is written that the Moors in Spain displayed to some extent the grandeur of African culture and civilisation. The Moors, during their civilising process, established schools and libraries that became famous throughout the medieval world; science and learning were cultivated and taught. The schools of Cordova, Toledo and Seville were world-famous. From these schools, the most famous African professors in medicine, astronomy and mathematics were produced.

From the above, it is clear that despite the attempt by Europe, from the sixth century, to sever all its historical links to Africa, the African Moors still continued, for some time, to assist in the civilisation process of Europe. Hence, despite the 'Dark Ages' when history was 'whitened', so to speak, and the fact that over time the idea has been fostered by some Europeans that Africa is a foreboding 'Dark Continent' (and this falsehood was greatly assisted much later in history by the confusion caused by the forced partitioning of Africa by the Europeans in the nineteenth century), the above facts of history are undeniable and should be known by all people. This is essential if we are to have a balanced view of history and "the Eternal Now" that is upon us.

Conclusion

Alkebulan or Africa is the cradle of humanity. From there, humanity spread East, North and subsequently West. On the breaking up of the original Plantation of God (the dry land on the planet that was habitable by man), Lemuria was separated from the east coast of Alkebulan or Africa as well as from Asia. Lemuria was said to have been a vast, great continent and civilisation. Unfortunately, as indicated earlier in this chapter, its physical environment was always volatile and this, coupled with esoteric causal factors, led to its eventual destruction. The remnants of this ancient continent are strewn across the Pacific, both above and below the ocean.

The continent of Atlantis was like a shooting star in comparison to Alkebulan, or Africa, and Lemuria. In the vast time frame of continents and civilisations, Atlantis came on the world scene, shone brilliantly, fizzed out and sank rapidly. Some authorities liken it to today's North America with all its wealth, power, aggression and unfortunate decadence.

There was great scientific advancement in Atlantis. The Atlanteans used geometrically cut crystals and solar energy to generate electro-magnetic energy; this was used for a multiplicity of purposes. Today's "Bermuda Triangle" in the Caribbean is a relic of the notorious Bestial or Terrible Crystal that is entombed in that area since the sinking of Atlantis. On the sinking of Atlantis (which tallies with the story of "Noah and the Flood"), the civilisation or high culture of the Empire of Kush endured and flourished, as it had from the beginning of time. The Empire of Kush, peopled by descendants of Adamic stock, always had a close (if not always friendly) relationship with the Atlanteans; this relationship or interlinkage of blood, science and culture was of mutual benefit to both civilisations or high cultures.

The Empire of Kush and, by extension, Africa (Alkebulan) has endured through the ages, unlike Lemuria and Atlantis. The ancient culture, religion and Wisdom Teachings of Northeast Africa have, by Divine Providence, been systematically spread to the rest of the world via the doorways of Egypt and the west coast of Africa. The west coast of Africa is referred to as a 'doorway', like Egypt, in light of the above-mentioned East/West religious and cultural interlinkage that took place between Egypt and the west coast, and the fact that millions of those Africans were forcibly taken from the west coast of Africa across the Atlantic to work as slaves in the Caribbean islands (island remnants of Atlantis), North and South America and other parts of today's Western world.

These Africans in Diaspora, be they in the Caribbean or America, went through a process of slavery, which was the worse form of human degradation and pressure. These Africans or people of melanin went through a process, at the human level, that is akin to the one that coal goes through to form diamond. Melanin, which is the dark-brown or black pigment in the hair and skin of the coloured races of the world, is carbon-based just like coal, the mineral. Hence, the people of melanin or carbon, from the dehumanising pressure of slavery and their experiences thereafter, have been transmuted into 'Diamond Souls' at the human level.

These Diamond Souls of African descent in the Caribbean, America and other parts of the Western world, are primarily descendants of former slaves who not only got unfairly treated, but on occasion were brutally dehumanised, yet worked tirelessly for the master every day. They are the same ones who helped to build the British Empire and the magnificent and powerful America that we all know today.

Despite all these material, pertinent and sometimes painful facts about our history, the underlying realities of life, which are that life is a spiritual journey in the flesh and that one must live by the Law of Love, must never be forgotten; when this is forgotten that is when we all go astray and the Crown of Glory slips away. The further astray we go, the more pained, difficult, and unhappy our earth journey becomes.

Before moving on to the chapter entitled "The Eternal Now", it is noted that nowadays, as the ultraviolet rays of the sun wreak havoc with some temples of flesh that are not blessed with sufficient melanin, a great deal is being written about melanin. Black is therefore not only beautiful, as touted in the 1960's and early 1970's, but also healthy.

Although it is unfortunate that God's sun, which is known to be essential to life,[138] now causes skin cancer in some humans, this, I daresay, has been brought about by the spiritual turpitude and intellectual arrogance of some humans. These humans have, amongst other things, depleted the ozone layer by their unnatural and unwholistic approach to life and development process. This development process has not only espoused the use of chemical drugs (with deleterious long-term side effects) for most ailments, but also pumped poisonous, hazardous and deadly chemicals throughout our environment. Some modern-day scientists, who have seen the light, now desperately try to undo the sins of the past; however, some still continue to boastfully use and recommend the continued use of atomic and nuclear power. "It is a clean power source", they say, that is, except the horrendous, deadly nuclear waste, which we know not what to do with. They are bright materialists who have lost their way.

In conclusion, it is posited that the Africans of Africa, as well as their descendants in Diaspora, can aptly be referred to as the people of melanin or carbon; and as indicated above, in the same manner that coal or carbon turns to diamond from intense heat and pressure, those African Souls in Diaspora have been transmuted into 'Diamond Souls' of the New World. These Diamond Souls can be found throughout the Caribbean and the Americas, as well as other parts of the world where they have migrated.

CHAPTER 4

THE ETERNAL NOW

Introduction

The concept of "the Eternal Now" is one whereby persons who are genuinely dedicated to realising God in their lives are granted, daily, more and more knowledge, not only of man's distant past (as reflected in "Beyond the Veil of History"), but also of man's probable future. Those persons therefore live in what is called "the Eternal Now", in that 'present events' are seen in their true perspective, that is, based on a knowledge of the past and an attunement to the future. It is like a person who has seen the complete picture on the box cover of a jig-saw puzzle: the individual pieces of the jig-saw puzzle are neither puzzling nor mysterious to the person, as he or she immediately knows exactly where to place the pieces to complete the picture.

Those persons living in the Eternal Now can also be said to have an overview of life. As an illustration: if two persons are at the corner of a flat, concrete roof of a five-story building, they can comfortably look down at vehicular traffic on either side of the corner of that building. They could therefore see quite easily that two vehicles speeding along on either side of the building are about to collide, head-on; hence, because of their strategic position, which allowed them to have an overview of things, they could possibly forewarn the drivers of the avoidable, impending danger. The two people on the roof were not prophets, but merely had a strategic overview of things, like the students of the times, who live in the Eternal Now.

Having dealt with man's pursuit and realisation of Truth in chapters 1 and 2, as well as an insight into man's history in chapter 3, we will now complete the picture in this chapter by succinctly presenting relevant prognostications or prophecies of our times. After imbibing this chapter, you may be said to be one who lives in the Eternal Now.

Prophecy and the Times That We Live In

There are many books and ancient writings relating to prophecy. So, too, there have been many genuine prophets and seers from all corners of the world — both ancient and modern. With this in mind, this chapter merely reflects the consistency of prophecy for the times that we live in presently. It also reflects the consistency of prophecy with the findings and consequent predictions of some of today's scientists, be they astronomers, seismologists or physicists.

Most of us will admit that we live in trying, special times of rapid, if not drastic, change. Some people may say that some of those changes have been brought about by man, whilst some changes, such as the noticeable changes in weather patterns and seismological activity, have been brought about by nature. But for those who have eyes to see and ears to hear, even those changes that are related to nature have been strongly influenced, if not brought about, by man. Unfortunately, many of us overlook the holistic, inter-related nature of God's perfect science and design as reflected in His Creation.

That which we human beings think, say and do as we tread the path of life influences the physical world around us in ways we do not realise. The so-called 'primitive', indigenous people of the world always knew this and lived in harmony with this understanding; in many instances they tried to convince their aggressive, brutal 'conquerors' of this, but to no avail. It has taken their 'conquerors' hundreds of years of ignorant, brutish living to realise at last this simple truth. For that matter, it is only a few of the more illumined, modern scientists who have not only realised this, but openly accept the inter-related, holistic nature of our world. And, amazingly, this simple truth known from antiquity (taught by the indigenous people of the world from time immemorial) is reported as an incisive, new discovery.

As was written in chapter 2, God's will shall not — and for that matter cannot — be frustrated: 'Dhamballa' or 'Divine Balance' will be restored. Hence, to those who love God with all their heart, soul and mind, I say: fear no more because Divine Balance is coming. Remember, if health is to be restored, the great purge must be endured. We must brace ourselves for vast change.

Most citizens of this earth will accept that the New World Order is with us. The concept of the New World Order has been proudly proclaimed by political and institutional leaders of Europe and America for some years now. To many citizens of this earth, especially those of African heritage,[1] this New World Order, supposedly engendered to enhance peace, economic growth and world trade,[2] has spelt disaster to their economies, political stability, and in many instances their national sovereignty and autonomy. These people of colour who have no military or financial clout are seemingly of no significance to the self-appointed demi-gods of this New World Order. Those self-appointed rulers proudly make decisions that adversely affect millions of humble, God-fearing citizens of this planet.

It seemingly has been decided by the 'might is right' rulers of this world that people of colour must either become subservient, modern-day slaves, just better 'educated' today than a few hundred years ago, and their nations, vassal states. If those nations do not oblige, they risk being destroyed economically, politically and culturally; in other words, as a people. Those demi-gods of this New World Order, with their high-fangled financial and trade regimes, intend to plunge 'Third World' States into economic and social ruin. Thereafter, the master plan is to buy up those 'economically unviable States', and with their supposedly 'superior intellect and business acumen', transform those States into vibrant ones. Today anything goes; hence, hard drugs are fed to the youth of those hapless States that do not submit to the dictates of the 'self-appointed world rulers'. Tomorrow, the question is: who's next? Or what's next — outright genocide? Some would say it is already happening.

Undeniably, the people of the world are suffering despite the New World Order and man's purported high ideals, as reflected in lofty legal instruments such as the International Bill of Human Rights. Since the hurried dismantling of the Soviet Union (which is all part of the Master Plan of the New World Order),[3] there has been great instability in some of the former Soviet Union countries. For example, there has been ethnic cleansing and war in Bosnia-Herzegovina, as well as war in Serbia, Chechnya and Albania, and recently, the biggest war in Europe since the Second World War, in Kosovo. To add to the chaos, there has been a frightening resurgence of terrorist activity throughout the world and bloodletting in parts of Africa.[4]

Seemingly oblivious to all this, the rich of the world continue to get richer as they live their 'soap opera lives' of vanity and decadence; and as reflected above, economic and trade regimes have been institutionalised to perpetuate and further enhance this. It is therefore no surprise that despite the inherent wealth of God's planet, people still die of abject poverty and starvation. With such unconscionable disparity throughout the world, people have turned upon themselves, brutally destroying each other; self-hate, frustration, decadence and despair have become the order of the day. Social and political strife has spread throughout the world. As usual, nothing has changed in Israel and the Middle East region: from time immemorial, the festering hatred and strife continue; the consequent unfortunate violence and senseless killings continue unabated. This region is the present focal point of planetary stress, and as will be reflected below, a great degree of biblical prophecy relates to this region.

It is true to say that in the times in which we live, no part of this earth has been spared the scourge of social and political strife and violence. Even in the once peaceful, some may say, paradisical Caribbean islands, economic decline, social strife and decadence have started to set in. The cultural sewage, to wit, the vanity, hard drugs, violence and immorality of the so-called 'First World' countries,[5] have not only washed ashore but washed all over these hapless islands.

The United States of America, proudly described by its politicians and media personnel as 'the only remaining superpower', has become the Police Force of the world and dictates to other countries (with the noted exception of China and to a lesser extent Russia) what can and cannot be done, even within their own national boundaries.[6] This seems to be the accepted 'order' of the day.[7] However, despite this unwholesome intimidation (some may say international terrorism), those who dwell on the mountainous peaks of ancient Atlantis, that is, today's islands situated in the Caribbean and Atlantic Ocean, should take solace, in that it is written: "the Lord shall (in that day) set his hand again this second time to recover the remnant of his people, ... from Egypt, ... from Cush (A/Ethiopia) ... from Shinar (Sumer) ... and from the islands of the sea".[8]

Relevant Biblical Prophecies

With the above in mind, a succinct insight into biblical prophecy, as it relates to our times, is presented below.[9] Most scholars and adherents of the Bible are aware that the majority of the prognostications of the ancient Hebrews have already taken place, except those relating to the much anticipated times of the "last days" that many accept we are presently living in.

The key event in prophecy of the ancient Hebrews as it relates to our times is the rebirth of Israel as a nation.[10] Moses, the great Lawgiver, foresaw that the Jewish Nation would be destroyed and scattered all over the world.[11] He, however, predicted that before the end of this age, the Jews would return to Palestine and become a nation-state once again. Without going into what went on 'behind the scenes' to bring this into reality, suffice it to say that a new nation of Israel came into being on the 14th of May, 1948. Christian authorities throughout the world are of the view that the countdown of the end of this age began from that day in 1948. In Ezekiel one reads: "I will take you from among the nations and gather you out of all countries, and bring you into your own land".[12]

Since the rebirth of Israel as a nation in Palestine, many authorities are of the view that many other prophecies relating to the last days have in fact taken place and are presently taking place. The so-called Middle-East Confederacy of Islamic Arab States formed after the Second World War, which brought into being the Middle East region, is seen as an integral part of the prophetic jig-saw puzzle, in that this confederacy of states is supposed to play an important role in the attempted destruction of the new Nation of Israel at the time of the Armageddon. The rise of the Soviet Union, more specifically Russia, as a great military power is also seen as a very significant part of the prophetic jig-saw puzzle. It is interesting to note the overnight dismantling of the Soviet Union so that the name Russia, which has direct significance in biblical prophecy, has now come back to the fore.[13]

The nation to the extreme north of Israel, which is predicted to invade Israel with its allies in the latter years, has been identified by many authorities as today's Russia. In Ezekiel the ruler from the north is described as "Gog" of "the land of Magog, the chief prince of (Rosh), Meshech and Tubal".[14] Incidentally, "Gog" is said to be the symbolic name of the ruler who controlled the land of Magog as well as the people of (Rosh), Meshech and Tubal.[15] Magog, Meshech and Tubal are referred to in the Bible as sons of Japheth.[16] Ancient authorities such as Josephus, the first-century Jewish historian, Herodotus, the Greek philosopher and historian, and Pliny, the Roman writer of the early Christian era, all link Magog, Meshech and Tubal to the Scythians or Muschovites. The Scythians, also called the people of Magog, are generally accepted to make up a good portion of the people who now inhabit today's Russia; and need it be said that some authorities are of the view that the city of Moscow derived its name from the Hebrew name "Meshech", and that today's Russian people derived their name from the ancient people of "Rosh".[17]

Another important part in the prophetic jigsaw puzzle is the reference in the Bible to the kings of the East that will command an army of two million soldiers.[18] The kings of the East are accepted to embrace the Orient, and many authorities interpret this to mean China and its allies from Asia. China, with the world's biggest population and mammoth army, is seen as capable of fulfilling prophecy in this regard. This dreadful prophecy reflects that this huge Eastern army, when loosed, will destroy a third of the world's population by fire, smoke and brimstone.[19] Some authorities attribute this biblical description to the use of thermonuclear warfare by this powerful army from the East.[20]

The exhumation or revival of the ancient Roman Empire is yet another integral part in the prophetic jigsaw puzzle. Most authorities and scholars of biblical prophecy see today's European Union, more specifically, the European Economic Community and the European Common Market, as the prophesied exhumation or revival of the ancient Roman Empire.[21] It must be remembered that the prophet Daniel had a vision in this regard; hence we read: "And four great beasts came out of the sea".[22] The fourth beast was described as "dreadful and terrible, and strong exceedingly; ... it was diverse from all the beasts that were before it; and it had ten horns".[23]

The prophet Daniel not only had those visions, but also received interpretations of them. Hence, we learn that "these beasts" represent "four kings, which shall arise out of the earth".[24] Therefore, the four beasts are four kings or rulers of four kingdoms. And the ten horns of the fourth beast or kingdom, "which shall be diverse from all kingdoms, and shall devour the whole earth," represent "ten kings" or ten rulers that join together to form one kingdom.[25] The European Economic Community accepted Greece as its tenth member and is undeniably comprised of countries heavily influenced in their culture and traditions by the ancient Roman Empire. It should be noted that the European Economic Union has had its own Parliament since July 1979 and has since January 1999 a single currency.[26]

Having clearly identified the major players in biblical Apocalyptic prophecy, it must be remembered that in prophecy this new Roman Empire is eventually to be ruled by the Anti-Christ or "the Beast", as he is also referred to in the Bible. This dictator of the world, with the support of a ten-nation (kingdom) confederacy, will be supported by the 'biblical Whore or Harlot', which represents a religious system that will give support and authority to the Beast.

Although it is generally accepted that both Napoleon Bonaparte and Adolph Hitler tried their utmost to exhume the ancient Roman Empire, but to no avail,[27] the World Dictator is to have much greater success. He is to be a dynamic, magnetic authoritarian. Initially, he will be relatively unknown but eventually has to come to prominence when he seemingly receives a mortal head wound which heals. It is written that from then, "all the earth followed the beast with wonder".[28] It is posited that the present social, economic, and political environment of the world is ideal for such a World Dictator. He will thrive in the chaos and sense of helplessness that pervades this so-called "Global Village" of Nation-States. Despite the endemic hypocrisy, racism, decadence and planetary stress that we now experience, we are forced to speak glibly of "the Global Village", "the Global Economy" and "the New World Order".

The Anti-Christ or Beast, empowered by "the dragon" (the Forces of Evil or Satan), is going to be an unparalleled negotiator, who will, according to some authorities, quickly rise to prominence and leadership in the European Economic Community.[29] It must be noted that this bestial political leader is joined by two other forces of evil: the second beast of Rev. 13:11 (also referred to as the False Prophet in Revelation 19), as well as the notorious "Harlot" of Rev. 17:1-18, which represents this powerful, religious system, with its headquarters in a "great city, which reigneth over the kings (or nations) of the earth". This evil triumvirate will hold sway over the world for a short while. This unholy trinity will be comprised of the Gentile political leader or first beast,[30] the False

Prophet or second beast,[31] who is supposedly not a Gentile but a descendant of Abraham from the land of Palestine,[32] and the powerful, world-wide religious system called "Mystery, Babylon the Great, Mother of Harlots", who is portrayed in the Bible as having "a golden cup in her hand" and "arrayed in purple and scarlet", as well as being "decked in gold, precious stones and pearls".[33] It should be noted that Isaiah also condemned the daughter of Babylon, referred to in the Book of Revelation as the "Mother of Harlots", when he said, "Come down, and sit in the dust, O ... daughter of Babylon.... Sit thou silent, and get thee into darkness, ... for thou shalt no more be called, the lady of kingdoms".[34] This Babylonic religious system is portrayed as extremely powerful in that she not only supports the Beast but also sits on him and, by inference, controls him.[35]

Before dealing with the fall of the Beast and the Babylonic system, which is on the horizon, we must deal briefly with the biblical signs of the end for which we were told to look. The Messiah of the Bible, Yashua or Jesus the Christ, was specifically asked: "what shall be the sign of thy coming, and of the end of the world?"[36] And he clearly forewarned of a time of great deception. He spoke of numerous deceivers who will come in his name,[37] "of wars and rumours of wars,"[38] of nations and kingdoms rising up against each other,[39] of an increase in plagues,[40] "famines, and pestilences", as well as "earthquakes in divers places".[41] It is written that "(a)ll these things are the beginning of sorrows".[42]

In these times it is written that many shall betray and hate each other,[43] but those that endure (by living lives of faith and love) until the end shall be saved.[44] It is also noteworthy that it is prophesied that before the end, the Gospel of the Kingdom would be preached throughout the world, as it has been.[45] It is also written that "there will be terror and great signs from heaven",[46] and that "men shall faint from terror, apprehensive of what is coming to the world, for the heavens ... shall be shaken".[47]

Strictly speaking, "the time of trouble" or "the tribulation" is prophesied to last for seven years,[48] the last three-and-a-half years being referred to as "the great tribulation".[49] In biblical prophecy these seven years are commonly accepted to immediately precede the second coming of Yashua or Jesus the Christ, the Messiah of this age.[50]

We will now deal briefly with the fall of the evil triumvirate, as well as the Armageddon and the time of spiritual harmony and peace that is biblically prophesied to follow.

As inferred above, from the malaise of world-wide political and social chaos (with the assistance of modern telecommunications technology), the evil triumvirate (led by the Beast) is predicted to enjoy almost absolute control of the world for three-and-a-half years.[51] It is therefore written that "all who dwell on the earth shall worship him, every one whose name has not been written from the foundation of the world in the book of the Lamb who has been slain".[52] Incidentally, the slain Lamb represents Yashua or Jesus the Christ, the Messiah, who was crucified for all sinners.[53]

In Revelation 18 and 19, there is a vivid portrayal of the ultimate fall of Babylon the Great, the Beast and his False Prophet, who helped him to institutionalise (in those last days) that all who trade (buy and sell) in the world must accept the mark of the Beast.[54] In Revelation 18, we read of an angelic being with a mighty voice saying: "Babylon the great is fallen ... she has become a den of demons, a haunt of devils and every ... evil spirit, ... for all nations have drunk the wine of her passion (immorality). The kings (rulers) of the earth have committed fornication with her, and the merchants (businessmen) of the earth have grown rich from the wealth of her wantonness.... And the kings (rulers) of the earth who committed fornication and were wanton with her (enjoyed her luxuries and favours), will weep and wail over her (will mourn).... Alas! alas! ... thou mighty city, Babylon! In one hour has thy judgment come".[55]

And the merchants (businessmen) of the earth will also be in confusion in that Babylon, the Harlot (this powerful world religion), is said to have been the biggest customer of their cargo, which included inter alia: gold, silver, jewels, fine linen, purple, silk and scarlet, all kinds of scented and costly wood, articles of ivory, marble, spice, incense, wine, oil and even slaves and the Souls of men.[56] It is written that Babylon's merchants (businessmen) will be known throughout the world, and all nations will be taken in by her sorcery. She is also said to be responsible for the blood of all the prophets and saints. Hence, in harmony with the kings (the rulers of the world), the merchants (businessmen) shall also mourn unashamedly: "Alas, the great city, so beautiful — like a woman clothed in finest purple and scarlet linens, decked out with gold ... precious stones and pearls! In one moment, all the wealth of the city is gone!"[57]

In Revelation 19, we read further: "Hallelujah! Praise the Lord! Salvation is from our God.... His judgments are just and true. He has punished the great prostitute who corrupted the earth with her sin; and he has avenged the murder of his servants.... Then I heard what seemed to be like a voice of a great multitude, like the sound of many oceans, and like the sound of mighty thunder-peals crying: Hallelujah! For the Lord our God the Almighty reigns! Let us be glad and honour him, for the time has come for the wedding banquet of the Lamb, and his bride has prepared herself".[58]

"Then I saw heaven open and a white horse standing there; and the one sitting on the horse was named Faithful and True, the one who justly punishes and makes war.... He was clothed with garments dipped in blood and his title was The Word of God.... On his robe and thigh was written this title: King of Kings and Lord of Lords".[59] "And I saw the beast and the kings of the earth (rulers of the world) with their armies gathered to make war against him that sits on the horse and his army. And the beast was captured and ... the false prophet, who in the presence of the beast worked miracles (signs) by which he deceived those who had received the mark of the beast and those who worshipped the beast's image. Both (the Beast and the False Prophet) were thrown alive into the lake of fire that burns with brimstone (sulphur). And their entire army was killed with the sharp sword in the mouth of the one riding the white horse, and all the birds ... were gorged with their flesh".[60]

For further details and insight into the great purge or blood bath called the Armageddon, which many believe is on our doorstep, one may read: Dan. 11:40-45; Ezek. 38 and 39; Joel 3:2-2; Isa. 34 and 63; Zech. 12 and 14; and finally, Rev. 16:12-21, where one reads, inter alia, of a great earthquake of a magnitude unprecedented in human history ... of countries, islands and mountains vanishing ... and hailstones weighing hundreds of pounds falling from the sky onto people on earth.[61] These are the times when, if the days were not shortened, all would perish.

All the major players in Apocalyptic prophecy that were identified earlier become involved at some stage in the battle of the Armageddon that commences in the middle of the Tribulation period, and culminates at the end of that period. The Armageddon begins with the invasion and destruction of the city of Jerusalem by the kings (rulers) of the North and South (Russia and the Middle-East Confederacy of Arab States), and culminates at the end of the Tribulation period, when the Son of God returns to establish control on Earth thereby destroying the Beast, the kings (rulers) of the earth, and their armies (the head of the Federated States of Europe and the armies of Europe, as well as the 200 million strong army from the East, purportedly China and other Asiatic Nations).[62] Only at that stage of world history, it is posited, can it truly be said that "(t)he kingdom of this world now belongs to our Lord, and to his Christ; and he shall reign forever".[63]

In Revelation 20, we read inter alia that the devil, Satan, is bound and thrown into a bottomless pit for a thousand years. During this heavenly period of peace, the blessed and the holy (the true Israelites), who are the chosen of the Lord, live and reign for a thousand years with the Messiah in his Earthly Kingdom.[64] In that we are dealing with prophecy as it relates to the times that we live in, the loosing of Satan after a thousand years[65] and the second resurrection,[66] followed by the final judgment and the appearance of a new heaven and earth, are not dealt with.

Before moving on to other relevant prophecy, it should be noted that in chapter 2 we had an esoteric insight into the meaning of the seven seals in Revelation and the part they play in spiritualising the body-temple of an initiate of Christ,[67] but in this chapter, the literal interpretation of the Book of Revelation has been given according to the keys of prophecy as reflected in the Bible itself.

Other Relevant Prophecies

Having dealt with biblical prophecy, other sources of relevant forewarning and prophecy will be briefly examined. As indicated at the outset, there have been well-acknowledged prophets, saints, seers, visionaries and even remarkable buildings, such as the Pyramid of Giza, that reflect prophecies and crucial insights into the times in which we live.

We will first examine what can only be described as paranormal or what some may refer to as supernatural visitations of Mary that are presently happening frequently throughout the world. For example, there have been visitations all over Europe, such as the former communist countries of Russia, Yugoslavia, Ukraine and Poland, as well as Ireland, Asia, Japan, the Middle East, Egypt and other parts of Africa, Mexico, North and South America (including visitations in Argentina, Ecuador, Colombia, Nicaragua and Venezuela), to name but a few places. Over the last century, but more so, over the last ten to fifteen years there have been numerous reports of very vivid appearances or apparitions of Mary, the Mother of Jesus, with messages or forewarnings for the world.[68] Those clear appearances or manifestations of Mary have been acknowledged by multitudes of people of all different religious backgrounds, such as followers of Judaism, Muslims, Catholic and Protestant Christians, as well as Pentecostal Christians. Some people, who have acknowledged seeing and hearing her message, had not before their paranormal experience acknowledged Mary or her importance. This may seem strange to some of us in that it is obvious that the mother who bore Yashua or Jesus the Christ, the Son of the Most High God, must be of great importance. The womb of such a being was immaculate, her virtue exemplary and her love and mercy fathomless. God chose her above all women.

As indicated before, the Immaculate Mother has appeared more in the twentieth century (and more so during the last ten to fifteen years) than ever before.[69] Prior to the last century, her appearances in the nineteenth century in Rue du Bac and LaSallette, France, introduced a new era of her visitations, as it supposedly heralded in the times referred to in Revelation 12 that speaks of a great sign in heaven of a woman clothed with the sun, with the moon under her feet, and her head encircled by a garland of twelve stars ... and there was also purportedly a great red dragon having seven heads and ten horns, with seven crowns on his heads ... and war supposedly broke out in heaven.[70] This war is said to represent the Immaculate Mother and her spiritual battle (with the assistance of Michael and his angels) to overcome Satan and his bestial allies on Earth.

In a nutshell, the message of all the visitations of Mary indicate clearly that the world is about to go through massive change through storms, floods, famine, earthquakes and fire; asteroids and comets are also mentioned.[71] The dominance of evil is being broken, but first great calamity and death is to take place; the forces of evil are having their last stand, but a great purge is coming. Her tireless plea to the world, sometimes with tears streaming down her face, is to repent and ceaselessly pray from the heart for forgiveness and mercy; repentance, prayer and fasting are said to be the means by which we can reduce the chastisement that is coming to the world.[72] She advises "purity of intention, humility and simplicity".[73] We are advised to "(r)ise and fight with the weapons of love and purity" and to forsake our "obsession with material success".[74] The clergy, priests and religious leaders are said to have angered God with their impiety and "obsession with money, honors, and pleasures".[75] Russia is also mentioned in a few apparitions not only as a place that will cause great woe to the world, but also as a place that will be eventually converted to the teachings of Christ. The Immaculate Mother also indicated that the West has caused civilisation in some ways to progress, "but without God, as if they were their own creators".[76] Religion has become a business in the West and Truth has long become secondary; further, it may be said, in these times Truth (in some instances) is an offence.

The visions and miraculous messages that occurred in Medjugorje, Yugoslavia throughout the eighties, and those which took place in the 1990's throughout the world, are seen to be the close of the era of forewarnings that began with the appearances of Mary in Rue-du-Bac and LaSallette in France.[77] This is gleaned from the tone of her more recent messages, such as this is the "hour of decision for humanity",[78] as well as we are on the "edge of catastrophe".[79] She has spoken of a Great Warning to be witnessed world-wide in the sky and on Earth, which will be the final warning before the chastisement. Due to the magnitude of the experience, no one will doubt that it is from God. In a flash, each Soul will hear the eternal voice of the Divine Spirit within them; they will see themselves as God sees them; and all that are capable of changing before the final chastisement will change.[80]

In keeping with the above, the consistency of prophecy for the times that we live in will be briefly considered. We will start with a well-known prophet of the Middle Ages, Michele Nostradamus, who was born in 1503 in France.[81] In the quatrains of Nostradamus, he foretold future events, even down to naming relevant places as well as names of people who played significant parts in history long before they were born. This he did in anagram form. For example, Nostradamus referred to Paris as Ripas, Henric or Henry as Chren, and aircraft were symbolically referred to as grasshoppers and locusts. Aircraft, it must be remembered, did not exist in his day.[82] This form of symbolism is also reflected in the writings of Daniel and in the Book of Revelation.

The king of the prophets, as he is referred to by some authorities, predicted the rise of three Anti-Christs: the Frenchman, Napoleon Bonaparte, was accurately described as the first, and Adolph Hitler, whom he referred to as "Hister", was clearly identified as the second. Nostradamus accurately described the Second World War — when it would begin as well as when it would end. He even wrote of the oven-like gas chambers of Hitler and prophesied about the use of atomic bombs in two bays, clearly referring to Hiroshima and Nagasaki. Nostradamus foresaw the development of submarines, space travel, man's trip to the moon, the space shuttle Challenger disaster, and the assassination of President John F. Kennedy; he even foresaw that a modern-day psychic would forewarn the great man. The modern-day psychic was Jeanne Dixon, who tried, in vain, to warn the late president.

Nostradamus also foresaw a great pestilence like AIDS sweeping over the earth at the end of the twentieth century, as well as super hurricanes and earthquakes in the late 1990's, and a terrible third world war to finish off the century. The super earthquakes are supposed to begin on the west coast of India and rise to a crescendo in the western United States.[83] He also predicted that "East Africa is to be split into three pieces and New York and Florida will be flooded".[84] Hence, Nostradamus foresaw vast changes to take place in the times in which we live. There are countless books on the quatrains of Nostradamus, but a few easily available ones for those interested in his prophecies are: *Countdown to Apocalypse*, Volume I, and *Nostradamus 2: Into the Twenty-first Century*, by Jean-Charles de Fontbrune; *Nostradamus and the Millennium: Predictions of the Future*, by John Hogue; and *After Nostradamus: Great Prophecies for the Future of Mankind*, by A. Woldben. It must be remembered that, although Nostradamus' quatrains are seemingly full of dreadful predictions, he also predicted that after the great changes to come in the late 1990's and early years of this century, there will be a golden era of peace for the remnants of humanity.[85]

Although there are numerous saints and seers of note who made similar predictions about the times that we live in, mention must be made of the Irish Bishop, St. Malachi, who predicted the names and character traits of all the remaining popes of Rome up to the last pope, who is prophesied to witness great calamity in this time culminating in the destruction of Rome, the city of seven hills.[86] Examples of other Christian saints and seers who made predictions about the desperate times that we live in were

St. Augustine; Anna Katherine Emmerich; St. Brigit; the Madonna to Berthe Petit in Belgium; the Blessed Anna Maria Taigi; St. Odilia; Elisabetta Canori; the Venerable P. Berbardo M. Clusi; sister Bertine Bouquillon; and sister Elena Aiello, to name but a few.[87]

Of the modern-day psychics and seers, Jeanne Dixon, who successfully predicted the re-election of President Truman and the assassinations of Martin Luther King, President John F. Kennedy and Robert Kennedy, is certainly worthy of mention. She, too, has spoken of the sinister Liar or Anti-Christ, whom she sensed to have been born in February of 1962; she also made many predictions about natural disasters and war in our immediate future. Like many others who foretell of things to come, she speaks of a comet striking the earth and doing tremendous damage. Her prophecies involve the U.S., Russia, China, the Middle East, and Israel, as well as some predictions about the Catholic Church.[88] Two other outstanding modern psychics or prophets who are also worthy of mention are Edgar Cayce, considered by many to be the best modern-day prophet, and Gordon-Michael Scallion, whose visions tend to support Cayce's prophecies.

Edgar Cayce, the 'sleeping prophet', always went into a trance when he diagnosed ailments and healed people as well as when he prophesied. There are numerous books written about the amazing accuracy of Edgar Cayce's diagnosis of disease as well as the efficacy of the remedies that he prescribed. Many people who came to him could not be helped by the medical profession, and in those days some of that profession tried to discredit him. Today many medical doctors not only endorse his findings but recommend and write highly of his remedies. To this end, one may read *The Edgar Cayce Handbook for Health through Drugless Therapy* by Dr. Harold J. Reilly and Ruth Hagy Brod, and *The Edgar Cayce Remedies* by William A. McGarey, M.D.

Among the many pertinent prophecies for the times that we live in, Edgar Cayce, who many years ago identified the Caribbean and Atlantic area as the resting place of ancient Atlantis, prophesied the rising of Atlantis in those last days.[89] In connection with the rising of ancient Atlantis, Cayce speaks of vast new tracks of land emerging from the Caribbean Sea and Atlantic Ocean.[90] In the writings of Cayce, a great deal is written about the Bahamas and Bimini Island as well as the ancient Sargasso Sea and the notorious Bermuda Triangle, which are all connected to the ancient continent of Atlantis.[91]

The Bermuda Triangle, where three-dimensional objects have been reported to have disappeared, is linked by some authorities such as Edgar Cayce to the Great Crystal of Atlantis, and by extension the Terrible or Bestial Crystal referred to by Ezekiel in the Bible.[92] This Bestial or Terrible Crystal, which was geometrically cut, was said to build up electro-magnetic energy from the sun and was the main, multi-faceted energy or power source for Atlantis; it was initially a blessing, but in time a curse. In time it was used for dominance and evil; hence, its burial today in the tongue of the ocean off Bimini Island.[93] It is said to be reactivated from time to time, which explains the periodical disappearance of three-dimensional objects in the Bermuda Triangle.[94] Edgar Cayce also predicted that the world and the continents as we know them presently shall be quite broken up before finally settling down into more stable times.

Edgar Cayce spoke of new land rising in the Pacific as he predicted for the Caribbean, but he foresaw portions of Japan and Northwest America going into the sea. Great changes are predicted to take place "in the North Atlantic Seaboard" of America.[95] Los Angeles, San Francisco, New York, as well as the southern portions of Carolina and Georgia, are all predicted to disappear. Safe areas are identified, such as "Norfolk, Virginia Beach, parts of Ohio, Indiana, and Illinois", as well as the southern and eastern portions of Canada. As part of the vast changes to take place, the Great Lakes are predicted to empty into the Gulf of Mexico.[96] The coup de grace of the prophecies of Edgar Cayce relating to those changes to come, is an earth-rending axis shift, which will change the electro-magnetic field of the earth and cause tremendous geophysical change.[97]

We will now briefly deal with another modern-day American seer, Gordon-Michael Scallion. He, too, has had visions of great change in the early years of the new millennium. In one of his visions he perceived that the earth became unusually quiet; then, suddenly, the wind picked up from the East and the sun seemingly abruptly reversed its direction in the sky, the oceans buckled, and a landmass from beneath the sea thrust into the sky. This seer's vision could clearly reflect the immediate effects of an axis or polar shift as predicted by Edgar Cayce.

This modern-day seer, Gordon-Michael Scallion, has attracted a fair amount of attention due to the accuracy of his visions thus far. Before becoming this well-known seer, he was a communications consultant. In 1979, whilst making a presentation, he lost his voice and was therefore hospitalised for observation. During the night, for the first time in his life, he got a vision of a woman seemingly floating into the room; she gave him certain instructions relating to prophecy. The next morning when the nurse came to check on him, his voice had returned. Mr. Scallion indicated on an A&E television programme called "Ancient Prophecies" that from that morning he could see what is known as the aura around all people and animals, as well as what I would refer to as the etheric or electro-magnetic field around plants. At first, he thought something was wrong with his eyes. He was not one who had read or had taken an interest in anything like the human aura and such things; therefore, he took all kinds of eye examinations. Mr. Scallion, like Cayce, has seen in his visions great geological upheaval. Incidentally, his visions include tremendous calamity: buildings collapsing almost everywhere and walls of water covering whole communities.

In 1991, Mr. Scallion and his wife started publishing his prophecies in a newsletter called the "Earth Changes Report". He supposedly had predicted Hurricane Andrew and the path it would take; the only worrying thing is that it came one year earlier than predicted. He also predicted accurately the earthquake in California in early 1992 as well as the flooding that has occurred in the Midwest of North America. In one of his vivid visions, he saw a map of the future North America: California becomes a series of islands; the West Coast will be Nebraska, Boulder and Denver; the Mississippi expands; and the Great Lakes up north merge. Some of New Jersey is also predicted to be under water.

Having dealt with prophets and seers both ancient and modern, it is interesting to note that the Great Pyramid of Cheops also has prophecy inscribed in its very structure. The Great Pyramid of Cheops and two other large pyramids are located on a man-made plateau known as Giza in Egypt.[98] In the introduction to *Secrets of the Great Pyramid* by Peter Tompkins, one reads that whoever built the Great Pyramid of Cheops clearly knew "the precise circumference of the planet, ... the length of the year...", and its architects very likely knew "the mean length of the earth's orbit round the sun, the specific density of the planet, the 26,000-year cycle of the equinoxes, the acceleration of gravity and the speed of light".[99]

With the above in mind, pyramidologists and other authorities, such as the English mathematician John Taylor, all agree that the Great Pyramid in Egypt, besides being originally an initiation centre, amongst other things, also contains for all humanity "divine revelation or ... prophecy". Although there are many books, an excellent book on the subject is *The Dramatic Prophecies of the Great Pyramid* by Rodolfo Benavides. This book, as well as others on the subject, indicates that based on the symbolism of the Great Pyramid, the internal corridors, various sizes of passages, rooms and steps represent "the measurement of time and the phases in the history of humanity until the end of time".[100] Both history and prophecy are engraved in the stone structure of the Great Pyramid. It deals with the past, from the commencement of the Adamic epoch, and the future up to the end of this epoch.[101]

In that many of the prophecies inscribed in the Great Pyramid have already come to pass, like the prophecies reflected in the Book of Revelation,[102] we will merely reflect one salient fact that should be known about the remaining years ahead in our time. In dealing with the years ahead, we are dealing with "the Chamber of Chaos ... found at the end of the Descending Passage", or a dead-end alley extending beyond the Chamber of Chaos, where it is dark and silent; many authorities claim that death reigns there.[103] The book *The Dramatic Prophecies of the Great Pyramid* should be read by those who desire details.[104]

Scientific Support of Prophecy

The advancement of computer and telecommunications technology, as well as optic fibre technology, make certain things possible as regards prophecy that would not have been physically possible before. This is well illustrated in books like *When your Money Fails* and *The New Money System* by Mary Stewart Relfe, Ph.D. These books, like many others, reflect the nightmare of the intellect (and by extension technology), outstripping the heart or spiritual nature in man. If the heart of man is dominated by the materialistic intellect, then science and technology will be used, as it is being used, deviously and selfishly for the dominance of others by a powerful minority.

In *When Your Money Fails*, we read inter alia that the 666 system referred to in Rev. 13:18 is already here. From pages 15 to 31, one reads of the world-wide usage of that dreaded prophesied number 666. For example, the number "666" is said to be the World Bank's code number and appears on Australia's national bank cards.[105] New credit cards in the U.S. are also being assigned the dreaded number, and it is commonly used by computer systems such as Olivetti Computer Systems and by central computers of huge business concerns such as Sears, Belk, J.C. Penney and Montgomery Ward. Those business concerns prefix their transactions with the number "666", "as necessitated by computer programs", it is explained.[106] The inside label of shoes made in European Common Market countries; the seal on the side of computers made by Lear Siegler; the employee badges of the IRS Alcohol, Tobacco, and Firearms Division; as well as purchasing paperwork of U.S. state governments and many IRS instructions and forms, all strangely use the number "666".[107] The dreaded number is now commonly used throughout the world, including Israel, where the people there are being prepared like the rest of the world to accept the number of the "False Messiah".[108]

A few other examples of the seemingly perverse use of the number 666 are as follows: the McGregor Clothing Company for a collection of men's wear; the encoded number of credit cards of some telephone companies; the identification tags on foreign-made Japanese parts for the Caterpillar Company, Peoria, Illinois; fertilisers; gloves; ID tags; MasterCard statements; computer receipts; record albums; IBM supermarket equipment; tanks built by the U.S. Chrysler Corporation for President Carter's Secret Security Force; some U.S. Navy helicopters; and other products in the U.S. Some metric rulers distributed throughout the U.S. have the number in the centre. Even the U.S. school system for junior high students is using a 666 system, to wit: 6 subjects, 6-week report periods, and 6 report periods a year.[109]

The rapid advancement of the Cable Network system, along with the electronic fund transfer system and the extensive use by computer giants such as IBM of a numerical coding system, has brought the 666 system silently and efficiently upon us. Many of our bank account numbers and goods that we buy are all encoded with the prefix 666. The Universal Product Code or UPC (black strips or lines of varying thickness plus a number) that we all see on many goods, cards and items that we purchase these days is said to be an 18-digit number, to wit, 666, which the computers can all decipher. The "latest evolution in the Universal Product Code is a horizontal 'F' and 'H' at the bottom, which is conjectured to be relevant for the future mark of the Beast, that is, whether the code or mark will be inserted on the 'F'orehead or the 'H'and".[110] It is written that since 1977 a Dr. Elderman of the European Economic Community announced that he was ready to give a number to everyone on Earth and that they plan to use "a three six digital unit, 18 numbers".[111] The said Dr. Elderman of the Common Market Confederacy in Brussels, in fostering a world-wide cashless society, is said to have unveiled a gigantic, three-story, self-programming computer. This computerised restoration system, he boasted, is supposedly capable of giving every human being a number.

Before moving on from technology and its implications as regards prophecy, we should also be made aware that cable TV, which has linked the world these past two decades and has ensnared millions of us (as we waste hours before our TV sets), has a sinister side that many of us have not realised. We all cherish our privacy, but soon by dint of modern optic fibre technology used in our telephone and cable systems, that cherished human right will be a thing of the past.

As regards cable TV making inroads into our privacy, it is posited that our TV sets are going to be used to monitor us, as is already the case in certain states of America.[112] Dr. Patrick Fisher is quoted by Dr. Mary Stewart Relfe as indicating that by the use of an optic fibre fish lens in the cable (that is attached to the back of our TV sets), the cable becomes a two-way light pipe. Everybody in the room watching TV can thus be monitored.[113] "Televisions will monitor work, earnings, food eaten, leisure hours, and programs watched. They will store in memory banks the analysis of each person's day"; the programming you watch will be known and stored in memory.[114] As regards telephones, there are modern computer programmes that programme certain key words into a computer, so that any time those words are used in a telephone conversation, the conversation is automatically taped. We can therefore thank optic fibre and computer technology as well as our advanced telephone systems (that have been designed specifically for such surveillance) for our loss of privacy in the world today. This clandestine, nefarious invasion of privacy will be fostered by the 'might is right', 'all-powerful', 'benevolent' New World Order as a necessary security device.

We will now link the spate of natural disasters that we are now experiencing, which were prophesied to occur, with the findings of some scientists. We, the people of the world, need no convincing that nature is seemingly in transition and change is at hand. The news is replete with the daily reports of natural disasters such as unprecedented, devastating hurricanes, storms, tornadoes, blizzards, floods, volcanic eruptions and earthquakes. Some time ago, *Time* magazine carried a series of feature articles on the "Killer Volcanoes" of the world.[115] The articles, under the heading "Science", were entitled: "Volcanoes with an Attitude";[116] "Apocalypse Someday, when the Volcanoes wake up";[117] and "Restive Warrior: After 70 years, Popocatepetl is stirring. How seriously? Countless lives depend on the answer".[118]

In the article entitled "Volcanoes with an Attitude", one reads that there are some 550 smouldering volcanoes right now in the world. In the words of Smithsonian Institution volcanologist Richard Fiske: "You can't stop them. You can't control them. All society can do is learn to co-exist with them".[119] Besides the threat of those smouldering volcanoes, the recent spate of earthquakes, for example, in Turkey, Greece and Taiwan, are vivid reminders of the times that we live in.

As thousands of people over the past few years have lost their lives, others their properties, via hurricanes, floods, storms, blizzards, volcanic eruptions, lava mud slides and earthquakes, many scientists — be they climatologists, archaeologists, geologists, physicists, seismologists, volcanologists or astronomers — are starting to wonder whether this increase in natural disasters is not in fact a prelude of disastrous things to come. Many climatologists are of the view that we are moving rapidly into an ice age. Ice and snow cover at the poles is said to be increasing in size and weight and will certainly contribute to the instability of the earth, which in turn could help to move the earth on its axis.[120] This is in keeping with the prophecies of Edgar Cayce and other seers, who have predicted such an axis shift at the end of the twentieth century or early in this century.

To add to the above, many scientists predicted a planetary alignment of most of the visible planets around the end of the twentieth century. When all the planets line up, it is predicted that the gravitational distortion or pull will cause further instability and could trigger a chain of events culminating in a planetary cataclysm. There are many scientists who now agree that they have greatly underplayed the part played by catastrophic events in shaping our planet and its development. Some seismologists predict that the coming global catastrophe will begin with a series of earthquakes in Japan, Italy, the Caribbean and the West Coast of the United States.

Finally, some scientists refer us to the ancient civilisation of Sumer. The Sumerians not only have detailed writings but pictorial evidence that depict our whole solar system with one extra planet between Mars and Jupiter of which we (of this era) were not aware before. This extra planet supposedly has a large, long, elliptical orbit, almost comet-like, which brings it once every 3,600 years between Mars and Jupiter and into our system. The recent appearance of a new large planet orbiting beyond Pluto has been verified by astronomers in the U.S. Naval Observatory in Washington. This planet is believed to be three to five times larger than our planet, and with its gravitational pull has the potential to cause global, cataclysmic disaster.[121]

Conclusion

The above undeniably reflects to the materialist a fairly gloomy, cataclysmic picture.[122] However, to the true Israelite or initiate of Christ, the times ahead, although trying, will be glorious times when Dhamballa or Balance will be restored on Earth. Life on this earth was ordained by God, the All-Father, to be a spiritual journey in the flesh; the ultimate journey for Souls in search of growth and development; the realm of the slowest vibrating substances of the All-Father. The need to restore Divine Balance has become absolutely necessary at this juncture because of mankind's ignorance (lack of spiritual knowledge) and consequent abuse of natural laws. If this abuse is permitted to continue, mankind's unwholesome behaviour and gross mismanagement of the earth's resources would do permanent damage to the earth and its biosphere, thus making it unsuitable for human habitation.

In that most people will accept that the times are definitely upon us, the priority advice at this time must be "repent, the kingdom of heaven is at hand".[123] To all those dedicated to Truth, you are advised to stay steadfast on the Path; be not side-tracked at this juncture by the nefarious ways and horrendous habits of evildoers. Develop daily a deep love of the Truth that you might be saved.[124] Remember, "God has from the beginning chosen you to salvation through sanctification of the spirit and belief of the truth".[125] Everlasting consolation and hope is said to be assured through grace; therefore, comfort your hearts, you lovers of Truth, and establish yourself with good thoughts, words and deeds.[126] Do this "that ye be blameless and harmless, the sons (and daughters) of God, without rebuke, in the midst of a crooked and perverse nation, among whom ye shine as lights in the world".[127] God is neither mocked nor fooled and His Laws are immutable. Hence, we read that evildoers will be cut off and the wicked shall be no more, whereas, on the other hand, the righteous will possess the earth, and will reside forever.[128]

To the rabid racists of the world that perpetrate this perverse 'social cancer' via international trade regimes, gunboat diplomacy and hypocrisy, they are advised to repent because their days are numbered. We must all understand that we are of one race, the human race, with the same divine potential. Nevertheless, truth must be told; hence, the chapter entitled "Beyond the Veil of History". How can you say that you love God and hate the first of God's Creation? Consequently, in the years ahead, may all of us humans who love God learn to love each other. We are all members of God's human family, so from hereon let us live that way. We must treat each other honestly, truthfully, lovingly and respectfully.

The Messiah and Christ of this age communicated to all of us when he said: "I have come to show you the way, the truth and the life. The things that I do, you can do also". And in Philippians we are advised in these times to let our moderation be known to all men because the Lord is at hand. As regards our thoughts, we are further advised: "whatsoever things are true, whatsoever things are honest, whatsoever things are just, whatsoever things are pure, whatsoever things are lovely, whatsoever things are of good report; if there be any virtue, and if there be any praise, think on these things".[129] And having thought of those things we must live love, because love is the fulfilling of the law.

To those who doubt the efficacy of the timing given for prophesied events, it is submitted that the pulsation of prophecy must be understood as a wave within the ocean of life and consciousness that is flowing towards the shoreline of the times that we live in. That the wave crashes against the shoreline a little earlier or later than predicted does not change the fact that the wave is coming in. A prophecy that is five, ten or even fifteen years off from the time predicted is like a few seconds in the vast eternity of time.[130]

Finally, "listen, I tell you a mystery: we shall not all sleep (die), but we shall all be changed (translated like Enoch) in a flash, in a twinkling of an eye ... the dead (the mortal body) will be raised imperishable, and we (those of us that are alive in the mortal, physical body) shall be changed. For the perishable must clothe itself with the imperishable, and the mortal with immortality".[131] For those who have ears to hear, let them hear; and may all those who have imbibed the Word be indelibly blessed and encircled with light in these trying but glorious times ahead. And so it is![132]

EPILOGUE

In that some people may seek to misconstrue for their own ends what I have written, I would like to state categorically that I have no desire to hurt or destroy any organisation, institution, race of people or anyone. On the contrary, the message is one of love, of hope, and of mutual respect for one another, but the truth must be told. We are all of the human race, God's creations, each and every one of us. Historical or spiritual truth must not be an offence; Truth is like the milk within the coconut, the essence of our being that nurtures our Souls, our minds and by extension our bodies. We have made use of the shell and the husk for long enough; we now need to be nurtured by the milk, the essence.

We can live together in harmony. God's plan for the human race cannot be frustrated. Truth must be told and known before true understanding and forgiveness can take place. "My people are destroyed from lack of knowledge: because thou hast rejected knowledge, I will reject thee". Only Truth shall set you free. The times are upon us. God bless you. *And so it is.*

Ray C. M. Harris

A SHORT INSIGHT INTO PRAYER AND MEDITATION

My people are destroyed for lack of knowledge.[1] For you have taken away the key of knowledge; you did not enter in yourselves (where at the centre of your being, the Indwelling Divinity or Christ dwells).[2] Nevertheless always remember, things you desire when you pray, believe that you receive them, and you shall have them.[3] And so it is!

From the outset it is submitted that both prayer and meditation are essential to the growth and development of the spiritual aspirant or initiate on the Path of Truth. Some may say prayer is speaking to God and meditation, on the other hand, is quietly listening to God. Some spiritual teachers compare prayer to a young monkey that grasps frantically with its hands, in times of crisis, to its mother's neck, as the mother makes good their escape; whilst meditation is compared to the young cat or kitten that stays quiet and still in a crisis so that the mother can grasp it at the back of the neck carrying it to safety — the kitten submitting totally to the care its mother. Some are of the view that prayer is paramount, preferring the monkey's approach. The young monkey that grasps its mother's neck represents the spiritual aspirant or initiate on the Path who constantly prays to God — God being represented by the mother, which carries the young monkey to safety in times of crisis. Others feel that meditation is paramount, preferring the cat's approach in times of crisis, whereby the kitten, representing the spiritual aspirant, depends totally on the mother by sitting still with total faith in its mother — representing God — to do what is necessary to ensure its safety.

The truth is, we human beings should use both prayer and meditation. We, being neither monkeys nor cats, behave differently in a crisis. Hence, a child in a crisis clutches around the neck of the mother and the mother simultaneously wraps her hand or hands around the child. This human method of clutching each other represents ultimate security, combining the cat and monkey method. Hence, we are advised to use both *prayer* and *meditation* in realising the fullness of God's grace: they complement each other.

The need to pray and meditate is as essential to your spiritual life as breath is to your physical life on Earth. And the same way that breath is inter-related to Spirit, whereby we became 'living Souls' when God breathed into our nostrils,[4] so too is prayer inter-related to meditation. For example, some spiritual teachers teach that every breath is a prayer unto God; and the sound of your breath as you inhale and exhale is your sound (song) or prayer unto God. And by extension, if you put your mind one-pointedly on the mild sound (song) or resonance of the breath as it flows in and out of the nostrils, you become immersed in the sound of your breath or song unto God. That is a form of simple meditation.

There are all types of prayer, for example: prayers of petition, of consecration, of dedication, for binding and loosing, for praise and thanksgiving; but the ultimate prayer is "Our Lord's Prayer" or the "Our Father", as it is also referred to. Hence, we will briefly analyse and present the ultimate prayer, "The Lord's Prayer", before dealing with a few simple meditation techniques. The commonly used version as appears in any authorised (King James) version of the Bible reads as follows:

Our Father which art in heaven, Hallowed be thy name.
Thy kingdom come. Thy will be done in earth, as it is in heaven.
Give us this day our daily bread.
And forgive us our debts, as we forgive our debtors.
And lead us not into temptation, but deliver us from evil:

For thine is the kingdom, and the power, and the glory, for ever. Amen.[5]

The above version has served humanity well in that, besides teaching deep esoteric truths, it has emphasised humility; this was necessary in that humanity has lived, especially over the last thousand years, in a very brutish, aggressive, unspiritual manner, whereby might is right and truth is an offence. In some circles, such as the Christian Brotherhood, it is pointed out for those who have ears to hear that our Heavenly Father waits patiently to give us our daily bread, if we would just accept it. Furthermore, the Heavenly Father implores us to feed on the bread of life (the Christ spirit substance), because if we do not we will surely die.

Before presenting the Lord's Prayer as originally taught by Yashua, or Jesus the Christ, it is posited that asking the Heavenly Father to "lead us not into temptation" is infra dig; that is not even something we would ask our earthly father not to do! Hence, for those of us who know that to live humbly is the only way to live, and that God is Everything, a more intimate, original version of the Lord's Prayer, as recorded in the Akashic "Records of Nature," is presented:[6]

My Father who art in Heaven: Adorable One.
Thy kingdom is come. Thy will is done in me, as it is in Thee.
Thou giveth me, each day, my daily bread, and
Thou forgiveth my debts, and I forgive my debtors.
Thou maketh me strong against temptation;
Thou delivereth me from evil, for Thine is the Kingdom
and the power, and the glory, forever. Amen.

The more intimate version above when said by the initiate reflects an affirmed faith that is essential in bringing about the spiritualisation of the three-fold body, which in turn culminates in the "Mystic Marriage" of the three-fold Soul to the three-fold Spirit. As Paul of the Bible indicated, you must persevere "until Christ be formed in you", whereby there is a transmutation of mortality into immortality.

After the initial words of salutation, the words of the Lord's Prayer relate to the purification and spiritualisation of the Dense, Vital and Desire bodies as well as the mind, the link to the three-fold Spirit.[7] For example, the words "Thou giveth me, each day, my daily bread" relate to taking care of the Dense or physical body; and the words "Thou forgiveth my debts, and I forgive my debtors" relate to the purification of the Vital body, in that the subconscious records of all thoughts, words and deeds (good or bad) are imprinted on the reflecting and light ether of the Vital body. By repeating those words of purification, a Soul is saved a lot of post-mortem misery in the afterlife; that is, if a Soul does not realise during a lifetime (here on Earth) the "Mystic Marriage" to the Christ within. And, finally, the words "Thou maketh me strong against temptation; Thou delivereth me from evil" relate to the Desire body and the mind, respectively. Desire is the great tempter as well as the great incentive to action;[8] hence, one's Desire body must be purified to work in unison with the Christ mind, as distinct from the carnal mind. The mind, it must be remembered, is the faculty of discrimination, which must in time deliver us from evil. Hence, the initiate must purify his mind and become high-minded through prayer and meditation.

There are many forms of meditation. For example, there is TM or Transcendental Meditation and Ananda Marga meditation, both of which have become fairly well known in modern times. For Catholic Christians there is a form of meditation known as "Centering Prayer", taught by a Catholic Monk called Father Pennington, which is excellent. He has many books on prayer and meditation, which you may wish to obtain. This meditation or centring prayer is done by consciously thanking Christ for his Indwelling presence and thanking him for allowing you to sit in silence in his Divine presence. Thereafter, when any disturbing sound is heard or distracting thought comes to your mind you merely replace it by mentally repeating the word "Love", "Christ" or "Jesus", according to your preference. This should be done sitting upright in a quiet place for twenty minutes. The spiritual attunement and peace that you experience when you do this cannot be denied.

Another very simple meditation technique, which may be referred to as the "So Hum" breath meditation, may be done by anyone. You merely sit in a quiet place and consciously put your mind on your breath. I say "consciously put your mind on your breath" because we tend to breathe in a very shallow manner, subconsciously. Concentrate on breathing deeply and·rhythmically. You should consciously breathe in and out slowly and completely. To start your meditation you must first exhale slowly, comfortably and completely, then whilst you inhale meditate on or mentally hear the sound "So", and as you exhale meditate on or mentally hear the sound "Hum". The mantra "So Hum", literally translated, is said to mean, "I am That".[9] "That" may be said to mean the "Divine Spirit" or, if you are a Christian, "the Christ Spirit". You should do this for twenty minutes. Alternatively, instead of seeding your breath with the mantra "So Hum", you may exhale "Fear" and inhale "Christ spirit substance".

As indicated above, there are many forms of meditation that are more complex than the above two simple examples. These more complex forms are taught by teachers of meditation. However, do not necessarily overlook the simple for the complex, because there is godliness in simplicity.[10]

In conclusion, you are advised to pray ceaselessly and to meditate at least once a day for twenty minutes, but it is preferable to meditate twice a day. However, if you seed your breath with a one- or two-word prayer or mantra, you can pray and meditate whenever the opportunity presents itself throughout the day. For example, before doing anything of importance in your life, pause for a few minutes and consciously do some slow rhythmic breathing and meditation with your mind held steadfast on a chosen mantra or prayer as taught above. You are advised to also use affirmations as taught in chapter 2, preferably as you arise in the morning and as you go to sleep at night. All that you require in life is yours for the asking. Awaken! The science of life is given to you, but it is up to you to use it. God is always ready to give, but you must be a conscious, willing recipient. Remember always: you are the children of the light and the children of the (new) day.[11]

APPENDIX II

RASTAFARI: TODAY'S NAZARITES

Introduction

On some of the remaining peaks of ancient Atlantis, to wit, today's Commonwealth Caribbean,[1] there was born a new breed of prophets, a new sect of Nazarites called the Rastafarians. The nucleus of this new movement originated in the island of Jamaica. From there the burning message of Truth, Love and Black heritage spread throughout the Caribbean and the world; where there are Africans in Diaspora, the message spread. Their prophecy, lamentation and social commentary presented as poetry in song has captivated the hearts and minds of the world. Their natural, innate simplicity, profound philosophy and dread-locked mane demand attention; sometimes, however, as will be explained below, the attention they have received, they could have done without.[2]

The Heart of Rastafari

The 'heart of Rastafari' can be said to be 'the Spirit and Soul of the African experience' from the beginning of man: from the Adam and Eve story. In modern times, 'the Spirit and Soul of the African experience' enlivened the consciousness of a modern-day prophet known as "Marcus Mosiah Garvey".

Marcus Mosiah Garvey was born on the 17th of August, 1887 in St. Ann's Jamaica. Some authorities say that his name "Mosiah" was a compromise between his father and mother and was linked to the name "Moses" of the Bible. His mother hoped he would lead his people like Moses; and, indeed, very much like Moses he led his people, as will be seen below.[3] The father of Marcus was a descendant of the famous Maroons and his mother was a God-oriented Black woman who was a regular churchgoer at the Wesleyan Methodist Church.[4]

By age twenty, Marcus Mosiah Garvey had become a master printer. In 1907 he was involved in the Printer's Union strike in Jamaica. Incidentally, the Printer's Union was the first labour organisation established in that island.[5] From such humble beginnings in the Labour Movement, Garvey's life blossomed. Seemingly, against all the odds, his life was filled with tremendous accomplishments; a few will be mentioned below.

During his life, Marcus Mosiah Garvey was involved in the publication of numerous periodicals and papers such as *Garvey's Watchman* and *Our Own* in Jamaica; *La Nacional* in Costa Rica; *La Prensa* in Panama; *The Negro World* in America; and with the well-known Pan-Africanist and publisher Duse Mohammed, *The African Times and Orient Review* in England, to name but a few. He travelled through many countries in South and Central America and worked tirelessly to improve the plight of the workers in those countries.

Garvey left England in 1914 after having spent two years there. After these two years of work, study and reflection, he was inspired with the idea of "uniting all Negro (Black) peoples of the world into one great body … envisaging not peons, serfs, … and slaves, but a nation of sturdy men *making their impress upon civilization and causing a new light to dawn upon the human race*". Thus was his vision.[6] Garvey also expounded the Eternal Truth of One God, One Aim, One Destiny — and consistently advocated the dignity and rights of all men.

Shortly after his arrival in Jamaica, he established the Universal Negro Improvement Association and African Communities League (UNIA). All people of African heritage were encouraged to contribute to the "rehabilitation of the race"[7] — so that, in turn, the Black race could further contribute to the development and advancement of the human race.

The potent seeds of Garvey's philosophy and opinions found fertile soil in the hearts and minds of the downtrodden Negroes (Black people) in America when he arrived there in 1916. By 1917, he had established a branch of UNIA in Harlem. The UNIA eventually built to a membership of several million Negroes in the United States, Africa, Latin America and the West Indies.[8] Garvey's economic program for the upliftment of his race also included the establishment of the Black Star Line Steamship Corporation and the Negro Factory Corporation.[9]

Support for Garvey and his organisation grew daily, and he is said to have addressed twenty-five thousand Negroes in Madison Square Garden on the 2nd August, 1920, with delegates coming from the West Indies, Central and South America and Africa. It was a great day of hope for all Black people in America and, by extension, the world over.

However, the Aryan rulers would not tolerate such power, dignity and organisation as exemplified in Madison Square Garden; neither were they prepared to listen to the truth about the ill treatment of Black people. Hence, with the able assistance of some 'brain-washed' 'Negro elite' and the 'Uncle Toms' of the Black race, the racists resolved to destroy Marcus Garvey and all he stood for. The forces of evil and racism were then led by the notorious J. Edgar Hoover, who was then U.S. Attorney General. Hoover was in the forefront in the battle against Garvey and all oppressed Black people. Unjustly, Marcus Garvey was accused and convicted of knowingly and with criminal intent, using the mail service to promote the sale of the stock of the Black Star Line Steamship Corporation, that is, after he knew the venture was hopeless. After Garvey was convicted of mail fraud in 1923, the forces of evil rejoiced; they felt that they had got "their pound of flesh", as Garvey had been an affront to white racists. He always rejected white supremacy as well as the injustices and lies it perpetuates; he saw it as a crime against humanity, as it is indeed.[10]

In 1927, Garvey's sentence was commuted, and he was immediately deported to Jamaica. In 1929, he began a new political party in Jamaica known as "The Peoples Political Party". The 'war' against Garvey was however continued by the Aryans and their 'lackeys' in Jamaica. Unfortunately, as bad as it may sound, some of us Caribbean people, from the days of slavery have been taught well to grovel for acceptance and to vehemently oppose our own; all this for some small monetary benefit or feigned acceptance by the white power structure.[11] It is not surprising, therefore, that opposition to Garvey's advanced thinking as regards the development of the Black race was so strong that he had to leave Jamaica and go to England. There, in exile, this Black leader, organiser, philosopher and prophet ended his life sojourn as "Marcus Mosiah Garvey".

It is posited that the following books relating to Marcus Garvey, to wit: *Philosophy and Opinions of Marcus Garvey or Africa for Africans*, compiled by Amy Jacques Garvey (2nd edition); *Black Moses* by E. D. Cronon; and *Garvey's Children* by Tony Sewell, should be required reading for all Africans on the continent and in Diaspora — for that matter, for all lovers of righteousness and Truth.[12]

Marcus Mosiah Garvey's "Back-to-Africa" philosophy brought about not so much a physical movement back to Africa, but a movement of consciousness, that affected the hearts and minds of all people of African heritage, especially those in the Caribbean, as well as North and Central America.[13] The revered Garvey helped to organise and unite his people as no one else in modern times had ever done; he revived in them a new self-dignity and pride, which is evolving to this day. One of the many things of note he told his people was to look for a Black king to be crowned; this event was to mean that the 'day of deliverance' was close at hand.

Garvey had spoken those words in the 1920's; therefore, his words certainly seemed prophetic with the coronation in Ethiopia of Ras Tafari, as Emperor Haile Selassie I in 1930. With the designation King of Kings, Lord of Lords, Conquering Lion of Judah, Haile Selassie I, as a direct line descendant of King David, seemed to fit the prophetic words of Garvey perfectly; his bloodline can be traced back to Solomon and Sheba, who had a son named Menelik I. The deeply spiritual Africans in Diaspora, especially those in Jamaica, the land of Garvey's birth, searched their Bibles for proof of this prophecy; many were satisfied that they had found sufficient proof in biblical writings that Haile Selassie I was the fulfilment of prophecy. Some biblical references usually cited are as follows: Rev. 1:14-18, 5:2-5, 19:19-20; Isa. 43:1-15, 24-28, 65:9; and Ezek. 37:19 and 22-25.[14]

Almost immediately after the coronation in Ethiopia, some spiritual and religious leaders of Jamaica started to spread the faith that His Imperial Majesty Emperor Haile Selassie I, King of Kings, Lord of Lords, Lion of the Tribe of Judah, with 'hair like lamb's wool' (Rev. 1:14) and 'feet like burnt brass' (Rev. 1:15), was the manifestation in this time of the living God referred to in the Bible[15] and spoken of by Marcus Mosiah Garvey. Some of the early advocates were Leonard Howell, Robert Hinds, Joseph Hibbert, Altamont Reed and Archibald Dunkley. The early founders and followers referred to themselves in honour of Haile Selassie I as "Ras Tafari", utilising his name prior to his coronation, "Ras Tafari", when incidentally, he was also called by his countrymen "the Golden Prince".[16]

Those early preachers and religious leaders above mentioned were also supported by secular leaders like Paul Ervington, Vernal Davis and others, who supported the philosophy of Marcus Garvey and recognised Haile Selassie I as the Living Christ. The attack by Mussolini on Ethiopia (utilising chemical warfare with the unfortunate blessing of the Head of the Roman Church),[17] and *Haile Selassie I's defiant stand as he led his warriors on a white horse against the invaders* only confirmed what his followers already felt was self-evident. Rev. 19:19 was to them fulfilled: "*And I saw the beast and the kings of the earth, and their armies, gathered together to make war against him that sat on the horse and against his army*". King Selassie I's inspired plea at the League of Nations on behalf of his people and subsequent triumphant return to Ethiopia in 1941 was seen as the fulfilment of Rev. 19:15 and 19:20, respectively.[18]

Incidentally, this feat of the exiled king who returned to Ethiopia to lead his army of 250,000 Black soldiers to victory over their 'Bestial' enemies won the grudging respect and admiration of the world.[19] Some racist writers tried, as they had done before, to sever the Ethiopians from the Black race by calling them 'Caucasian brunettes'; but as an ancient elder and prophet once said, an "Ethiopian cannot change his skin".[20]

In keeping with the statement of the ancient elder and prophet, Ethiopia's children in Diaspora cannot change their skin; hence, Ethiopia's children in the Caribbean identified with and rejoiced at the Ethiopian king's victory. The 'long hair' or 'locks' of Ethiopian warriors, who fought alongside the Emperor, made an immediate impression on the early followers in Jamaica known as "Ras Tafari". Incidentally, the well-publicised success of the 'long-haired' Niyabingi Order of Warriors in Ethiopia over white oppression is seen by some authorities as the reason why some Rastafarians were related to violence in their initial years of development; it was felt that those Rastafarians were of the view that the oppression and racism in Jamaica could likewise be overcome by violence. From the late 1930's to the early 1960's, many Rastafarians were unfortunately involved in and arrested for crimes of violence. Frequently, they were also charged for growing cannabis (marijuana), which was and still is illegal.[21] It should be noted, however, that from the inception there were always many Rastafarians of the movement that dedicated themselves to natural living and spirituality, emphasising purity of mind, body and Spirit; there are many to this day who are so dedicated.

Before moving on with the development of Rastafari, it is important to realise that from the inception there were certain aspects of Rastafari that alienated the movement from the established social order:

- They proudly stood up for Africa, the Motherland of all Black people, and by extension all people, if we are to take biblical or scientific accounts of the creation of man and his development seriously;

- They represented the downtrodden, the poor and disenfranchised, those with no political or financial clout;
- They stood up and vociferously denied the Eurocentric view of life that was, and still is, the order of the day;
- They not only grew, but used cannabis (marijuana) medicinally, recreationally and as a sacrament; and
- They also used the 'spoken word' with uncanny power, which was, and still is, an aggravation to the authorities of the established social order.

In those early days, too, the British Colonial rulers were worried about the movement's allegiance to, as strange as it may sound, a 'Foreign King'. In 1934, the above-mentioned Leonard Howell, the first known advocate that propounded the view that Emperor Haile Selassie I was the Divine King referred to in Revelation of the Bible, was sentenced to imprisonment for "sedition and blasphemy".[22]

Another development of note in the early years that influenced the development of Rastafari was the establishment in 1937 of the Ethiopian World Federation; this was accomplished with the blessings of His Imperial Majesty Emperor Haile Selassie I. In 1938, a branch of the Ethiopian World Federation was set up in Jamaica. The Ethiopian World Federation was organised inter alia to bring about greater unity, solidarity, freedom and self-determination of all Black people of the world; to secure justice and maintain the integrity of Ethiopia, as well as to realise the brotherhood of man under the auspicious Fatherhood of God.

The doctrine of the Ethiopian World Federation spread rapidly among the masses of Jamaica. Over the years, tens of thousands of Rastafarians in Jamaica, and by extension, in the Caribbean and the world, developed an alliance, if not an allegiance, to the Spiritual Home of all Black people, "Ethiopia", the 'land of the Blameless Race'. Over the years the establishment in Jamaica of an Ethiopian Orthodox Church has further enriched and strengthened the link between Ethiopia and Ethiopia's children in Jamaica, and by extension, the Caribbean and other distant lands.

An Insight into Certain Aspects of the Religious Beliefs and Theology of Rastafari

The religious beliefs and theology of Rastafari are generally not emphasised or understood. Hence, a brief insight is in order.

As indicated above, Rastafarians trace their origin to Africa generally, but more specifically to Ethiopia. The physical as distinct from the spiritual link to Ethiopia follows from two beliefs: one is that Black people are the reincarnation of ancient Israel,[23] and the other is that they see themselves as the 'flesh and blood' descendants of the original ancient Israelites, in that many of their ancient forebears from Northwest Africa were either "Jewish at least in faith, and perhaps too in origin",[24] or at the very least well-versed in the religious beliefs and theology of the Hebrews. This seems well founded if one reads the scholarly work of Joseph Williams, to wit, *Hebrewism of West Africa.*[25]

The followers of Rastafari therefore represent those incarnate Israelite-souls who had seen the Light of salvation since the days of Yashua, the Christ, also called Yeshai or Jesus, pronounced by Rastafari as "Jess-us", after the root "Jesse".[26] Today, it is well known and acknowledged by most historical and religious authorities that the original Israelites were Black people; and even in fairly recent history, during the Second World War, the European Jews, many of whom had adopted Judaism, were seen by some 'purist-blue-eyed-blonde-white Germans' as 'tainted' with black blood. For that unforgivable 'impurity', as well as for other reasons, they were mercilessly persecuted by the world-renowned racist fanatic, Adolph Hitler, close associate of the above-mentioned fascist, Mussolini.

Rastafari, as the seers or prophets of those Black Israelites in Diaspora, not only accept Christ Jesus, unlike the European Jews, but recognise King Haile Selassie I of Ethiopia as the returned Messiah, the Christ-man of this era. As above mentioned, they proudly trace Haile Selassie I's lineage to the union of King Solomon and Sheba, or Makeda as she was called in Africa.[27] It is believed by Rastafari, as well as by some other authorities, that Menelik I, the fruit of that union, took the original Ark of the Covenant to Ethiopia where it is secretly held to this day.[28]

It is very evident that Rastafari accept Christ in the flesh and look to the Bible, more specifically to 1 John, chapter 4, verses 1-3, to support this. The origin of the House of David and Rastafari's link thereto is said to be reflected in Isaiah, chapter 2, verses 1-4, which is supported in Jeremiah 23, where one reads inter alia: "Behold the day is coming, said the Lord, that I will raise unto David a righteous branch, and a king shall reign and prosper, and shall execute judgment and justice in the earth";[29] "In his day Judah shall be saved and Israel shall dwell safely";[30] "And I will gather the remnant of my flock out of all countries whither I have driven them, and will bring them again to their folds; and they shall be fruitful and increase".[31] The biblical prophecy in Revelation 5 and Jeremiah 23 was believed, as indicated above, to have been fulfilled in the coronation of Haile Selassie I as King of Kings, Lion of the Tribe of Judah. He is seen as the prophesied appearance of Christ as king in this time through the lineage of David.

We read inter alia in Revelation 5: "And I saw a strong angel proclaiming with a loud voice, Who is worthy to open the book, and to loose the seals thereof? And no man in heaven, nor earth, neither under the earth, was able to open the book, neither look thereon.... And one of the elders saith unto me, Weep not: behold the Lion of the Tribe of Judah, the Root of David, has prevailed to open the book, and to loose the seven seals thereof".[32]

Specific biblical references in Isaiah and Ezekiel have been shown earlier, according to Rastafari theology, to refer to King Haile Selassie I; and, by extension, to the children of Rastafari in Diaspora, who are seen as that "righteous Branch" of David, that "remnant of God's flock", the modern-day Nazarites or Nazarenes of "the children of the Kingdom of God".[33] Before moving on, it would be good for the reader, especially those of us Souls in temples of flesh commonly referred to as "Black Folks" or "Negroes", to realise that whereas the Tibetans accept their Dalai Lama as the God-king and many of us respect this, as we should, we may be the first without any investigation, to reject the consciousness and beliefs of Rastafari.[34]

Before delving further into the religion and theology of Rastafari, it would be remiss of me not to mention two things. One is the pre-eminence of the Bible in the life of a Rastafarian; the Bible to the Rastafarian is a Sacred Book written primarily about Black people.[35] The other is that the religious beliefs and views of Rastafari are certainly not racist, although there are some misinformed people who may be of that view. Undeniably, Rastafari's religion and theology propounds and engenders great racial consciousness and self-dignity. This is a natural, necessary response to the rank racism that is the order of the day in Western societies. Fortunately, the perverse reverse racism is not meted out by Rastafarians to white people to counteract white racism. On the contrary, like their prophet Garvey, they preach One God, One Aim, One Destiny; their racial self-consciousness merely stands firm in the face of white racism and flatly negates it.[36]

Rastafari's theology can be said to go beyond racial boundaries because it teaches of the inherent dignity of all men, that is, the doctrine of the living Christ or divinity in man. To Rastafari, Christ is alive, incarnate within man; and your soul, mind and body must become one with Christ. They emphasise that the physical body is the temple of God and de-emphasise the large concrete structures emphasised by other Christian religions. Besides preaching love, which is the key theme of Jesus, they preach that

Jesus Christ destroyed death and not the other way around; also, Rastafari, as the followers of the living Christ, must in this time "perpetuate this victory over death ... and by so doing ... verify the existence of Christ's life within" them.[37]

The esoteric teaching about the divinity in man is as ancient as time. Within the framework of Christianity and the Holy Bible, "The Brotherhood", "The Ancient Order of the Divine Brotherhood", "The Order of Melchizedek", and since the coming of Jesus Christ, "The Secret Order of the Christian Brotherhood and School of Christian Initiation", have all taught and in the case of the latter order, still teaches the reality of the divinity or Christ within man. This Christ or divinity within must be realised here on Earth and not, as Rastafari would say, as a 'duppy in the sky'. The teachings of Rastafari are therefore in keeping with the highest esoteric teachings of the Massu,[38] Jesus the Christ, as well as the ancient prophets, high priests and elders.

Incidentally, a key concept of Rastafari, to wit, the "I-n-I" concept, refers to the Indwelling Divinity or Eternal "I" Spirit of "Jah Rastafari" that dwells in the hearts of all men. This Eternal "I" within man is the uniting "I-n-I" Spirit of Rastafari — in Christian parlance, the Christ in man, the true Self, the son or daughter of God.[39]

Although Rastafari teaches the divinity of man coupled with man's direct link to God — man being made in the image and likeness of God — Rastafari acknowledges the Absolute Supremacy and Primacy of God, man being His humble creation and subordinate. Rastafari justifies man's life and existence only in terms of God and justifies man's existence only if he serves God. "For the whole purpose of man is to serve God (Daniel)".[40]

The main name and appellation of God used by Rastafarians is "JAH RASTAFARI" or simply "JAH". "JAH" is possibly derived from the Hebrew "Yahweh". The name "Jah" is used in certain Bibles, and is similar to words like Eli-jah or Hallelu-jah.[41] As indicated above, the word "Rastafari" is derived from Haile Selassie I's appellation before his coronation as Emperor. In Amharic, the word "RAS" means Prince, Head or Self, and the word "Tafari" reflects His Imperial Majesty's proper name prior to coronation. Hence, to a Rastafarian "Jah Rastafari" is God, the Creator, the One who brought the world into existence and maintains it. They believe that "Jah dwells everywhere and has existed from the beginning of time; (H)e knows man's innermost thoughts and can accomplish all things". To them "the spirit of the King lives within all things".[42] Obviously, to the Rastafarian the impersonal all-pervading God is personalised in the persona of King Haile Selassie I. The strict Rastafarian devotee teaches that those who recognise Haile Selassie I as king will receive a kingly reward, and those who recognise him as God will receive a godly reward.[43]

It must always be remembered that the God of Rastafari is first and foremost a God of life. To them, death certainly does not come from God, but comes from man's evil ways. Rastafari teaches that man was created to conquer death, which comes to man as 'the wages of sin'. To conquer death, you must live a life full of hope and faith in the God within yourself.[44]

It can be said that the doctrine of Rastafari evolved from the crucible of oppressed African Souls in Diaspora, who, grovelling in material poverty, realised the Eternal Truth of the divinity and peace within man. As the Rastafarian would say: "Jah dwells within I-n-I". The movement of Rastafari did not only quest to 'resurrect' for themselves the fullness of their own humanity, but sought to achieve this for all oppressed Black people. In discovering the depth, length and breadth of their own humanity, they realised their divinity, and by extension the divinity of all human beings. To Rastafari, to be completely human one must also be divine; and for God to be completely Divine, which He is, He must also be within man.[45]

With the foregoing in mind, Rastafari had to deal with what most would have thought was a telling blow to the root of the movement, that is, the passing away of Haile Selassie I from the Physical Realm. However, Rastafari responded with typical intuitive insight to the dethronement and death of King Haile Selassie I, who was undoubtedly "one of the most revered monarchs in history".[46] Hence, to Rastafari the

King of Kings was above politics; political events in Ethiopia didn't affect their belief "in the divinity and invincibility of the King".[47] Further, the concept of "death does not figure in Rastafarian theology, so the death of the King would only be a transformation from the temporal body".[48] In *Members of a New Race: Teachings of H.I.M. Haile Selassie I*, by Junior "Ista J" Manning, one reads: "H.I.M. Haile Selassie I disappeared from His socialist back stabbing enemies in 1975. No one knows where he has gone to...."

Ras "D", in response to a question from Professor Leonard Barrett, said inter alia: "God is a God of the living, not of the dead. So we do not think about death. Even so, take Christ, when the Messiah first revealed himself in the person of Christ, he said at his departure that he would come again. He did not die, he gave *up* of himself".[49] To Rastafari, "the King had not died, he had only moved away from the temporal scene in order to carry out his work as God and King in the spiritual realm. As spirit, he will be much more accessible to his followers.... (o)ne needs only to call his name and enter into his spiritual vibrations to feel his power".[50]

In the words of a Rastafarian from Portland Cottage in Clarendon, Jamaica: "I accept Selassie as I personal father, I personal teacher, I personal master. Jah, the most high, who is King Alpha and Omega, first and forever, beginning without last. Selassie-I liveth in the hearts of I-n-I I-dren, as creator of Zion and earth and all things and all people...."[51]

In October 1975, within five weeks of the reported death of Haile Selassie I, there was a massive extravaganza of sound at the Jamaican National Stadium, where thousands of people not only heard 'one of the seven wonders of the world', Stevie Wonder, but also heard the legendary Prince of Reggae, Robert Nestor "Bob" Marley O.M., sing: "Jah live, children, yeah!" The song, like an anthem of the people, was felt and understood by all present.[52]

The fact that the death and burial of King Haile Selassie I was covered in secrecy, with "no details of where the burial took place", is also alluded to by Rastafari.[53] As Professor Barrett correctly points out on pages 215-216 of his book *The Rastafarians*: throughout history, "the death of founders does not severely affect religious movements; it often deepens the faith of the followers". Further, he posits that the king concept "played ... a unifying function in the development of the movement, a collective self-discovery device.... The real force of the movement is the concept of Ethiopianism, Haile Selassie being only part of the Godhead". Nevertheless, in the hearts and minds of Rastafari "Jah-Jah Live".[54] And in the words of a Rastafarian: "Jah liveth within all who have life upon the face of this earth.... Jah in the white, Jah in the black, Jah in the red. In any colour you want to name, Jah in him". In the theology of Rastafari, "Jah Rastafari" lives within the hearts of all human beings.[55]

An Insight Into the Lifestyle of Rastafari

The followers of Rastafari are naturalists who feel a tremendous affinity not only to Jah Rastafari, but also to Mother Earth, the Realm of our present existence. The earth and nature are seen as a unit and both are identified with God.[56] The key to understanding Rastafari is being "natural".[57] They are down-to-earth people. That is why they do not preach about "duppies in the Sky", but of a living God here on Earth. Likewise, Rastafari's view is that eventually heaven must be realised on Earth and requires that man's morals and lifestyle be in accord with natural law. Their natural living is reflected in the way they grow their hair, the way they relate to the land, the way they eat and use herbs, the way they communicate, work, write songs and make music.

The growing of one's hair and beard is simply an expression of naturalness. Certainly, as Rastafari would say: "Jah, the Creator made no mistake when Jah Rastafari created I-n-I and bestowed upon I-n-I hair as Jah Rastafari knew to be necessary". It is noteworthy that from ancient times, it was normal for people to speak of 'the long-haired spiritualist'. It is said that when people become truly spiritual and immersed in God they have an innate desire not to act unnaturally by cutting their hair.

Rastafari, moving away from the traditional 'vanity of vanities' lifestyle, grow their hair naturally into locks. They do not cut, comb and style their hair like most people do (which is seen as mere vanity), but wash it with an assortment of herbal plants; this they do to demonstrate their commitment to naturalness and the righteous path of Rastafari. They see this commitment to growing locks as a covenant with God similar to the covenant between the ancient Hebrews, known as the Nazarites and later the Nazarenes, and their God, Jahovah. Incidentally, the Nazarites, the Nazarenes and later still "the Essenes", represented the elect of God, the spiritual 'eye' or 'nucleus' of the ancient Hebrews.

In that the Rastafarians see themselves as the Nazarites of today, they try to conform to the Nazarite vow set out in the Holy Bible. Num. 6:5 reads: "All the days of the vow of his separation there shall no razor come upon his head: until the days be fulfilled, in which he separateth himself unto the Lord, he shall be holy, and shall let the locks of the hair of his head grow". Amongst the Hebrews the ancient Nazarites were set apart by their exemplary pure living. They did not cut their locks, drink alcohol or deal with the dead. Locks are said by Rastafarians to serve as antennae to receive inspiration from God, Jah Rastafari. This reasoning, incidentally, is by no means far-fetched but is substantiated by authoritative writings relating to esoteric Truth.[58]

Traditionally, locks symbolise "wisdom" and "authority". This is well reflected in the "wigs of locks" that judges and lawyers wear. Other people expected to exhibit wisdom and authority, like a Speaker of the House, on occasion proudly wears his or her "wig of locks". One would think that "real locks" would get, at least, as much acceptability and respect as the "false locks". Finally, the "locks" of Rastafari symbolise "the Conquering Lion of the Tribe of Judah", Haile Selassie I, who is said by some to have been a "Natty" as a youth.[59]

The above reasoning in no way denies that there are many 'dreadlocks' who are not genuine Rastafarians or Locksmen.[60] Some merely grow locks as a style to attract attention to themselves or as a matter of youthful defiance; others are mere criminals under the guise of Rastafari: 'wolves in sheep's clothing'. Some Rastafarians would say those criminal elements are 'rascals' not Rastas.

In that Rastafari is of the view, in harmony with scriptural text, that "the earth is the Lord's and the fullness thereof", this has influenced their attitude to the land and the use they make of it. Some of them have the view that no one should claim absolute ownership of land. The scriptural text above mentioned has been used by some Rastafarians to assert their rights as squatters to the tiny pieces of God's land that they see as necessary for their survival.[61]

Today, Rastafarians are to be found in all professions, trades and business ventures, but I think it fair to say that many are farmers; and even those that are not farmers have a great affinity to the land. The general view of Rastafari is that presently Mother Earth is in travail due to the abuse and total ignorance exhibited by 'Chemical-Western' man. Western man is said to have created an imbalance and is seen to have spread pollution throughout God's earth. Rastafari is firmly of the view, however, that balance and harmony — "Dhamballa" — will be restored to God's earth shortly.

In that the physical body is seen as the temple of the living God,[62] that which feeds the temple is of great importance to the Rastafarian. Hence, they use the land to cultivate sustenance for the holy temple. Throughout the Caribbean, they therefore produce fruits, vegetables and provisions that are indigenous to their island. These include oranges,[63] grapefruits, limes, papayas, coconuts, sugar apples, pineapples, mangoes, sour sops, bananas,[64] plantains, avocado pears, bread-fruits, watermelons, ginger, pumpkins, yams and other ground provisions. Obviously, some land is usually used to produce good quality cannabis, 'the holy herb' or 'incense' for the body-temple.[65] This practice, as indicated above and which will be discussed below, has caused a great deal of conflict with the authorities.

Rastafarians' fidelity to nature and Mother Earth is reflected in the food they eat, which they call "Ital" food. "Ital" food basically means clean, vital, organic food, grown without chemical fertilisers.[66] Many strict Rastafarians, in keeping with the idea of eating clean, pure food, abstain from blood foods and are vegetarians. In Gen. 1:29 we read: "And God said, Behold, I have given you every herb bearing seed, which is upon the face of the earth, and every tree, in which is the fruit of a tree yielding seed; to you it shall be for meat (food)". Some Rastafarians eat fish, however, as you also find that quite a few of them are fishermen. It is interesting to note that in an authoritative book entitled *The Essene Gospel of Christ*, vegetarianism is encouraged, but the eating of fish and birds in season is acceptable. Some Rastafarians have a strong aversion to pork and to meats generally, referred to as "deaders". The non-eating of meat is also related to the principle of non-violence, as meat eating involves violence and the shedding of blood.[67]

The preparation of "Ital food" is an art in itself; basically, it is the art of cooking tastily but simply without salt. This art is shared by both the brothers and sisters of Rastafari. They use a great deal of other herbs and spices in cooking their food. They also grate coconut quite often to make coconut milk to flavour their "Ital dishes", such as rice and peas. As most Caribbean people would know, the coconut milk gives certain dishes a delightful flavour.

Moving on, we will now deal with the burning question of the growing and use of the herb "cannabis sativa" by Rastafarians. No presentation dealing with Rastafari would be complete without some short, yet serious insight into their perspective on the herb.

It is noteworthy that Rastafari's view and understanding as regards the growing and use of cannabis sativa does not represent the current accepted view of the authorities in the Commonwealth Caribbean. As proof of this statement, it is presently a criminal offence throughout the Commonwealth Caribbean to grow or use cannabis sativa, also called 'marijuana' or 'ganja'.[68]

It is interesting, however, that in recent times Rastafari's view and understanding on the matter has received support and substantiation by many authorities, including those with a medical and scientific background.

Rastafari's view on the matter can be said to be as follows: Despite the categorisation of the herb "hemp" or "cannabis sativa" as a drug, to Rastafari, it is not a drug. The hemp plant, cannabis sativa, has a recorded use of thousands of years, and the hemp plant is entwined with the history of the world. Some believe that it originated somewhere to the north of the Himalayan Mountains. Some say it originated in Asia, others Africa.

Rastafari points to history to support their use of cannabis (hemp). "The earliest known woven fabric was apparently of hemp, which began to be worked in the eighth millennium (8000-7000 B.C.)".[69] There is also recorded reference to the cultivation and use of hemp in China as far back as 3000 B.C. Also, as far back as the fifth century, its use as a euphoriant is recorded by the Greek historian Herodotus. He wrote that the ancient Thracians and Scythians used hemp (cannabis) for clothing and also inhaled the vapours of the burning seeds.[70]

The Thracians and Scythians were not the only recorded users. The sacred writings of India, to wit, the Atharva-Veda, mention the plant as "bhanga", and the Zend-Avesta, written centuries before Christ, also mentions it along with its euphorigenic properties. The fourth book of the Vedas called hemp "vigahia": the source of happiness. The Iranian tribes from time immemorial are said to have used it and so, too, do many of the holy men of India to this day: some Yogis and other contemplatives either eat or smoke it "to quiet the distractions of the world and to put their thoughts into an egoless trance".[71]

By A.D. 500, the plant had spread all over Europe. However, it is said that hemp (cannabis sativa or marijuana) was known in the New World before the arrival of the

Europeans. It was known to be used by the Aztecs and other indigenous people of the New World in religious rites. After the Europeans' arrival in the New World and their introduction of forced labour and slavery, the East Indian workers and African slaves were known to have used cannabis.

In more recent history, many of the great thinkers and philosophers of Western civilisation, such as John Stuart Mill, Alexander Dumas, Fitzhugh Ludlow, Walter de la Mare, Aldous Huxley and William James, are said to have used the herb. So, too, it has been written about by many ancient and modern writers, such as: Pliny, Lucilius, Celsus, Cato, Columella and Titus Livius, to name a few ancient ones, and Allen Ginsberg, G. Jung, Lewis Carroll, Alan Watts and Herman Hesse, to name a few modern ones.[72] It is also recorded that George Washington and Thomas Jefferson, both presidents of the United States of America, grew cannabis on their plantations.[73]

Rastafari also points to the plant's economic and medicinal value throughout history. In February 1938, an influential journal *Popular Mechanics* published an article about cannabis entitled the "Billion-Dollar Crop". Due to the fact that in those days the hemp plant was used to make paper, rope, ships' sails, canvas, fabric for clothing, oil for lamps, feed for animals, amongst other things, many thought that "hemp" was to become the billion-dollar crop to move America forward after the Great Depression. However, due to the fact that the best hemp is grown in the Equatorial regions of the world (where coloured people live) and the hemp trade at the time was controlled in America by Mexicans and Blacks, hemp (cannabis) was taxed in 1937. Immediately after legislation taxing cannabis was enacted, the production and sale of tobacco and liquor increased rapidly as vested interests worked overtime to gradually outlaw cannabis in America; nothing would now stand in the way of the tobacco and liquor sales.[74]

Despite the fact that since 1937 cannabis has been gradually outlawed, the medicinal value of cannabis is now almost common knowledge. Obviously, from around 1937 the use of cannabis as a medicine has been restricted. Recently, however, there has been a new upsurge of research and interest in the use of the herb.[75] Cannabis (hemp) is said to be useful in dealing with asthma, glaucoma, tumours, nausea (e.g., aids cancer therapy, seasickness), epilepsy, back pain and muscle spasms, migraine/headache/neuralgia, arthritis, herpes, cystic fibrosis and rheumatism, lung congestion (cleanser and expectorant), stress (by aiding sleep and relaxation), lack of appetite (appetite stimulant), and depression.[76]

It is also touted as an antibiotic/antibacterial, disinfectant, oxytocic, an aid to psychotherapy, as well as an agent to ease withdrawal from alcohol and opiates.[77] Some Rastafari would say: a great deal more could be said as regards the potential positive uses of cannabis, especially as a healing agent. However, enough has been said to show the other side of the story.[78]

With the foregoing in mind, Rastafarians generally grow and use cannabis in many ways. As indicated above, they use it as a religious ritual or sacrament, for healing, socialising, reasoning[79] and "grounation". The word "(g)rounation" means the affirmation of life through the earth".[80]

The Rastafarians' use of cannabis as a religious ritual or sacrament has attracted much scholarly and legal discussion and debate, as throughout history it has been so used by cultures throughout the world. In support of their general use of the plant, they cite the above-mentioned Gen. 1:29 as well as Gen. 1:12, which reads: "And the earth brought forth grass, and herb yielding seed after his kind, and the tree yielding fruit, whose seed was in itself, after his kind: and God saw that it was good". They also cite Gen. 3:18: "... thou shalt eat the herb of the field"; Exod. 10:12, which exhorts us to "eat every herb of the land"; and Prov. 15:17, where we are reminded that: "Better is a dinner of herbs where love is, than a stalled ox and hatred therewith". Ps. 104:14 is often cited to show that God in His Wisdom created herb to serve man. We read: "He causeth the grass to grow for the cattle, and herb for the service of man...."

As regards the Rastafarians' use of the cannabis herb for healing, they cite Rev. 22:2: "... the leaves of the tree were for the healing of the nations". They also point to the medicinal history of the plant, coupled with up-to-date scientific research and findings as regards the healing properties and medicinal value of the plant.

In light of the foregoing, Rastafarians see no need to defend their use of the herb socially and during grounation.[81] They posit that the effects of cannabis have been found over centuries to be mainly anti-crime unless some other drug is taken along with cannabis (usually alcohol, crack or cocaine).[82] They also point to the fact that there is no recorded death in history caused by cannabis; this, they point out, cannot be said about alcohol, tobacco, LSD, heroin and the dreaded cocaine and crack, all of which have literally claimed millions of lives.

Some of the elders of Rastafari and other knowledgeable Caribbean people are even of the view that America's drug policy (War on Drugs) in the Caribbean was intentionally organised to replace cannabis with cocaine and crack. Cocaine and crack are both deadly and seriously addictive; cannabis is not. Cannabis for years has earned foreign exchange in the Caribbean and would be said by many to have assisted in giving insight and wisdom to the masses. Cocaine on the other hand takes money from the Caribbean and destroys the minds and lives of our youth and corrupts whole societies by the 'blood money' it generates.[83]

Despite the foregoing reasoning and the fact that some Rastafarians may be of the view that cannabis cannot be abused, it is submitted that like most things it can be,[84] especially by those who are undernourished and smoke all day long for years. And although for thousands of years cannabis has been used and does seem to cause users to introspect and gain a closer akinship to their God, the leaves, as distinct from the flowering tops or buds, contain a fair amount of tar, which obviously is not the best thing for the lungs.[85] The best thing for the lungs, and by extension the body, is Jah's clean fresh air, which has all the oxygen, cosmic energy and Christ spirit substance necessary for enduring survival, illumination and unity with God. Hence, the advice is: if you have not smoked cannabis, do not start; and if you do, you should think of stopping. Breathing exercise and meditation is a purer and healthier way for introspection and communion with God. Incidentally, it should be pointed out that not all Rastafarians or Locksmen smoke or use cannabis, although I think it fair to say that the majority does.

Before dealing with the legacy of Rastafari to the Caribbean, and by extension the world, it should be noted that Rastafarians, in keeping with the spirit of love, give great priority and respect to the family. They may not all get married in the orthodox churches or under the law, although some do, but they are very family conscious and take pride in raising their children in the ways of Rastafari. Usually joined by common-law marriage, Rastafarians generally live prayerful, simple lives without great emphasis on material wealth.

The female members of Rastafari are generally referred to as "daughters" or "sisters". This is in keeping with the feeling of affection, respect and protectiveness felt by the male members towards their female counterparts. The sisters of Rastafari are supposed to present themselves as "positive female role models to the community".[86]

The sisters are usually involved in bearing and rearing the children of the family. And although they are experts at preparing Ital food and looking after the family, it is not uncommon for the brothers to do those chores while the sisters spend some value time with the children or in other pursuits, such as developing their own talents and abilities. Nowadays Rastafarian sisters also pursue a variety of careers. With the new world-wide movement towards natural foods and ways of living, some Rastafarians, male and female, are in the forefront in developing business enterprises in their respective countries to provide local herbal teas, remedies, tasty alternative foods, cereals and nutritious snacks.[87]

The Rastafarian family tends to conform to Deut. 22:5 as regards their mode of dress. We read: "The woman shall not wear that which pertaineth unto a man, neither shall a man put on a woman's garment: for all that do so are an abomination unto the Lord thy God".   Sisters usually wear their dresses from mid-calf to the ankles; and form-fitting apparel is not condoned.   The sisters and daughters of Rastafari tend to move with a certain serenity and dignity.[88]

As naturalists, the brothers of Rastafari discourage the sisters of the movement from using birth control devices.   In the words of Ras Hu-I: "A woman start to hate the seed of a man by killing them ... woman becomes the sexpool of corruption and man become the sexamaniac.   That's what a society of intellectuals produces.   Them na can't produce more than corruption".[89]   Obviously, Rastafari is strongly against abortion, and if a daughter gets pregnant outside of a legal marriage or common-law marriage, the Rasta community usually tries to assist the sister to prevent her "dependence upon Babylon ... in time of need".[90]   The Rastafarian lifestyle can be said to reflect a strong moral emphasis and communal spirit.

Legacy of Rastafari to the Caribbean and the World

From the hearts, souls and minds of Rastafarians have flowed the fresh, pure lyrics and music of Rastafari.   Their word-sound (lyrics) and music (instrumentation and harmony) have conscioutised the people of Jamaica, the Caribbean and the world. Their God-centred way of thinking: their love for Jah, humanity and Mother Earth is clearly reflected in their songs; so too is their love for Truth, as regards history, religion, social norms and politics.   Their social and political commentary in song, coupled with prophecy and guidance for living, have greatly influenced the cultural development of Caribbean people over the past 20 to 30 years.[91]

Caribbean people love their Reggae music; not that they do not love their Calypso, Soka, Cadence, Zouk, Bouyon or whatever other music that is played and enjoyed in the Caribbean, but they love their Reggae music with a passion.[92]   Some would say it represents the modern-day, musical heartbeat of the Caribbean; the sound of the rhythmic march forward of Caribbean people.

Jamaican Reggae has swept the Caribbean and the world with its simplicity, purity of lyrics and magical sound.[93]   Reggae music can boast of hundreds of top-class, world-renowned artists.   The following names represent but a few outstanding "singers of songs and players of instruments": Robert Nestor (Bob) Marley O.M., Peter Tosh, Bunny Livingstone Wailer (all members of the original Bob Marley and the Wailers), Jimmy Cliff, Dennis Brown, John Holt, Ziggy Marley, Joe Higgs, Pablo Moses, Max Romeo, Freddie Mcgregor, Gregory Isaacs, Ken Booth, Eric Donaldson, Maxi Priest, Nasio Fountaine, Lucky Dube, Big Youth, U-Roy, I-Roy, Rita Marley, Marcia Griffiths, Judy Mowatt, Sandra Jones, Carlene Davis, and J. C. Lodge; and groups such as: Black Uhuru, Frederick "Toots" Hibbert and the Maytals, Burning Spear, Culture, Ras Michael and the Sons of Negus, The Mighty Diamonds, The Third World Band, Steel Pulse, and Aswad, to name just a few that come to mind.   Obviously, Reggae music has evolved over the years in Jamaica, the Caribbean, Africa and other parts of the world and has not been an overnight phenomenon.[94]

Moving on from the musical contribution of the Rastafarian "Psalmists", it would be folly to think that their artistic and cultural talent ends there.   In Jamaica, the rest of the Caribbean and the world, Rastafarians have made outstanding contributions in art, literature and sports.   Some of the best artists, painters and sculptors are Rastafarians; their art is filled with religious inspiration, vibrancy and beauty.[95]

In keeping with their religious, God-centred way of thinking, *their natural way of living* has influenced the Caribbean masses to have a greater self-respect and godliness even in their material poverty.   Their closeness to nature and simplicity of life coupled with their exhortation "to eat natural, get off the chemical" has been translated into island-wide governmental campaigns and slogans of "buy local" and "eat what you grow".[96]   Regional governmental meetings have been held to discuss and develop these ideas in real terms. We need to eat what we grow and, obviously, the other side of the coin is we need to grow what we eat.

Over the last 30 years, there has generally been a trend throughout most of the Caribbean islands to move away from the land. Rastafari's philosophy and natural "back-to-the-land" lifestyle tended to counteract this. Some attributed this trend 'to move away from the land' to more job and training opportunities, coupled with what some saw as the 'stigma attached to working the land': like you had not progressed from slavery, so to speak. Others saw this trend as a mere sign of 'development'. Whatever was the major reason for this trend, Rastafari helped to counteract it and de-stigmatised the land; there is certainly a new respect and understanding of the need to plant and grow something and to identify with and relate to the land. This contribution should not be underestimated, because a complete movement away from the land could have spelt disaster to many agro-based economies of the Caribbean.

Although a great deal more could be said about the positive contributions of Rastafari, suffice it to say that Rastafari has given the masses of the Caribbean, and by extension all Africans in Diaspora (wherever they are in the world), an incisive look into Black history, a greater self-dignity and confidence, as well as a healthy respect for a simple, natural, God-fearing lifestyle — Caribbean style.

Some will say that the above is a glorified view of Rastafari, but the truth is, what has been written is the essence of Rastafari; it is the heart and soul of Rastafari: the spiritual essence, which should be known. On the crude, material level, there are many people with locks or 'rough tops' that may not adhere to the essence of Rastafari; it takes great self-discipline to do so. Many are now involved in the cocaine trade, destroying their own people. Some have made a name for themselves in America as modern-day gangsters and hitmen. This is unfortunate, but true. But it must also be realised that many men, well dressed in 'jacket and tie', who do not have locks, perpetuate the same nefarious crimes. All are products of the same society.

Relating his mind to certain criminal activity in America, a Jamaican Rastafarian in New York, who is quoted by Professor Barrett in *The Rastafarians*, posits that some of those bad elements who pass off as Rastafarians are merely "sent to the United States in 'mothball' by party officials to hide away until the time when election should come". "Political refugees", he calls them. As Professor Barrett rightly points out: "(i)n every religion there are many counterfeits".[97] And in the words of the said Rastafarian: "(a) true Rastafarian does not condone violence, robbery, murder, rape, stealing, and things like that".

Although a whole book could be dedicated to the study of Rastafari, I think it best to end with ten biblical directives that Rastafarians tend to identify with, if not adhere to:[98]

1. He that smiteth a man, so that he dies, shall surely be put to death.[99]
2. And he that smiteth his father, or his mother, shall surely be put to death.[100]
3. If men strive, and hurt a woman with child, so that her fruit depart from her, ... he shall be surely punished, according as the woman's husband will lay upon him; and he shall pay as the judges determine.[101]
4. And if a man entices a maid that is not betrothed, and lie with her, he shall surely endow her to be his wife.[102]
5. And ye shall be holy men unto me: neither shall ye eat any flesh that is torn of beasts of the field; ye shall cast it to the dogs.[103]
6. And every creeping thing that creepeth upon the earth shall be an abomination; it shall not be eaten.[104]
7. Whatsoever (that) goeth upon the belly, and whatsoever goeth upon all fours, or whatsoever hath more feet among all creeping things that creep upon the earth, them ye shall not eat; for they are an abomination.[105]

8. For I am the Lord your God: ye shall therefore sanctify yourselves, and ye shall be holy; for I am holy: neither shall ye defile yourselves with any manner of creeping thing that creepeth upon the earth.[106]
9. Ye shall not eat any thing with blood: neither shall ye use enchantment, nor observe times.[107]
10. Ye shall not round the corners of your heads, neither shalt thou mar the corners of thy beard.[108]

In closing, it is interesting to note that the author was present at a lecture and film presentation in the basement of the Seminary at Mount Saint Benedict, Trinidad and Tobago by the Jesuit priest Joseph Owens, the author of *Dread: The Rastafarians of Jamaica*. At that candid, intriguing lecture he said, inter alia, that in all his travels throughout the world, Rastafarians represent the group of people whose lifestyle is most similar to that of the ancient Nazarene, Jesus the Christ/Yashua, and his followers. With that having been said, I commend the above to all who genuinely wish to understand Rastafari better.[109]

NOTES

Chapter 1:

1. Max Ehrmann, *Desiderata* (1927; reprint, Crown Publishing Group, 1995).
2. Joseph Owens, *Dread: The Rastafarians of Jamaica* (Kingston: Sangster's, 1976), p. 177.
3. Deut. 4:29, John 15:4, Matt. 11:28 and Isa. 30:15, respectively.
4. Owens, n. 2 supra, pp. 177-178.
5. 1 John 2:4.
6. Ps. 119:97.
7. Rom. 8:1.
8. Heb. 13:18. Incidentally, the word "conscience" is used over 25 times in the Bible; see also chap. 2 text leading up to nn. 67, 92 and 122.
9. See *Dhammapada: The Path of Perfection*, trans. Juan Mascaro (Middlesex, England: Penguin Books), p. 9.
10. Ibid.
11. Matt. 5:48. See too *Dhammapada*, pp. 9-10.
12. Read Luke 11:33-35. It is interesting to note that the words "eye" and "eyes", etc. are used over 300 times in the Bible.
13. See Edward Lewis Hodges, "The Everywhereness of God", chap. xix in *Teachings of the Secret Order of the Christian Brotherhood and School of Christian Initiation* (Santa Barbara, CA: J. F. Rowny Press, 1952), pp. 106-118.
14. Isa. 1:18.
15. See Mark 4:39 as well as Ps. 46:10.
16. Ps. 91:1.
17. James 4:8.
18. See George James, *Stolen Legacy* (Newport News, VA: United Brothers Communications Systems, 1989), p. 3.
19. See reasoning as regards H_2O in Richard Ingalese, *The History and Power of Mind* (Romford Essex: L. N. Fowler & Co.), p. 30.
20. Referred to as the Christ within you in Christian parlance.
21. See Appendix I — "A Short Insight Into Prayer and Meditation".
22. Ingalese, *History and Power of Mind*, pp. 14-15; 34-35.
23. Ibid., p. 118.
24. James 1:5.
25. Eccles. 2:26.
26. See chap. 2, especially text to nn. 4, 6, 11, 24-41, 58, 72-86 and 92-104.
27. See reference to chap. 2 at n. 26 supra.
28. John 8:31-32.
29. John 14:17.
30. 1 John 2:17.
31. See chap. 2 text to nn. 156 and 255.
32. See text to nn. 157-159 and text to n. 205 in chap. 2 for the esoteric meaning of 'the fresh pure waters', Bible ref. Jer. 2:13; Isa. 58:11; Ps. 65:9; John 4:10 and 7:38; Heb.10:22; and Rev. 21:6, 22:1 and 17.

Chapter 2:

1. As regards GOD being the <u>G</u>enerator, <u>O</u>perator and <u>D</u>estructor, see *The Thoughts of P. R. Sarkar*, ed. Avadhutika Anandamitra, Acarya (Tiljala, Calcutta: Ananda Marga Publications, 1981), p. 10. For an interesting short presentation on "Nija: The Way", see Molefi Kete Asante, *Afrocentricity: The Theory of Social Change* (Trenton: Africa World Press, 1988), pp. 21-24; and on the meaning of "God", see Janheinz Jahn, *Muntu: The New African Culture* (New York: Grove Press, 1961), pp. 104-105; also see Frank L. Riley, "The Way", in *Biblical Allegorism: A Key to the Mysteries of the Kingdom of God* (Los Angeles: Phillips Printing Company; reprint, Mokelumne Hill, CA: Health Research), pp. 95-128.
2. As regards Melchisedeck, see Heb. 7:10-11 and 7:15-26; see too Heb. 11:5 for reference to the translation of Enoch so that he should not see death.
3. See John 14:2.

4. See Hodges, *Teachings of the Secret Order*, chaps. 8 and 9; also Max Heindel, *Rosicrucian Cosmo-Conception or Mystic Christianity*, 3rd ed. (London: L. N. Fowler & Co., 1974), chaps. 1 and 2; and Vera Stanley Alder, *The Finding of the Third Eye* (New York: Samuel Weiser, Inc., 1986), p. 45, as regards the realms, planes or mansions of God. See too C. W. Leadbeater, *Man Visible and Invisible* (Wheaton: Quest Books), Illustration Plates nos. II-IV, dealing with the planes of Nature, which appear between pp. 22-23.
5. Heindel, n. 4 supra, p. 29.
6. Ibid.
7. It should be noted that in Ingalese, *History and Power of Mind*, it is said that there are forty-nine states of consciousness; see too text immediately before and after n. 49 below, relating to the consistency of the number "forty-nine".
8. Reflect on the text to this footnote after studying Diagram I; consider the seven main Realms or Mansions and their subdivisions — from the REALM of GOD to the REALM of MAN; reflect too on the text beneath Diagram I and to nn. 1 to 4 supra. See too Heindel, n. 4 supra, p. 188.
9. Hodges, n. 4 supra, p. 107.
10. Ibid., pp. 58 and 59.
11. Ibid.
12. Heindel, n. 4 supra, p. 703; for a profound presentation on "Nommo", the Word, see Jahn, *Muntu*, pp. 121-155, especially pp. 132-133.
13. Hodges, n. 4 supra, p. 59; as regards "the Word" being inherent in the creation and manifestation of all "form" that we perceive in the material world that we live in; see too chap. 3, subheaded "The Materialisation of the Heavens and the Earth".
14. Heindel, n. 4 supra, p. 54.
15. See Hodges, n. 4 supra, pp. 108-109.
16. Ibid., p. 109.
17. See Heindel, n. 4 supra, p. 189, where he explains why the Earth Realm or 'Schoolroom of the Earth' must be attended and victory finally realised; the Earth Realm must be overcome.
18. See Hodges, n. 4 supra, p. 58; see too Diagram I.
19. Heindel, n. 4 supra, p. 216; Hodges, n. 4 supra, p. 110.
20. Heindel, ibid.
21. Heindel, ibid.; Hodges, n. 4. supra, p. 110.
22. See Hodges, ibid. See too text to nn. 229-233 re: Love as a science.
23. See Hodges, n. 4 supra, p. 111.
24. See Heindel, n. 4 supra, pp. 48-55; see too Hodges, ibid., p. 108.
25. Hodges, ibid.
26. Ibid.
27. Ingalese, *History and Power of Mind*, pp. 128-130.
28. See Hodges, n. 4 supra, pp. 108, 113; also Heindel, n. 4 supra, pp. 54, 113-121.
29. Hodges, ibid.
30. Ibid., pp. 108 and 115.
31. Incidentally, the Eternal "I" is the same "I-n-I" Spirit in the theology of Rastafari; see Appendix II entitled "Rastafari: Today's Nazarites".
32. Hodges, n. 4 supra, p. 114.
33. Ibid., p. 111.
34. Ibid. See too Heindel, n. 4 supra, pp. 36-37 and pp. 143-144.
35. Hodges, ibid., pp. 116-117.
36. Ibid., p. 117.
37. See Heindel, n. 4 supra, pp. 35, 94 and 143.
38. John 14:2.
39. 1 Cor. 3:16.
40. Luke 17:21.
41. Diagram II reflects the three-fold spirit, the three-fold body and the three-fold soul linked by the mind; see Max Heindel, *The Vital Body* (London: L. N. Fowler & Co.); also *Rosicrucian Cosmo-Conception*.
42. See text to nn. 56, 71 and 73.
43. See Desmond Dunne, *Yoga Made Easy* (Frogmore, St Albans, Herts: Granada Publishing Ltd.), p. 34.
44. Some also include the spleen; see Hilton Hotema, *Awaken the World Within* (Mokelumne Hill, CA: Health Research, 1991), p. 233.
45. Ovaries in females and testes in males.

46. Although it should be noted that vitality is also realised at a more subtle and powerful level through our Vital or Etheric bodies, see Corinne Heline, *Occult Anatomy and the Bible* (New Age Bible and Philosophy, 1991), p. 163, as well as pp. 245-274 for a priceless presentation on the endocrine glands. On p. 246 the seven ductless glands are referred to as "the anatomical sphinx".

47. See Acarya Avadhu tika Anandamitra, *Beyond the Superconscious Mind* (Tiljala, Calcutta: Ananda Marga), pp. 7-8.

48. See Diagram III.

49. See Heline, n. 46 supra, pp. 161-162.

50. See Heindel, *The Vital Body*, p. 33.

51. Prov. 9:1.

52. See Geoffrey Hodson, *The Hidden Wisdom in the Bible*, 2 vols. (Wheaton: Quest Books, 1994), p. 146; see also Gen. 2:9 and 17.

53. Illumination, moksha in Hinduism and nirvana in Buddhism.

54. See text to n. 255 below for elaboration on Christ consciousness and the Mystic Marriage.

55. Exod. 3:1-4.

56. See Heindel, n. 4 supra, p. 97; see too nn. 126-133 and the text relating thereto. Also engraved on this seed atom, located in the left ventricle of the heart, is said to be the record of one's life on Earth, whereby the soul is judged. See, to this effect, Heline, n. 46 supra, p. 27.

57. Some authorities say Shiva instead of Vishnu.

58. See Hotema, *Awaken the World Within*, pp. 245-255; Hilton Hotema, *Sacred Wisdom of the Ancients: Living Fire and God's Law of Life* (Mokelumne Hill, CA: Health Research), pp. 18-23; Swami Vishnudevananda, *The Complete Illustrated Book of Yoga* (New York: Pocket Books, 1985), pp. 321-325. It should be noted that the Sahasrara Chakra is the seventh centre, another example of the 'complete' spiritual number "seven" which pervades the Bible and all religious and sacred writings. Note too: God, the Creator of all that there is, is the All-Father (Gen. 1:1, Acts 17:24-28); the Christ in Jesus/Yashua and in man is the Heavenly Father; and the man who begets a child on Earth is the earthly father. See too Appendix I relating to prayer and meditation.

59. See Edward Shook, *Advanced Treaties in Herbology* (Mokelumne Hill, CA: Health Research), Lesson 5, p. 4.

60. Ibid., p. 3.

61. Ibid., p. 4. Only recently, more specifically, August 5, 1996 on the CNN TV Channel, it was reported that a computer programme to assist in the prevention of heart attacks was being developed which was directly linked to understanding the electrical currents within the body. It was also stated in that report that every time the heart beats not only blood flows, but waves of electrical current flow through the whole body; other statements were also made about the research being done on the electrical currents in the brain and other parts of the body. For those who have eyes to see and ears to hear, this is in keeping with the inner teachings of Christ to his Apostles and close followers (see text to nn. 130-133 below).

62. As regards frugal eating and fasting, read Arnold Ehret, *Rational Fasting for Physical, Mental and Spiritual Rejuvenation* (Beaumont, CA: Ehret Literature Publishing Co.), and *Mucusless Diet Healing System* (Cody, WY: Ehret Literature Publishing Co.); as regards the use of herbs, read a simple but enlightening book by Jethro Kloss called *Back to Eden* (Santa Barbara, CA: Woodbridge Press Publishing Co., 1981) or Shook, *Advanced Treaties in Herbology*; and finally, as regards exercise, especially breathing exercise, read Yogi Ramacharaka, *The Hindu: Yogi Science of Breath* (London: L. N. Fowler & Co., 1960); Vishnudevananda, *The Complete Illustrated Book of Yoga*; and B. K. S. Iyengar, *Light on Yoga* (London: Unwin Paperbacks, 1976).

63. See Ingalese, *History and Power of Mind*.

64. See Heindel, n. 4 supra, p. 63.

65. See Edward Lewis Hodges, *The Scientific Procedure of Spiritualizing the Physical Body* (Santa Barbara, CA: J. F. Rowny Press), p. 12.

66. See n. 80 below and text relating thereto (Desire body); also, Lobsang Rampa, *Wisdom of the Ancients* (London: Corgi Books), p. 16; and his *You Forever* (London: Corgi Books), pp. 30-41.

67. See Heindel, *The Vital Body*, pp. 114-115; also, text leading up to n. 92, as well as text to n. 122 infra.

68. See Heindel, ibid., p. 124.

69. Ibid., pp. 145-146.

70. Ibid., pp. 159-168 and 434-435.

71. See Heindel, n. 4 supra, pp. 10 and 433.

72. Hodges, p. 113.

73. Heindel, n. 4 supra, p. 10.

74. See Heindel, n. 4 supra, p. 142.

75. Ibid. See Llaila O. Afrika, *African Holistic Health*, 3rd ed. (Beltsville, MD: Adesgun, Johnson & Koram, 1990), pp. 161-163, re: wholistic female/male puberty.

76. See Swami Narayanananda, *Brahmacharya for Boys and Girls* (Gyling, Denmark: N.U. Yoga Trust and Ashrama), p. 22.

77. Matt. 26:40-41.

78. See Heindel, n. 4 supra, pp. 462-464.

79. Re: Mantras and Yantras, see Acarya Bhavamuktananda Avadhuta, *The Way of Tantra* (Denver: Ananda Marga Publications, 1989), pp. 59-69 and 97-99.

80. See Heindel, n. 4 supra, pp. 66-67; also referred to by some as the "aura", which reflects the condition of the Soul; see too Ingalese, *History and Power of Mind*, pp. 101-106.

81. Heindel, ibid., p. 66.

82. Ibid., p. 67.

83. See Heindel, n. 4 supra, pp. 96 and 404, respectively.

84. Gal. 4:19 and 2:20; see also text to n. 70 and immediately thereafter relating to affirmations.

85. See Hodges, n. 4 supra, pp. 68-69; also 1 Cor. 15:52-54.

86. See text to n. 55 relating one's 'feet' to the cleansing of one's desires, and the text immediately following n. 83.

87. 2 Cor. 4:18.

88. See Acarya Avadhu tika Anandamitra, n. 47 supra, p. 9.

89. Hodges, n. 4 supra, p. 126.

90. This is illustrated in Diagram V.

91. Hodges, n. 4 supra, p. 126.

92. Re: death and purgatory, see Heindel, n. 4 supra, pp. 97-112; the exceptions to the text to this footnote are some Masters, who give up the use of their physical bodies after their missions on Earth are completed.

93. See text to n. 30 supra and Diagram I.

94. See text to nn. 4 and 30 supra.

95. See Heindel, n. 4 supra, pp. 113-121.

96. See Hodges, n. 4 supra, pp. 134-138.

97. In the words of Peter Tosh: "Live clean, let your works be seen".

98. Hodges, n. 4 supra, p. 114.

99. Heindel, n. 4 supra, p. 117; also Hodges, n. 4 supra, p. 136.

100. Heindel, ibid., p. 119; Hodges, Ibid., p. 137.

101. See Heindel, ibid., pp. 121-122.

102. See Hodges, n. 4 supra, pp. 138-140.

103. Ibid., p. 140.

104. Hodges, n. 4 supra, p. 142; and Heindel, n. 4 supra, pp. 129-133.

105. See Hodges, n. 4 supra, pp. 155-156; also, Lobsang Rampa, *Wisdom of the Ancients*, p. 109, and H. Spencer Lewis, *Mansions of the Soul* (San Jose, CA: Supreme grand Lodge of AMORC, 1986), pp. 125-139. The idea of returning home every day or at the end of every term or academic year can be equated to the different lifespans on Earth experienced by different people; after this, those Beings or Spirit-Souls return to the other Mansions (Realms or Rooms) of God in the Spirit World.

106. Hodges, ibid.; Rampa, ibid.

107. Prov. 4:9 and 16:31; 1 Pet. 5:4; Isa. 28:5 and 62:3; Jer. 13:8; see too James. 1:12 and Rev. 2:10 re: "crown of life"; also Rev. 3:11 and 6:2. There are numerous other references to "crown" used in that esoteric sense.

108. See Isa. 62:1-5 and 61:10-11; also Jer. 7:34, 16:9 and 25:10; Matt. 25:1; John 3:29; Rev. 18:23 and 22:17.

109. Ibid.

110. Lewis, supra, n. 105, pp. 149-157.

111. H. Spencer Lewis, *The Secret Doctrine of Jesus* (San Jose, CA: Supreme Grand Lodge of AMORC, 1995), pp. 141-146; also Heindel, n. 4 supra, pp. 125, 130, 136, 147-174, 282, 357, 471, 507-508; reconciled to Christ's atonement at p. 401.

112. Paramahansa Yogananda, *Autobiography of a Yogi* (Los Angeles: Self-Realization Fellowship, 1979), p. 199.

113. See Heindel, n. 4 supra, p. 167.

114. Referred to by some authorities as "a courtesan".
115. Yogananda, n. 112 supra.
116. Hodges, n. 4 supra, pp. 153-163.
117. Heindel, n. 4 supra, pp. 147-174. There are countless other presentations and real life stories on the subject; "seek and you shall find; knock and it shall be opened for you".
118. See text to n. 110 supra.
119. Yogananda, n. 112 supra, pp. 371-372.
120. Matt. 11:14-15.
121. Hodges, n. 4 supra, pp. 153-154; also Yogananda, n. 112 supra, n. 43.
122. Heindel, *The Vital Body*, p. 115; also Ingalese, n. 7 supra, p. 88. See too Heb. 13:18 and 1 Pet. 2:19 and 3:16-18 re: conscience.
123. Remember always: "Faith is the substance of things hoped for, the evidence of things not seen".
124. See Bunny Wailer's *Blackheart Man* album.
125. In other schools of thought referred to as the Shiva, Vishnu or NTU Essence within. NTU is the cosmic universal force or spirit that is inseparable from its manifestation: "NTU is Being itself". See Jahn, *Muntu*, p. 101; for an insight into "NTU", read chap. 4, pp. 96-120 of this illuminating book. See also Appendix I.
126. See Ingalese, n. 7 supra, pp. 94-96. See too Heline, n. 46 supra, pp. 18-20, where hereditary diseases are discussed; certain diseases are more related to past misdeeds of the incarnating soul.
127. Hodges, n. 4 supra, pp. 147-148; as regards the permanent or seed atom of the Dense body being placed in the semen of the earthly father, see Heindel, n. 4 supra, p. 137.
128. Mark 9:41: "...Ye belong to Christ"; also 1 Cor. 3:23: "Ye are Christ's; and Christ is God's".
129. Note the translation of Enoch cited in Heb.11:5; and the reference in 1 Cor. 15:51 to those who shall not sleep (meaning they will not know death; see too Ps. 13:3) when Jesus the Christ returns; see also Rom. 8:10-14.
130. In Eastern esoteric teaching, one learns of the mantra that reflects the above, to wit — "Om Mane Padme Hum": He dwells within the Lotus of the heart. Note too the concept of the "Sacred Heart of Jesus", with the Flame or Fire of Life in the Heart of Jesus/Yashua.
131. Blood nourished by wholesome food, fresh air and cosmic energy.
132. That is, thoughts that do not dishonour God, the All-Father or the Indwelling Christ.
133. See Hodges, *The Scientific Procedure of Spiritualizing the Physical Body*, which is a subsidiary booklet to the book *Teachings of the Secret Order of the Christian Brotherhood*.
134. Gal. 4:19.
135. See, for example, Mark 4:2; Gal. 4:24.
136. Encyclopaedia Britannica, vol. xvii. See too Riley, *Biblical Allegorism*, p. li; and Geoffrey Hodson, *The Hidden Wisdom in the Bible*, vol. II, pp. 19-21, as regards the esoteric nature of the Bible and other sacred writings.
137. See Riley, Ibid., pp. xlvii-lii.
138. Mark 4:11.
139. Mark 4:33-34.
140. See Lewis, *The Secret Doctrine of Jesus*, pp. 73-95.
141. See Gal. 4:19, Col. 1:27 and 1 Cor. 3:16; see too Hodson, n. 136 supra, pp. 27-28.
142. Hodson, ibid.; see too text between nn. 115-116 and the text to n. 111 re: karma; as well as Riley n. 136, p. xiv; also Mark 4:11-12.
143. More specifically, the Red Sea obstructing the path of the Israelites represents the carnal, materialistic, animal mind or lower state of consciousness that must be crossed before true freedom from bondage can be realised; Riley, n. 136 supra, pp. 9-10.
144. For a simple but excellent presentation on the Massu's experience in Egypt, see Levi, *The Aquarian Gospel of Jesus the Christ* (Marina Del Rey, CA: DeVorss & Co., 1979); see also Riley, n. 136 supra, p. 115.
145. Hodson, n. 136 supra, p. 29.
146. Another aspect of the David persona is that he reflects the "half-way house" of a living Soul's journey back to God; he represents the partially regenerated person who oscillates between high spirituality and Divine inspiration and the unregenerate or carnal mind that brings one down to the depths of sensuality, perversion and cruelty. See Riley, n. 136 supra, p. 17.
147. Hodson, n. 136 supra, p. 29.
148. See text immediately before and after n. 79 supra re: effective prayer as well as Appendix I.
149. Hodson, n. 136 supra, p. 30.
150. Mark 4:38.

151. Gal. 4:19.

152. Eph. 4:13; see too Hodson, n. 136 supra, p. 31.

153. Hodson, n. 136 supra, p. 32.

154. Ibid., p. 33; see too Matt. 7:13-14. That is why traditionally it has been said: 'wide is the path to destruction and narrow is the path to salvation'.

155. Matt. 13:18-23 and 24-53. See also Hodson, n. 136 supra, p. 33.

156. Hodson, ibid.

157. Gen. 16:7.

158. Riley, n. 136 supra, p. 6.

159. See, for example, Gen. 21:14-20.

160. Hodson, n. 136 supra, p. 41.

161. Riley, n. 136 supra, p. 6.

162. Hodson, n. 160 supra; see John 6:47-58.

163. 1 Kings, 6:38.

164. Dan. 3:19-25.

165. Riley, n. 136 supra, pp. 83-84.

166. Another example in Genesis is Gen. 7:1-4, when one reads about Noah being directed to collect within his ark seven clean beasts, seven fowls of the air and "for yet seven days" before it was to rain for "forty days and forty nights". See too Hodson, n. 136, pp. 169-171.

167. See Riley, n. 136 supra, p. 133; see as regards the numbers "ten" — pp. 101-102, "twelve" — pp. 102 and 118, and "thirty" — p. 119.

168. Riley, ibid., p. 69.

169. Rev. Ishakamusa Barashango, *God, the Bible and the Black Man's Destiny* (Silver Spring, MD: Fourth Dynasty Publishing Co.), p. 23; also read pp. 20-25.

170. Gen. 2:7.

171. See Hodson, n. 136 supra, pp. 51-52 (parthenogenesis), 59, 148-149; John P. Scott, *The Hidden Bible: Genesis*, p. 2; Riley, n. 136 supra, p. 69. See too Hotema, *Awaken the World Within*, pp. 199-201.

172. Gen. 2:21-25; Scott, ibid.; Hodson, ibid., p. 129; Riley, ibid.

173. See chap. 3, "Beyond the Veil of History", where this is developed and further insight into the Adam and Eve story is given.

174. See Scott, n. 171 supra, p. 2.

175. See Gen. 3:16-24.

176. Scott, n. 171 supra, p. 3.

177. Gen. 4:8.

178. Scott, n. 171 supra, p. 4.

179. Ibid.

180. Ibid., p. 5.

181. Hodson, n. 136 supra, pp. 161-162, but read pp. 161-165 for the dual esoteric meaning of the above.

182. Hodson, ibid., p. 171; Scott, n. 171 supra, pp. 5-6.

183. Scott, ibid., p. 6.

184. Gen. 6:9.

185. Also referred to as the "Robe of Glory", "Auric Envelope" or "Causal Body"; Hodson, n. 136 supra, pp. 177 and 180.

186. Scott, n. 171 supra, pp. 6-7. Incidentally, Christ-conscioutised Spirit-Souls (Masters) can consciously leave and return to the body at will; this is called astral travelling.

187. Hodson, n. 136 supra, p. 181; also pp. 200-203.

188. See text to nn. 92-96 supra.

189. Gen. 8:2-3.

190. Gen. 8:4.

191. Hodson, n. 136 supra, p. 179.

192. Ibid.

193. Ibid.

194. See Hodson, n. 136 supra, p. 249.

195. Riley, n. 136 supra, pp. 4-5.

196. Ibid., p. 4.

197. Exod. 3:1.

198. Exod. 3:2-5.

199. Riley n. 136 supra, p. 5; see too Exodus chap. 5.

200. Riley, ibid.

201. See text to n. 161 supra; and Riley, n. 136 supra, p. 6. See too Exodus chap. 12.
202. See text to n. 143 supra, where the esoteric meaning of the "Red Sea" is mentioned.
203. Riley, n. 136 supra, pp. 6-7; also Exod. 14:13,14.
204. Riley, ibid., p. 7; Ps. 14:10.
205. Riley, ibid., pp. 11-12.
206. See text to n. 201 supra.
207. Riley, n. 136 supra, pp. 12-14.
208. Rev. 6:1-2.
209. Hotema, *Awaken the World Within*, p. 125.
210. Rev. 6:3-4.
211. Hotema, n. 209 supra.
212. Rev. 6:5-6. The bracketed words reflect the slight variations in wording one finds in different Bibles.
213. Hotema, n. 209 supra, p. 126.
214. Ibid.
215. Rev. 6:7-8.
216. Hotema, n. 209 supra, pp. 126-127.
217. Ibid.
218. Rev. 6:9-11.
219. Hotema n. 209 supra, pp. 127-128.
220. Rev. 6:12-17.
221. Hotema, n. 209 supra, p. 128.
222. Ibid.
223. Rev. 7:17.
224. See Rev.7:3; also, Hotema, n. 209 supra, pp. 129-132.
225. Rev. 8:1-6.
226. Hotema, n. 209 supra, pp. 132-133.
227. Ibid.
228. Hodges, n. 4 supra, pp. 68-69.
229. Spiritual or Natural Laws of God not commonly known or consciously considered.
230. See Ingalese, *The History and Power of Mind*, pp. 114-115.
231. See, for example, 1 Cor. 13 and 14:1.
232. As an aside, in these times of rapid change, even this simple 'rule of thumb' could, in the exceptional case, lead to difficulties. We do have some people with weird or 'warped desires', who may do to you strange things that they may not mind you doing to them! That is why a 'rule of thumb' is not absolute, but a guide to be used intelligently.
233. See Sri Aurobindo, *On Yoga I: The Synthesis of Yoga*, vol. IV (Sri Aurobindo International Centre of Education Collection), p. 565; read pp. 559-565, chapter entitled "The Mystery of Love".
234. See Ingalese, n. 230 supra, p. 77.
235. Ibid.
236. Ibid., pp. 77-78.
237. See an excellent tiny pamphlet by Enoch Penn entitled *Sex and Spiritual Development* (Applegate, CA: Esoteric Publishing Co.).
238. Matt. 5:8.
239. Titus 1:15.
240. For a profound understanding and distinction between "orgasm" and "ejaculation", see Afrika, *African Holistic Health*, pp. 176-177.
241. This will also be dealt with in the Adam and Eve story in chap. 3.
242. See Hotema, n. 209 supra, pp. 234-235.
243. See text to n. 52 supra.
244. See Swami Narayanananda, *Sex Sublimation* (Gyling, Denmark: N.U. Yoga Trust and Ashrama), as well as his *Brahmacharya for Boys and Girls*; see too Samael Aun Weor, *The Perfect Couple* (New York: American Institute of Universal Charities), re: sex magic.
245. Purification of the blood comes about when one eats frugally — pure, wholesome food — or by being a Breathatarian.
246. When one's thoughts are purified, the mind is free of thoughts that dishonour the Indwelling Christ Spirit or divinity within.
247. See Jess Stearn, *Yoga, Youth, and Reincarnation* (New York: Bantam Books, 1981), pp. 123-134. There are whole books written on the preservation of the life force, even if you are sexually active, by the masters of non-ejaculation; see also Weor, *The Perfect Couple*.

248. Incidentally, for an illumined, balanced, wholistic view of sex, that is, if one does not practice celibacy, or sex magic, one should read pp. 172-190 of Afrika, *African Holistic Health.*
249. See Zech. 4:12: "the two golden pipes empty the golden oil out of themselves".
250. See Ps. 23:5: "thou annointest my head with oil; my cup runneth over".
251. See John 6:35 and 6:41 and Matt. 2:1.
252. See Rev. 11:8; and Hotema, n. 209 supra, pp. 318-320.
253. Mark 16:19.
254. See Isa. 60:19; Matt. 6:22; Luke 11:34; also Hotema, n. 209 supra, pp. 320-330.
255. Luke 17:21.
256. 1 Cor. 3:16-17.
257. 1 Cor. 5:1.
258. 1 Cor. 6:18.
259. 1 Cor. 6:9-10.
260. Rom. 6:20-22.
261. Rom. 8:13.
262. Ezek. 18:23.
263. Ezek. 18:31.
264. Ezek. 18:32.
265. Ezek. 33:11.
266. John 6:49-51.
267. John 3:14-15.
268. John 8:51; also see John 5:24-25.
269. Rom. 8:14.

Chapter 3:

1.   Gen. 1:2.
2.   John 1:1.
3.   Gen. 1:7-10. This in no way runs contrary to the "Big Bang" scientific theory; the whole evolutionary process of the planets flowed from an initial Divine Ideation and an impulse that was put in motion to materialise this Ideation.
4.   Epeirogenesis.
5.   See W. S. Cerve, *Lemuria: The Lost Continent of the Pacific* (San Jose, CA: Supreme Grand Lodge of AMORC, 1997), p. 72; and Ingalese, *History and Power of Mind*, pp. 19-20.
6.   Gen. 2:10-14.
7.   See Rev. Cain Hope Felder, introduction to *The Original African Heritage Study Bible: King James Version*, ed. James W. Peebles (World Bible Publishing Co., 1993), pp. ix-xi. For that matter, at certain stages of history Europeans referred to all of what they knew of Africa as Aethiopia or Ethiopia.
8.   Ibid., p. 94, where it is pointed out that those two rivers in Africa/Aethiopia, "following a Latin designation ... have been known as the Blue and White Nile" of Northeast Africa.
9.   Ibid., p. x.
10. It must be remembered that the Suez Canal was only built in 1869; this effected a physical severance of what became known as "the Middle East" from Africa. The term "Middle East" was popularised by European World War II correspondents; ibid., p. xi.
11. Gen. 1:27.
12. Gen. 2:7.
13. Gen. 2:15.
14. Ruth Montgomery, foreword to *The World Before* (New York: Fawcett Crest Books, 1990), p. 11. The skull, which was unearthed at Olduvai Gorge in today's Northern Tanzania, Tanganyika, dated back to between 1,750,000 years and two million years. They christened the find "Zinjanthropus" or "East African man".
15. Marcellin Boule and Henri Vallois, *Fossil Men* (AMS Press, 1978), p. 466.
16. Cheikh Anta Diop, *The African Origin of Civilization: Myth or Reality* (Westport, CT: Lawrence Hill, 1983), p. 273.
17. "The Search for Adam and Eve", *Newsweek — The International News Magazine*, Jan. 11, 1988, p. 36.
18. Ibid.
19. Ibid.
20. Ibid.
21. Ibid.

22. Ibid.
23. Ibid., p. 40, where we read that "our cells carry the history of mankind's development, a path scientists followed to Eve".
24. See text to nn. 40 and 41.
25. *Newsweek*, n. 17 supra, p. 40.
26. Aeschylos, *Prometheus Bound*, translation (Great Books of the Western World). Quoted in *Crucial Insights Into African History*, p. 79.
27. See Yosef Ben-Jochannan, *Black Man of the Nile and His Family* (New York: Alkebu-Lan Books, 1970), p. 128; also Diop, n. 16 supra, p. 169.
28. See *The Lost Books of the Bible and the Forgotten Books of Eden: Gospel of the Infancy of Jesus Christ* (A Meridian Book, New American Library), chap. 17:9, p. 54.
29. See *The Evolution of Primitive Man*, pp. 11-12.
30. See too Diop, n. 16 supra, pp. 56-57.
31. See Gen. 1:26-27.
32. For such a view, see Montgomery, *The World Before*.
33. Cerve, n. 5 supra, pp. 153-154.
34. Montgomery, n. 32 supra, p. 36.
35. See Cerve, n. 5 supra, pp. 98-99.
36. See Montgomery, n. 32, p. 32.
37. Cerve, n. 5 supra, pp. 134-135; see too p. 153.
38. Mark K3364 British Museum Pre-Adamites referred to in Sterling Means, *Ethiopia and the Missing Link in African History* (Harrisburg, PA: Atlantis Publishing Co.), p. 12.
39. See Means, ibid., p. 36.
40. However, today this may be due to the interbreeding of Black people (people of African heritage) with other people such as Asiatics and Europeans.
41. Cerve, n. 5 supra, p. 26.
42. Ibid., p. 125.
43. Montgomery, n. 32 supra, p. 44.
44. Cerve, n. 5 supra, p. 124.
45. Ibid., pp. 123-126.
46. Ibid., pp.135-136.
47. Ibid., p. 161.
48. Cerve, n. 5 supra, p. 151.
49. Montgomery, n. 32 supra, p. 67.
50. Cerve, n. 5 supra, p. 132.
51. Ibid.
52. Eccles. 12:6.
53. Montgomery, n. 32 supra, p. 66.
54. Cerve, n. 5 supra, pp. 108 and 115.
55. Isa. 14:12-15.
56. See Montgomery, n. 32 supra, p. 25.
57. Ibid.
58. Ibid.
59. Cerve, n. 5 supra, p. 108
60. Ibid., p. 81.
61. Ibid.
62. Ibid., p. 82.
63. See Montgomery, n. 32 supra, p. 118.
64. Ibid.
65. Cerve, n. 5 supra, pp. 105-106.
66. Ibid., pp. 83-84 (bracketed word inserted by the author); see also Heindel, *Rosicrucian Cosmo Conception*, p. 291; Ignatius Donnelly, *Atlantis: The Antediluvian World* (New York: Gramercy Publishing Co.); and Montgomery, *The World Before*, chap. 6.
67. See Charles Berlitz, *The Mystery of Atlantis* (Frogmore, St. Albans, Herts: Panther Books, 1977), p. 16.
68. See Donnelly, *Atlantis: The Antediluvian World*; also Berlitz, *The Mystery of Atlantis*; Cerve, n. 5 supra, pp. 83-84; Ingalese, n. 5 supra, pp. 20-23; see too *Dialogues of Plato* — to wit, "Timaeus and Critias" — supposedly written around 350 B.C.
69. Cerve, n. 5 supra.
70. See reasoning thereon by Cerve, n. 5 supra, p. 85.
71. Ibid.

72. Ibid., pp. 85-86.
73. See Montgomery, n. 32 supra, p. 70; also, Ingalese, n. 5 supra, p. 20.
74. Berlitz, n. 68 supra, pp. 16, 66-69; better still, read pp. 57-69.
75. See Montgomery, n. 32 supra, pp. 85-86; although mistakenly identified with the Phoenicians.
76. See Ivan Van Sertima, *They Came Before Columbus* (New York: Random House, 1976), p. 162.
77. Heindel, supra, n. 66, p. 291.
78. Ibid., p. 292.
79. Ibid., p. 300.
80. Montgomery, n. 32 supra, p. 69.
81. Although some authorities would point out that Atlas was the oldest son of Poseidon, who preceded him.
82. Note reference to similar manifestations in the life of young Jesus/Yashua cited in *The Missing Books of the Bible* (Halo Press, 1996), pp. 52 and 53.
83. See Montgomery, n. 32 supra, p. 107, re: Lemuria.
84. For example, see Mary Ellen Carter, *Edgar Cayce on Prophecy*, ed. Hugh Lynn Cayce (New York: Paperback Library, 1982), p. 55; or Ezek. 1:22.
85. As regards the link between the Sargasso Sea and Atlantis, read, for example, Berlitz, n. 67 supra, pp. 54-56.
86. Ezek. 1:22.
87. See Montgomery, n. 32 supra, p. 96.
88. See Ingalese, p. 22.
89. These Asians interbred with the descendants of the Atlanteans (that is, Atlanteans who had sought refuge in America on the destruction of Atlantis) and were the ancestors of the Sioux, Cherokee, Maya, Aztecs and all the other Native Americans. See Michael D. Lemonick, "The World in 3300 B.C.", *Time*, Oct. 26, 1992, p. 41, reported by Andrea Dorfman/New York and Marlin Levin/Jerusalem, with other bureaus. See too Van Sertima, *They Came Before Columbus*, pp. 53-54, where he refers to the Asian influence via the Bering Strait.
90. Ingalese, n. 5 supra, p. 23; as regards the submergence of Atlantis generally, see pp. 21-23.
91. Hence, the need for spurious books such as the one entitled *Chariots of the Gods* by Erich von Daniken (Berkeley Publishing Group, 1999). Not that I reject the possibility of alien beings visiting Earth 40,000 years ago, but I do reject the typical white racist need to 'whiten' greatness wherever it is found, even if it be found in the heart of Africa. Even their Tarzan and Jane comic book story reflects this dire need.
92. See Diop, n. 16 supra, pp. 145-153.
93. Ethiopia and Egypt have sometimes been referred to interchangeably by Europeans when it suits their purpose.
94. Observe, for example, the endemic racism (even today) that runs through the fabric of the so-called 'bastion of democracy and freedom' in the Western world: America; see *Newsweek*, Oct. 16, 1995, pp. 7-21.
95. See Herodotus, *The Histories* (Middlesex, England: Penguin Series), p. 138; and in Penguin Classics, pp. 134-135; see too Homer, *Odyssey* — 4xii; and George O. Cox, *Crucial Insights Into African History* (New York: African Heritage Studies), pp. 83-86.
96. Diodorus Siculus, *Histoire Universelle*, 3.1; Cox, p. 79.
97. Strabo, *Geography*, 1.2.xxxiv; Cox, ibid.
98. Cox, n. 95 supra, p. 83.
99. Ibid., p. 81.
100. Ibid.; the word "Britain" was used by Prof. Cox instead of the words "the British Empire".
101. Ibid., p. 87.
102. Ibid.
103. See Herodotus, *The Histories*, p. 167, but read pp. 166-168; see too Cox, n. 95 supra, pp. 81 and 82.
104. Herodotus, p. 167.
105. Ibid.; it should be noted that other Syrians that lived near the rivers and their neighbours the Macronians were said to have learnt this practice later from the Colchians.
106. Cox, n. 95 supra, pp. 83-84; see too V. Gordon Childe, *The Dawn of European Civilization*, 6th ed. (Alfred A. Knopf, 1996), p. 19; also Rudolph R. Windsor, *From Babylon to Timbuktu: A History of the Ancient Black Races Including the Black Hebrews* (New York: Exposition Press, 1969), pp. 31-32.
107. See Means, *Ethiopia*, p. 38.

108. Cox, n. 95 supra, p. 92.
109. Ibid.; see also pp. 101-102.
110. See Indus Khamit-Kush, *What They Never Told You in History Class* (Bronx, NY: Luxor Publications, 1983), p. 51.
111. Ibid.
112. To this effect, one should read Khamit-Kush, *History Class*. See too Herman Brame, *The World Records of Black People*, 4th ed. (Sudan Publications, 1979), p. 49; Sir Godfrey Higgins, *Anacalypsis*, 2 vols. (1840; reprint, Kessinger Publishing Co., 1998); Gerald Massey, *Book of the Beginnings*, 2 vols. (1930; reprint, Kessinger Publishing Co., 1992), as well as his *Ancient Egypt: The Light of the World* [New York, 1932]; Albert Churchward, *Origin and Evolution of Religion* [London, 1921]; Count C. F. Volney, *Ruins of Empires* [France, 1792]; Sir Wallis Budge, *Egyptian Book of the Dead: The Papyrus of Ani*, 2 vols. (New York, 1895); John G. Jackson, *Man, God and Civilization* (Citadel Press, 1983); and Gaston Maspero, *The Dawn of Civilisation*, 3 vols. (London, 1888].
113. See J. A. Rogers, *Sex and Race*, vol. 1 (Helga Rogers, 1967); see too Khamit-Kush, n. 110 supra, p. 47.
114. See Khamit-Kush, ibid., p. 48.
115. See Khamit-Kush, n. 110 supra, p. 60. See too Alan Landsburg and Sally Landsburg, *In Search of Ancient Mysteries* (London: Corgi Books, 1974), p. 94: "Egyptian medicine was the root of modern western medicine".
116. See Khamit-Kush, n. 110 supra, p. 49.
117. Ibid., p. 50.
118. See Yosef Ben-Jochannan, et al., *The African Origins of the Major Western Religions*, ed. Amon Saba Saakana (New York: Alkebu-Lan Books, 1973).
119. To substantiate this, one can read Kersey Graves, *The World's Sixteen Crucified Saviors*, 6th ed. (Book Tree, 1999), as well as Jackson, *Man, God and Civilization*.
120. In support of this, read Rogers, *Sex and Race*, vol. 1; see Khamit-Kush, n. 110 supra, p. 89.
121. Khamit-Kush, n. 110 supra, p. 91.
122. Ibid., p. 81.
123. Ibid., pp. 73-87.
124. The same year President Ronald Reagan was also wounded.
125. See Ben-Jochannan, et al., n. 118 supra, pp. 25-27.
126. Khamit-Kush, n. 110 supra, p. 92.
127. James, *Stolen Legacy*.
128. Ibid.
129. Ibid.
130. Heindel, n. 66 supra, p. 517.
131. See Isa. 11:11, 19:18 and 27:13; also Windsor, n. 106 supra, pp. 76-80; see too *Edgar Cayce on Prophecy*, p. 168.
132. Windsor, ibid., p. 78.
133. Read of the Tabiban Kamant and Wasambara Jews of Northeast Africa in Allen S. Godbey, *The Lost Tribes a Myth* (Durham, NC: Duke University Press, 1930), p. 201; and Windsor, n. 106 supra, pp. 80-82.
134. Windsor, ibid., pp. 130-131.
135. Ibid., pp. 131-133.
136. Ibid., pp. 127-130; also referred to as the "Mavambo, Ma-Yomba, Ma-yumba and Mavumbu".
137. Windsor, n. 106 supra, pp. 87-92.
138. Although much maligned by the press of late.

Chapter 4:

1. And by extension all non-Caucasian citizens of the earth who find themselves in those areas referred to as 'Third World Countries'.
2. Eurocentric, stark materialism, others would say outright racism under the guise of economic and trade regimes to further pauperise so-called 'Third World' countries of the earth.
3. Despite the host of players who behind the scenes orchestrated these grand changes in the former Soviet Union and by extension Europe, the two front-runners in this exercise were undeniably Mikael Gorbachev and His Holiness, Pope John Paul II.

4. The blatant hypocrisy of the 'White Power Structure' led by America is painful in these last days. When Hutus were slaughtering Tutsis in Rwanda, Africa, everything possible was done to ensure the safety of white people living in Rwanda, whereas nothing was done to stop the genocide. Further, the arrangements for ensuring the safety of white people ensured that no black people were to be included, even if their slaughter was certain. Strangely, whereas the President of America was like an 'angelic' crusader against genocide in Kosovo, the Americans, with their 'super-power' influence, ensured that no one, not even at the UN, was permitted to use the word "genocide" as regards what went on in Rwanda. However, in keeping with the sham of today's world politics, as soon as the genocide was complete, none other than the President of America used the word "genocide" (more than ten times) in a short speech when referring to what had transpired in Rwanda. Today, white World Leaders, like incarnations of Christ, speak of peace and love for all humanity as they drop bombs on hapless people and destroy economies of non-white communities throughout the world. Is this what the New World Order is all about?

5. Especially from the United States of America.

6. Whilst the mighty U.S. takes the economically impoverished, ultra-democratic States of the Windward Islands to the World Trade Organization over bananas, the Republic of China is granted "Most Favoured Nation" status by the U.S. The author has nothing against the Republic of China or, for that matter, that China is granted "Most Favoured Nation" status, but such double standards must be exposed.

7. Even the United Nations conforms to the dictates of the United States of America. For example, note the U.S.-orchestrated war waged against Iraq some years ago, and to this day the way the U.S. decides what can and cannot be done in Iraq; note as well the events leading up to the election of the present Secretary General of the United Nations.

8. Isa. 11:11. Note the text to nn. 89-97, where prophecy reflects that parts of ancient Atlantis are to re-emerge in the Caribbean and Atlantic area. See Edgar Evans Cayce, *Edgar Cayce on Atlantis*, ed. Hugh Lynn Cayce (Warner Books, 1999), as well as Carter, *Edgar Cayce on Prophecy*; also Berlitz, *The Mystery of Atlantis*. In Donnelly, *Atlantis: The Antediluvian World*, it is interesting to note that he finds it extraordinary the number of times mention is made of "the islands in the sea" in the Old Testament, especially in Isaiah and Ezekiel, thus linking the ancient Hebrews and Ethiopians to the Atlanteans and the islands that remained after the initial destruction; to this effect, see pp. 28-29.

9. Two good books on the subject are *The Late Great Planet Earth* (London: Marshall Pickering, an imprint of HarperCollins, 1970) and *The 1980's: Countdown to Armageddon* (New York: Bantam Books, 1983). Both of these books, which are easily available, are worthy of being read by all who are interested in biblical prophecy as it relates to our times. The first book is written by Hal Lindsey with C. C. Carlson and the other by Hal Lindsey.

10. See Ezek. chaps. 36-38; see too the prophecies of Daniel, Zachariah and Micah as well as Lindsey with Carlson, ibid., pp. 60-61.

11. Deut. 28:63-68.

12. Ezek. 36:24.

13. As regards the Arab Confederacy and the rise of the Soviet Union/Russia, see Hal Lindsey, n. 9 supra, pp. 12-13.

14. Ezek. 38:2; it should be noted that not all Bibles include the name in brackets.

15. Lindsey with Carlson, *The Late Great Planet Earth*, n. 9 supra, p. 63.

16. Gen. 10:2.

17. See Lindsey with Carlson, n. 9 supra, pp. 64-66.

18. See Rev. 16:12 and 9:14-16.

19. Rev. 9:18.

20. Lindsey with Carlson, n. 9 supra, p. 82, but read however pp. 81-87; see too Hal Lindsey, n. 9 supra, p. 14.

21. Hal Lindsey, n. 9 supra, pp. 14-15 as well as pp. 99-113; also Lindsey with Carlson, n. 9 supra, pp. 88-113. See too Herbert W. Armstrong, *Mystery of the Ages*, pp. 246-248.

22. Dan. 7:3.

23. Dan. 7:7.

24. Dan. 7:17.

25. See Dan. 7:23-24.

26. Lindsey with Carlson, n. 9 supra, pp. 93-97; also Hal Lindsey, n. 9 supra, pp. 15 and 106. See too J. Dwight Pentecost, *Prophecy for Today* (Grand Rapids: Zondervan Publishing House, 1984), pp. 69-79; also Dan. 2:31-45.

27. Lindsey with Carlson, ibid., p. 94. Incidentally, Nostradamus, the sixteenth-century prophet, identifies Napoleon and Hitler as two of the three Anti-Christs that he foresaw would try to dominate the world; some other authorities see Napoleon and Hitler as the forerunners to the ultimate Anti-Christ, who is shortly to come to the fore.

28. Rev. 13:3; however, read the whole of Revelation 13.

29. Hal Lindsey, n. 9 supra, p. 109; also, Pentecost, n. 26 supra, pp. 80-91.

30. Rev. 13:1-10.

31. Rev. 13:11-18.

32. Pentecost, n. 26 supra, p. 93.

33. Rev. 17:4.

34. Isa. 47:1-5; see also Lindsey with Carlson, n. 9 supra, pp. 118-119.

35. Rev. 17:3; Lindsey with Carlson, n. 9 supra, p. 123. Some authorities, such as J. Dwight Pentecost (n. 26 supra, pp. 127-138), claim that the "harlot" is a religious system or church (to wit, the Roman Church began by Emperor Constantine in the early fourth century) that professes to be the bride of Christ but in fact is an adulteress. The power and world-wide influence of this church or religious system is reflected in Rev. 17:15, where one reads: "The oceans, rivers and lakes that the (harlot) woman is sitting on represent masses of people of every race and nation". In some Bibles, for the last eight quoted words one may read instead: "peoples, and multitudes, and nations, and tongues".

36. Matt. 24:3.

37. Ibid., 24:4-5.

38. Ibid., 24:6.

39. Ibid., 24:7.

40. Luke 21:11.

41. Matt. 24:7.

42. Matt. 24:8; see too Hal Lindsey, n. 9, pp. 19-33.

43. Matt. 24:10.

44. Ibid., 24:13.

45. Ibid., 24:14. With the rapid advancement of telecommunications technology (i.e., via satellite and cable TV), millions throughout the world listen to the gospel simultaneously in a manner never before experienced in the world.

46. Luke 21:11.

47. Luke 21:26; Matt. 24:29.

48. See Dan. 9:27 and 12:1; Jer. 30:5-7; Rev. 11:3.

49. Matt. 24:15 and 24:21; see Pentecost, n. 26 supra, pp. 32-41.

50. As regards the period referred to as "the time of ... trouble" or "tribulation", see Matthew 24, Mark 13 and Luke 21.

51. See Rev. 13:5.

52. Rev. 13:8; see too Lindsey with Carlson, n. 9 supra, pp. 110-112.

53. Hence, for those who have ears to hear, let them hear: all who (in their hearts and minds) repent and accept the divine sacrifice of Yashua or Jesus the Christ (salvation through the blood of Christ), and who thereafter live by his dictates of faith and love, shall not be ensnared by the Bestial system. In other words, by the divine grace of God they shall be spared and live on after the forces of love and harmony have restored genuine peace and order throughout the world.

54. Rev. 13:16-18.

55. See Rev. 18:1-10.

56. Ibid., 18:11-13.

57. Ibid., 18:16-17.

58. Ibid., 19:1-7.

59. Ibid., 19:11-16; see Appendix II — "Rastafari: Today's Nazarites", as this appellation is related to H.I.M. Haile Selassie I, who defeated the fascist, Mussolini, the forerunner and close friend of Adolph Hitler.

60. Rev. 19:19-21.

61. Rev. 16:18-21. Incidentally, the seers of the indigenous or First Nation's People of North America predict that a Great Purge is imminent.

62. See Pentecost, n. 26 supra, pp. 114-124 and 139-149.

63. Rev. 11:15.

64. Rev. 20; see too Matt. 25:31-46 and Isa. 65:17-25.

65. Rev. 20:7-8.

66. Rev. 20:12-15; also see Revelation 21 and 22 for what comes thereafter.

67. As explained in chap. 2, in esoteric law, the seven seals are the seven centres or vortices of force in the Solar body of the Indwelling Christ Spirit.
68. See Byron Kirkwood, comp., *Mary's Message to the World: As Sent by Mary, the Mother of Jesus to Her Messenger Annie Kirkwood* (New York City, CA: Blue Dolphin Publishing). Also read Michael H. Brown, *The Final Hour* (Milford, OH: Faith Publishing Co.); for a chronology of some of the major apparition sites, see pp. 353-354. In Egypt thousands of people of a variety of religious persuasions and social backgrounds saw vivid apparitions of Mary; see pp. 164-170 and 173-174.
69. The first miraculous appearance of Mary supposedly goes back to the first century, when she manifested herself to St. James at Zaragoza, Spain; see Brown, n. 68 supra, pp. 4, 8-9.
70. Rev. 12:1-9; also Brown, n. 68 supra, pp. 10-11.
71. See Brown, n. 68 supra, pp. 134-140.
72. The advice to say the Holy Rosary and for devotion to the Immaculate Heart of Mary is also often repeated.
73. Brown, n. 68 supra, p. 271.
74. Ibid.
75. Ibid., p. 16.
76. Ibid., p. 251.
77. Some of the messages are said to have been kept secret as it supposedly relates in a negative way to the future of the Church, the Vatican in Rome and the papacy. For a discussion of this, see Brown, n. 68 supra, pp. 150-156 and 319; see also A. Woldben, *After Nostradamus: Great Prophecies for the Future of Mankind* (Frogmore, St. Albans, Herts: Mayflower Books, 1975), pp. 171-179 and 180-186.
78. Brown, ibid., p. 273.
79. Ibid., p. 255. Other books of interest as regards the apparitions of Mary are: Judith Albright, *Our Lady of Medjugorje* (Riehle Foundation, 1988); Fr. René Laurentin, *Nine Years of Apparitions* (Riehle Foundation, 1991); as well as three other books written by the same author entitled *Ten Years of Apparitions* (Faith Publishing Co., 1997); *An appeal from Mary in Argentina* (Faith Publishing Co., 1997); and *Our Lord and Our Lady in Scottsdale* (Faith Publishing Co., 1997). See also Josyp Terelya with Michael H. Brown, *Josyp Terelya — Witness* (Queenship Publishing Co., 1991).
80. See "The Warning in 97", *Rose Notes* 9, no. 23 (Jan. 1997) (Bayside, NY: Our Lady of Roses, Mary Help of Mothers Shrine).
81. Woldben, n. 77 supra, p. 55.
82. Ibid., p. 54.
83. John Hogue, *Nostradamus and the Millennium: Predictions of the Future* (Garden City, NY: Doubleday & Co., 1987), p. 202; see pp. 150-157 re: AIDS.
84. Ibid.
85. This is very similar to Rev. 20:1-5; see too Jean-Charles de Fontbrune, *Nostradamus 2: Into the Twenty-first Century*, trans. Alexis Lykiard (New York: Henry Holt & Co.), p. 154.
86. Woldben, n. 77 supra, pp. 99-104; in similar vein read what St. John Bosco had to say on the subject on pp. 91-95, and what Nostradamus foresaw on pp. 95-99.
87. Ibid., pp. 120-131.
88. See Woldben, n. 77 supra, pp. 107-118, about Jeanne Dixon and her prophecies and the book written about her, to wit, *On the Threshold of the Future*, or *La procellarie de futuro*, by A. Del Fante (Bologna, 1936); also read Jeanne Dixon, *My life and Prophecies* (London: Muller, 1971).
89. See Edgar Evans Cayce, *Edgar Cayce on Atlantis*; also Carter, *Edgar Cayce on Prophecy*, for example, pp. 57, 63, 116-122 and 125-126; as well as Jeffrey Furst, ed., *Edgar Cayce's Story of Jesus* (Coward-McCann, Inc., 1991), pp. 101-103, 348 and 350.
90. Ibid., for example, *Edgar Cayce on Prophecy*, pp. 63 and 61, respectively.
91. For example, ibid., pp. 57, 116-122 and 125; see too Montgomery, *The World Before*, pp. 125-142.
92. Ezek. 1:22.
93. See Montgomery, n. 91 supra, pp. 133-141, about this cataclysmic disaster.
94. Ibid., pp. 113 and 134. These disappearances in the Bermuda Triangle should be understood in the light of what was explained in chap. 2 as regards all life being of substance at different rates of vibration. At this juncture some of it can be perceived by the optic senses, whilst some of it cannot.
95. Carter, *Edgar Cayce on Prophecy*, n. 89 supra, p. 62.
96. Ibid.

97. Ibid., pp. 57-63. Incidentally, Edgar Cayce accurately predicted, amongst other things, the 1929 Stock Market crash, the beginning and end of the Second World War, the racial unrest in America in the 1960's, the invention of laser light and blood tests, the finding of the Dead Sea scrolls and the Fall of Communism. See too Montgomery, n. 91 supra, pp. 115-123.

98. There are countless books in a variety of languages on the pyramids of Egypt, especially the Great Pyramid of Cheops; see, however, Peter Tompkins, *The Secrets of the Great Pyramid* (New York: HarperCollins, 1978). See too Woldben, n. 77 supra, pp. 43-53; also *Edgar Cayce on Prophecy*, n. 89 supra, pp. 107-113.

99. Tompkins, introduction, pp. xiv-xv.

100. Woldben, n. 77 supra, p. 48.

101. Ibid., p. 4; see also in this regard Rodolfo Benavides, *The Dramatic Prophecies of the Great Pyramid.*

102. Benavides, ibid. For example, the spiritual descent of humanity from around 1913 was predicted, including the beginning of World War I. Many outstanding events in history were predicted as well as the changes in weather patterns and increases in natural disasters (melting of ice at the poles, earthquakes, volcanic activity, tidal waves, terrible hurricanes and other disturbances and storms) that we have experienced since the late 1970's. The deep interest in UFOs and other solar systems was also predicted as well as the possible threat of comets to the earth in the latter part of the last century.

103. Ibid., pp. 300-302.

104. Benavides, *The Great Pyramid*, pp. 303-332. Incidentally, since the events of September 11, 2001, the world that we knew certainly ended. What shall take place in the years ahead is anyone's guess; anything seems to be acceptable under the guise of security or to curtail the supposed scourge of 'terrorism'.

105. Mary Stewart Relfe, *When Your Money Fails* (Montgomery: Ministries, Inc., 1981), p. 15.

106. Ibid., p. 16.

107. Ibid.

108. Ibid., p. 17, where examples of a lottery ticket and an advertisement from the Education Department in Israel are displayed with the number 666; see also pp. 130-139 as regards the Age of "6".

109. Ibid., pp. 18-20.

110. Ibid., p. 30.

111. Ibid., p. 37. Dr. Relfe obtained this information from Rev. David Webber's "Point of No Return", Southwest Radio Church.

112. Ibid., pp. 117-125.

113. Ibid., p. 124.

114. Ibid., p. 117; see also p. 232 as regards a statement made by a Chief Executive Officer of Electronic Data Processing Inc., which indicated that cable TV is going to play an integral part in bringing into effect the cashless or paperless aspect of the new monetary system of the New World Order. The card is just the forerunner of the mark of the Beast referred to in the Bible.

115. *Time*, April 28, 1997, pp. 35-40.

116. By Jeffrey Kluger. Reported by Dan Cray/Los Angeles and Dick Thompson/Menlo Park, with other bureaus.

117. By Maryland Bird. Reported by Greg Burke/Rome and Helen Gibson/London.

118. By Tim Padgett, with reporting by Paul Sherman/Amecameca.

119. Quoted in Kluger, "Volcanoes with an Attitude".

120. Scientists explain that this off centre weight at the poles will cause a wobble very similar to tyres that are out of alignment. This exaggerated wobble, coupled with the buckling of the earth's crystal arches by the shrinking of its mantle, could be disastrous along the faults of the earth, which literally form a web worldwide.

121. The Sumerian writings in fact reflect the cataclysmic devastation that took place worldwide when that large planet approached the earth during their era. Much of the data relating to recent scientific findings that seemingly gives further credence to prophecy was obtained from a series of TV programmes entitled "In Search of".

122. Incidentally, according to Hindu scriptures this is the end of the era of the Goddess of Darkness, to wit, Kali. It is written that the people of the East consider the end phase of the Kali Yuga age as the interplay of the law of cause and effect, whereby account is taken of the past and all accounts are settled so that we (humanity) can "proceed into the future with a budget in the black". To this effect, see Woldben, n. 77 supra, pp. 16-19.

123. Matt. 4:17.

124. 2 Thess. 2:10.
125. 2 Thess. 2:13.
126. 2 Thess. 2:17.
127. Phil. 2:15; bracketed words are the author's insertion.
128. Ps. 37:9-10 and 37:29, respectively.
129. See Phil. 4:5-8.
130. See *Edgar Cayce on Prophecy*, n. 89 supra, pp. 182-205, as regards time and prophecy.
131. 1 Cor. 15:51-53.
132. It should be noted that this book, which is very relevant in these uncertain times in which we live, was completed prior to the events of September 11, 2001.

Appendix 1:

1.   Hos. 4:6.
2.   Luke 11:52.
3.   Mark 11:24.
4.   Gen. 2:6.
5.   Matt. 6:9-13.
6.   See Hodges, *Teachings of the Secret Order*, pp. 47-48.
7.   See chap. 2 re: the Dense, Vital and Desire bodies as well as the three-fold Spirit, the three-fold Soul and the mind link.
8.   Heindel, *Rosicrucian Cosmo-Conception*, p. 464; see too pp. 463-466.
9.   See Swami Rama, *Meditation and Its Practice* (Honesdale, PA: The Himalayan Institute Press, 1998), pp. 40-45, for an excellent insight into "So Hum" meditation; the whole book is worthy of being read.
10. Through meditation you become one with your inner being, with your inner self, your Christ or Divine Spirit within the body-temple; and through this doorway of "the Christ or Divine Spirit" you become one with the All-Father of Creation. Meditation brings you to the centre of the hurricane of life; and just like the centre or eye of a hurricane is blessed with infinite calm (in comparison to the rest of the hurricane), so too does the realisation of the Christ Spirit in the centre of your being bring a "peace that passeth all understanding". Meditation has been acknowledged by Western medical science as having a positive influence on all that take the time to do it. If nothing else, all agree on its positive effect on the nervous system and its calming effect on the mind. Other modern health research centres claim that the practice of daily meditation may assist you to live a healthier and longer life. People who meditate seem to maintain over the years a higher level of an age-related hormone cited as DHEA-S. Generally this hormone is most plentiful in the early twenties and lessens as one ages. (See article entitled "Meditation May Help You Live Longer," *Sun*, Jan. 5, 1993, p. 22.)
11. See 1 Thess. 5:5.

Appendix II:

1.   The Commonwealth Caribbean is comprised of English-speaking Caribbean countries that were former British possessions, such as Jamaica, Guyana, Trinidad and Tobago, the Bahamas, Belize, the Commonwealth of Dominica, St. Lucia, St. Vincent and the Grenadines, Grenada, Antigua and Barbuda, St. Kitts and Nevis and Barbados, which are presently independent countries. The term Commonwealth Caribbean also includes Anguilla, the British Virgin Islands, Montserrat, the Cayman Islands and the Turks and Caicos Islands, which are not independent countries. These countries have over the years established by Treaty the Caribbean Community with a Caribbean Community Secretariat. There is also an Agreement, which was attached as an annex to the Treaty, that established the Caribbean Common Market. The Treaty and Agreement have both been amended by a series of Protocols. The acronym for the Caribbean Community and Common Market is CARICOM. Recently, a CARICOM 'brainchild' called the Association of Caribbean States was formed, which includes countries such as Cuba, Venezuela, Mexico and Colombia. Although the Commonwealth Caribbean is comprised of English-speaking countries, many languages are spoken in the Caribbean, such as Spanish in Cuba, French in Guadeloupe and Martinique, and Dutch in St. Maarten (St. Martin) and Curacao. Kweyol is also spoken in some countries such as St. Lucia and the nature island of the Caribbean: the Commonwealth of Dominica. Kweyol is a French-based language with African syntax.

2. See text immediately preceding nn. 21 and 97 below.

3. See Adolph Edwards, *Marcus Garvey: 1887-1940* (New York: New Beacon Books, 2000), pp. 5-6; see too Amy Jacques Garvey, comp., introduction to *Philosophy and Opinions of Marcus Garvey or Africa for Africans*, 2nd ed. (London: Frank Cass & Co.), p. x.

4. Amy Jacques Garvey, ibid., pp. x-xi.

5. Ibid., p. xi.

6. Ibid., p. xiii.

7. Ibid., p. xiv.

8. Ibid., pp. xvi-xvii.

9. Ibid., p. xvii.

10. Ibid., p. 178.

11. See Rex Nettleford, *Mirror Mirror: Identity, Race and Protest in Jamaica* (Kingston: Collins and Sangster's, 1970), for an analysis of modern Jamaica.

12. See too Asante, *Afrocentricity*, pp. 10-12; Shawna Maglangbay, *Garvey, Lumumba, Malcolm: Black Nationalist Separatists* (Chicago: Third World Press, 1972), pp. 19-36; Edwards, *Marcus Garvey: 1887-1940*; Robert Athlyi Rogers, *The Holy Piby*, with a foreword by Ras Sekou Tafari and an introduction by Miguel Lorne (1924; reprint, Chicago: Research Associates School Times Publications and Frontline Distribution Int'l Inc., 2000).

13. Although, undeniably, it must be noted that physical repatriation is seen as important to many Rastafarians, common sense would dictate that if people are dragged away from their homeland by force, put in bondage and after hundreds of years emancipated, in all fairness, if the people so desire, they should be repatriated. Nevertheless, as indicated in the text above, the concept of repatriation also signifies a return of African consciousness and culture. Repatriation is also seen as "the earthly redemption which the Israelites have long sought in vain — the blessed state of living in peace in the kingdom of Jah". See Owens, *Dread: The Rastafarians of Jamaica*, p. 230; also pp. 232-242.

14. See Nicholas and Sparrow, *Rastafari: A Way of Life* (Chicago: Frontline Distribution Int'l Inc., 2001), pp. 22-25; Owens, ibid., pp. 90-124.

15. See Leonard E. Barrett, *The Rastafarians: The Dreadlocks of Jamaica* (Kingston: Sangster's Book Stores, 1977), pp. 104-111.

16. See Means, *Ethiopia*, p. 125; see too Owens, supra n. 13, pp. 14-21.

17. Re: the Catholic Church and the pope, see Owens, n. 13 supra, pp. 86-89.

18. See Nicholas and Sparrow, n. 14 supra, pp. 22-25; see too Means, n. 16 supra, pp. 150-156; see also Thomas M. Coffey, *The Lion by the Tail: The story of the Italian-Ethiopian War* (Viking Press, 1974); and Owens, n. 13 supra, p. 73.

19. See Means, n. 16 supra, pp. 126-127.

20. Jer. 13:23.

21. See Nicholas and Sparrow, n. 14 supra, pp. 24-25; also Barrett, n. 15 supra, pp. 86-89, captioned "Rastafarians Turned Maroons"; and text to nn. 68-85 below.

22. See Owens, n. 13 supra, pp. 15-17; for more on Howell, Joseph Hibbert and others, see Barrett, ibid., pp. 80-92.

23. Barrett, n. 15 supra, pp. 111-113.

24. See Joseph Williams, *Hebrewism of West Africa*, 2nd ed. (New York: Dial Press, 1931), p. 227; also, Windsor, *From Babylon to Timbuktu*, pp. 91-92.

25. Williams, *Hebrewism of West Africa*, ibid.: the whole book; see too Barrett, n. 15 supra, p. 104; and Windsor, ibid., especially pp. 76-92.

26. See Owens, n. 13 supra, pp. 106-107.

27. See Yosef Ben-Jochannan, *Makeda*.

28. Barrett, n. 15 supra, p. 205. There is another version of how the Ark came to be in Ethiopia, however, the authority who posits the other version is firm in his belief that the original Ark of the Covenant still is in Ethiopia to this day.

29. This King from the lineage of King David is seen to be H.I.M. Haile Selassie I.

30. Jer. 23:5-6.

31. Jer. 23:4; the whole of Jeremiah chap. 23, especially verses 1-15, makes interesting reading.

32. Rev. 5:2, 3 and 5.

33. It should be noted that "Nazarene" and "Nazarite" mean a native of Nazareth and "nazar" means to separate or consecrate oneself.

34. *Reggae International*, Stephen Davis and Peter Simon, an article entitled "From the Root of King David," by Rory Sanders, pp. 59-71.

35. Barrett, n. 15 supra, pp. 127-128; Owens, n. 13 supra, p. 3; preferably read pp. 30-38.

36. See Owens, n. 13 supra, p. 57.

37. Ibid., pp. 105-109.
38. Another word for "Messiah"; see Means, n. 16 supra.
39. See the reasoning of Christ Jesus in John 10:34-38.
40. Owens, n. 13 supra, p. 131.
41. Ibid., p. 109.
42. Ibid., pp. 112-113.
43. Ibid., pp. 110-111; and for a discourse on the divinity of Haile Selassie I, King of Kings, Conquering Lion of the Tribe of Judah, see pp. 90-124. See too Davis and Simon, n. 34 supra, pp. 70-71, article by Rory Sanders; also Barrett, n. 15 supra, pp. 104-111.
44. Owens, n. 13 supra, p. 133.
45. Ibid., p. 114 and pp. 130-131.
46. Barrett, n. 15 supra, p. 211.
47. Ibid., p. 214.
48. Ibid.
49. Ibid.; the italicised word is the author's insertion.
50. Ibid., p. 215.
51. Owens, n. 13 supra, p. 258.
52. Ibid., p. 279.
53. Ibid., p. 256.
54. Bob Marley — from the song of a similar name.
55. Extracts taken from taping of Rastafarian consciousness done by Joseph Owens referred to in text to n. 51 supra. See Owens, n. 13 supra, pp. 258, 276 and 257, respectively. It should be noted that strict Rastafarians always accepted King Haile Selassie I as the living God. They, as well as others, who did not acknowledge his divinity, accepted that he was the King referred to in the Bible; the King of Kings, the Lion of the Tribe of Judah: the opener of 'the seven seals', who from his arrival on the world scene marked the beginning of the end of the Babylon system, so that Truth could sweep the earth. His arrival also brought about the reawakening of the "Christ or Jah" Spirit within the hearts and minds of "the remnants of the righteous Branch of David", that is, those who are to inherit the earth when the final, fatal blow is dealt to Babylon.
56. Ibid., pp. 146-147.
57. Ibid., pp. 147-149.
58. As regards locks serving as "antennae" or "aerials", see Hiram E. Butler, *The Narrow Way of Attainment* (Kessinger Publishing Co., 1998).
59. See Davis and Simon, n. 34 supra, pp. 62-63; also, Nicholas and Sparrow, n. 14 supra, pp. 54-56; and Owens, n. 13 supra, pp. 153-157. See too Barrett, n. 15 supra, p. 142, re: the Symbolism of the Lion.
60. Davis and Simon, ibid., p. 63, where it is pointed out that "locks" may be a worldwide phenomena among ascetic and deeply spiritual people. Incidentally, in 1974, a law, to wit, "The Unlawful Associations Act", which was subsequently acknowledged to be unconstitutional, had been passed in Dominica that effectively outlawed "Locks". In the circumstances, under that law it was not a criminal offence to shoot and kill someone with locks seen in any public place; amazing but true.
61. Owens, n. 13 supra, p. 146.
62. 2 Cor. 6:16.
63. Oranges, incidentally, are said by some authorities on the subject of Atlantis to be the "golden apples" of that sunken continent; this is interesting in that the Caribbean islands are said to be part of the remnants of Atlantis.
64. The banana, a staple crop of the Caribbean, has also been linked to ancient Atlantis by some authorities; the banana plant is an ancient one.
65. See Owens, n. 13 supra, pp. 66-67, where commonly used "I" words are presented; incense may be pronounced "I-shence".
66. Owens, ibid., p. 166.
67. Ibid., p. 167 and pp. 168-169; see too Davis and Simon, n. 34 supra, p. 6; and Nicholas and Sparrow, n. 14 supra, pp. 58-62.
68. Strangely, this is not the case in some American states where it is decriminalised, despite the fact that America has supported the passage of draconian laws relating to cannabis throughout the Commonwealth Caribbean; all this in an effort to assist in the 'war against drugs'. Many Commonwealth Caribbean countries carry penalties of up to $200,000 and 14 years in jail for growing, trafficking and possession of cannabis. Cannabis is treated similarly with the deadly, addictive cocaine, crack, heroin and other chemical drugs, that within a few

years of use destroy societies. Further, even if one accepts that cannabis is bad, the movement from cannabis to cocaine is a clear case of 'jumping from the frying pan into the fire'.

69. *The Columbia History of the World* (1981), p. 54, referred to in Jack Herer, *The Emperor Wears No Clothes* (Van Nuys, CA: Hemp Publishing, 1992), p. 2.

70. See John Lust, *The Herb Book* (Simi Valley, CA: Benedict Lust Publications, 2001), p. 591.

71. John Roseyear, *Pot: A handbook of Marijuana* (Carol Publishing Group, 1973), p. 18.

72. Ibid., pp. 16-25.; also, Herer, n. 69 supra, p. 1. See too George Andrews and Simon Vinkenoog, eds., *The Book of Grass: An Anthology of Indian Hemp.*

73. Herer, ibid. Amusingly, even President Clinton has admitted trying it, but he did not inhale! Incidentally, this is in no way to detract from the American president, who has enunciated many positive ideas to improve his country.

74. Ibid., pp. 21-30. It is interesting to read in an article by John Hanson entitled "An Outline for a U.K. Hemp Strategy" in *The Ecologist* 10, nos. 8/9 (Oct./Nov. 1980), that:

    The United States of America's Marijuana Tax Act of 1937 was engineered by a powerful clique of vested, self-perpetuating interests ranging from government departments to the alcohol, tobacco, pharmaceutical and wood-pulp lobbies in the U.S. Administration. These baleful interests, now reinforced by international treatise and 'censorship of morality', persist to the present.

    See p. 260, where one also reads at footnote 6:

    By using the Freedom of Information Act, we have discovered that the reefer-madness hysteria of the early 1930's was nothing but a hoax perpetuated on the American people in order to take hemp out of competition with synthetic and other patent industries.

75. Herer, ibid., pp. 32-34.

76. Ibid., pp. 35-39; also Lust, n. 70 supra, p. 146.

77. Lust, ibid.

78. See Lust, ibid., pp. 145-146 and 591-592; also, Roseyear's book cited above, n. 71; and Herer's book, supra, n. 69; incidentally, pp. 35-42 thereof deal specifically with the herb's therapeutic use. A few other writings that make interesting reading are as follows:

    Dr. F. Hickling, *Ganja in Jamaica*; Sidney Cohen, "A progress report: Marijuana as Medicine", *Psychology Today* (April 1978); Vera Rubin and Lambros Comitas, *Ganja in Jamaica* (New York: Anchor Press/ Doubleday, 1976; research done by the Research Institute for the Study of Man); editorial of the world-acclaimed *The Ecologist* magazine 10, nos. 8/9 (Oct./Nov. 1980), entitled "The Cannabis Market—Present and Future" by Nicholas Hildyard. Also appearing in that volume of *The Ecologist* was the aforementioned article by John Hanson; James Graham, *Cannabis and Health*; Don Aitken and Tod Mikuriya, M.D., "The Forgotten Medicine: A look at the medical uses of Cannabis"; John Michell, "Grow Hemp ... Or Else" (dealing with the importance of hemp-cannabis, especially in sixteenth, seventeenth, eighteenth and to a lesser extent nineteenth-century England and America, considering that in both of those countries at some stage it was compulsory to grow cannabis; there was even a penalty for not growing it ... Imagine!); "War on Drugs is War on People" by Anthony Henman, a Tenetehara Indian from Brazil, who was brutally beaten by the authorities (this article posits that international anti-marijuana laws are used by the authorities to suppress traditional Indian cultures); Colin Moorcroft, "The Magic Weed" (its ecological value and ancient use in China are discussed); and Tim Malyon, "Just Another Cash Crop? The Cannabis Market, Present and Future". Also, for an extract of an official report of the National Commission on Marijuana and Drug abuse in Jamaica, see Barrett, n. 15 supra, p. 132. The report is entitled *Marijuana: A signal of misunderstanding, The Official Report of the National Commission on Marijuana and Drug Abuse* (New York: The New American Library, Inc., 1972).

    On the 2nd of September, 1993, Radio Caribbean International carried a news item reflecting new medical breakthroughs relating to the utility of cannabis as a healing agent. Lately, the news media, both radio and television, carry such news items quite frequently.

79. See Owens, n. 13 supra, pp. 185-187. Reasoning among Rastafari is of the highest order; sometimes they will ask Jah Rastafari to imbue "I-n-I" with Love, Wisdom and Overstanding to do Jah's Will. No frivolous talk is indulged in during serious reasoning sessions.

80. See Nicholas and Sparrow, n. 14 supra, pp. 68-71.

81. Grounation is celebrated in Jamaica on the 21st of April every year to affirm life through the earth and to commemorate the visit to Jamaica of King Haile Selassie I in 1966.

82. See Roseyear, n. 71 supra, p. 103. See too Nicholas and sparrow, n. 14 supra, pp. 49-52; Owens, n. 13 supra, pp. 157-166; Barrett, n. 15 supra, pp. 128-136; Davis and Simon, n. 34 supra, pp. 63-64.

83. This reasoning is consistent with the text to and substance of n. 74 supra, as well as with the present reality in many Caribbean states where cocaine/crack is rapidly replacing cannabis, and crimes of violence are on the increase. The question is, has this really been orchestrated? We pray that is not the case.

84. See Barrett, n. 15 supra, p. 130.

85. However, Donald Tashkin, M.D., UCLA, one of the world's leading cannabis researchers on pulmonary functions, is said to indicate that "the biggest health risk to the lungs would be a person smoking 16 or more 'large' spliffs a day of leaf/bud because of the hypoxia of too much smoke and not enough oxygen". In that not even the biggest cannabis smokers smoke 16 big spliffs a day, "Tashkin feels there is no danger for anyone to worry about protracting emphysema 'in any way' by the use of marijuana — totally different from tobacco". See Herer, n. 69 supra, p. 80; also pp. 80-81 re: THC metabolites attaching themselves to fatty deposits within the body, which the body disposes of later, and the actual benefit to emphysema sufferers due to the "opening and dilation of the bronchial passages".

86. Nicholas and Sparrow, n. 14 supra, p. 64.

87. For example, "Blow's Herbal Enterprises", "Calabasse Healing Centre" and "Shashamane Enterprises" in Dominica.

88. Nicholas and Sparrow, n. 14 supra, p. 64.

89. Ibid., p. 65; extract from quotation of Ras Hu-I.

90. Ibid., p. 66.

91. See Barrett, n. 15 supra, pp. 193-197 on "Rastafarian Music".

92. Calypso and Reggae music represent the paramount forms of music in the English-speaking Caribbean. Calypso evolved from slavery and has been a source of social and political commentary for years. In many of the islands of the Caribbean there are Rastafarians who are Calypsonians.

93. Some may cite the lyrics of artists such as "Yellowman" or some modern-day Dub-artist who sing songs that may not pass the test of "pure lyrics"; they are the exception to the scores of Reggae artists who have for years consistently sang "conscious lyrics".

94. See Rolston Kallyndyr and Henderson Dalrymple, *Reggae: A Peoples Music* (London: Carib-Arawak Publications, 1973); Davis and Simon, n. 34 supra, pp. 25-55 and 75-171; also Stephen Davis and Peter Simon, *Reggae Bloodlines: In Search of the Music and Culture of Jamaica* (London: Heinemann Education Books).

95. See Barrett, n. 15 supra, pp. 185-193.

96. This was very much the case in the Island of Dominica, where a good deal of Rastafarians and Dreadlocks are to be found. Dominica is like an altar in Zion to Rastafari as it is called "The Nature Island of the Caribbean"; naturalness thrives there; hence, so too does Rastafari. Prof. Barrett, n. 15 supra, p. 197, refers to the "Dreadlocks" of Dominica.

97. Barrett, n. 15 supra, p. 200.

98. See Nicholas and Sparrow, n. 14 supra, p. 45.

99. Exod. 21:12.

100. Exod. 21:15.

101. Exod. 21:22.

102. Exod. 22:16.

103. Exod. 22:31.

104. Lev. 11:41.

105. Lev. 11:42.

106. Lev. 11:44.

107. Lev. 19:26.

108. Lev. 19:27.

109. A study of the following books may be illuminating, to wit: Rev. Sterling Means, *Ethiopia and the Missing Link in African History*; Thomas M. Coffey, *The Lion by the Tail: The story of the Italian-Ethiopian War*; Junior "Ista J" Manning, *Members of a New Race: Teachings of H.I.M. Haile Selassie I* (Blantyre, Malawi: A Rastaman Vibration/Clarity Production); Joseph Owens, *Dread: The Rastafarians of Jamaica*; Amy Jacques Garvey, comp., *Philosophy and Opinions of Marcus Garvey or Africa for Africans*, 2nd ed.; Tony Sewell, *Garvey's Children: The Legacy of Marcus Garvey* (London: Macmillan Publishers, 1990); Leonard E. Barrett, *The Rastafarians: The Dreadlocks of Jamaica*; Prof. Rex Nettleford, *Mirror, Mirror: Identity, Race and Protest in Jamaica*; Carey Robinson, *The Fighting Maroons of Jamaica* (Jamaica: Collins

and Sangster); Joseph Williams, *Hebrewism of West Africa*; Chancellor Williams, *Destruction of Black Civilization: Great Issues of A Race From 4500 B.C. to 2000 A.D.* (Chicago: Third World Press, 1974); Yosef Ben-Jochannan, *Black Man of the Nile and His Family*; Cheikh Anta Diop, *The African Origin of Civilization: Myth or Reality*; Saint Claire Drake, *Redemption of Africa and Black Religion* (Atlanta: Third World Press, 1970); George O. Cox, *Crucial Insights Into African History*; and last, but by no means least, George G. M. James, *Stolen Legacy*.

SELECT BIBLIOGRAPHY

Afrika, Llaila O. *African Holistic Health.* 3rd ed. Beltsville, MD: Adesgun, Johnson & Koram, 1990.

Alder, Vera S. *The Finding of the Third Eye.* New York: Samuel Weiser, Inc., 1986.

Anandamitra, Acarya Avadhu tika. *Beyond the Superconscious Mind.* Tiljala, Calcutta: Ananda Marga.

Asante, Molefi Kete. *Afrocentricity: The Theory of Social Change.* Trenton: Africa World Press, 1988.

Aurobindo, Sri. *On Yoga I: The Synthesis of Yoga.* Vol. IV. Sri Aurobindo International Centre of Education Collection.

Avadhuta, Acarya Bhavamuktananda. *The Way of Tantra.* Denver: Ananda Marga Publications, 1989.

Barashango, Ishakamusa. *God, the Bible and the Black Man's Destiny.* Silver Spring, MD: Fourth Dynasty Publishing Co.

Barrett, Leonard E. *The Rastafarians: The Dreadlocks of Jamaica.* Kingston: Sangster's Book Stores, 1977.

Ben-Jochannan, Yosef. *Black Man of the Nile and His Family.* New York: Alkebu-Lan Books, 1970.

Ben-Jochannan, Yosef, Charles Finch, Modupe Oduyoye, and Tsegaye Gabre-Medhin. *The African Origins of the Major Western Religions.* Edited by Amon Saba Saakana. New York: Alkebu-Lan Books, 1973.

Berlitz, Charles. *The Mystery of Atlantis.* Granada Publishing Ltd. Published Frogmore, St Albans, Herts: Panther Books, 1977.

Bernard, R. W. *The Dead Sea Scrolls and the Life of the Ancient Essenes.* Mokelumne Hill, CA: Health Research, 1990.

Brown, Michael H. *The Final Hour.* Milford, OH: Faith Publishing Co.

Carter, Mary Ellen. *Edgar Cayce on Prophecy.* Edited by Hugh Lynn Cayce. New York: Paperback Library, 1982.

Cerve, W. S. *Lemuria: The Lost Continent of the Pacific.* San Jose, CA: Supreme Grand Lodge of AMORC, 1997.

Churchward, Albert. *Origin and Evolution of Religion.* London, 1921.

Coffey, Thomas M. *The Lion by the Tail: The story of the Italian-Ethiopian War.* Viking Press, 1974.

Cox, George O. *Crucial Insights into African History.* New York: African Heritage Studies.

Davis, Stephen, and Peter Simon. *Reggae Bloodlines: In Search of the Music and Culture of Jamaica.* London: Heinemann Education Books.

Diop, Cheikh Anta. *Civilization or Barbarism: An Authentic Anthropology.* Brooklyn: Lawrence Hill, 1991.

————. *The African Origin of Civilization: Myth or Reality.* Westport, CT: Lawrence Hill, 1983.

Dixon, Jeanne. *My Life and Prophecies.* London: Muller, 1971.

Donnelly, Ignatius. *Atlantis: The Antediluvian World.* New York: Gramercy Publishing Co.

Drake, Saint Claire. *Redemption of Africa and Black Religion.* Atlanta: Third World Press, 1970.

Dunne, Desmond. *Yoga Made Easy.* Frogmore, St Albans, Herts: Granada Publishing Ltd.

Edwards, Adolph. *Marcus Garvey: 1887-1940.* New York: New Beacon Books, 2000.

Ehret, Arnold. *Mucusless Diet Healing System.* Cody, WY: Ehret Literature Publishing Co.

————. *Rational Fasting for Physical, Mental and Spiritual Rejuvenation.* Beaumont, CA: Ehret Literature Publishing Co.

Fedler, Rev. Cain Hope. *The Original African Heritage Study Bible: King James Version.* Edited by James W. Peebles. World Bible Publishing Co., 1993.

Furst, Jeffrey. *Edgar Cayce's Story of Jesus.* Coward-McCann, Inc., 1991.

Garvey, Amy Jacques, comp. *Philosophy and Opinions of Marcus Garvey or Africa for Africans.* 2nd ed. London: Frank Cass & Co.

Heindel, Max. *Rosicrucian Cosmo-Conception or Mystic Christianity.* 3rd ed. London: L. N. Fowler & Co., 1974.

————. *The Vital Body.* London: L. N. Fowler & Co.

Herer, Jack. *The Emperor Wears No Clothes.* Van Nuys, CA: Hemp Publishing, 1992.

Herodotus. *The Histories.* Middlesex, England: Penguin Classics.

Higgins, Sir Godfrey. *Anacalypsis: An Attempt to Draw Aside the Veil of the Saitic Isis.* 2 vols. 1840. Reprint, Kessinger Publishing Co., 1998.

Hodges, Edward Lewis. *Teachings of the Secret Order of the Christian Brotherhood and School of Christian Initiation.* Santa Barbara, CA: J. F. Rowny Press, 1952.

————. *The Scientific Procedure of Spiritualizing the Physical Body.* Santa Barbara, CA: J. F. Rowny Press.

Hodson, Geoffrey. *The Hidden Wisdom in the Bible.* 2 vols. Wheaton: Quest Books, 1994.

Hogue, John. *Nostradamus and the Millennium: Predictions of the Future.* Garden City, NY: Doubleday & Co., 1987.

Holy Bibe, King James Version.

Hotema, Hilton. *Awaken the World Within.* Mokelumne Hill, CA: Health Research, 1991.

————. *Sacred Wisdom of the Ancients: Living Fire and God's Law of Life.* Mokelumne Hill, CA: Health Research.

Ingalese, Richard. *The History and Power of Mind.* Romford Essex: L. N. Fowler & Co.

Iyengar, B. K. S. *Light on Yoga.* London: Unwin Paperbacks, 1976.

Jahn, Janheinz. *Muntu: The New African Culture.* New York: Grove Press, 1961.

James, George. *Stolen Legacy.* Newport News, VA: United Brothers Communications Systems, 1989.

Kallyndyr, Rolston, and Henderson Dalrymple. *Reggae: A Peoples Music.* London: Carib-Arawak Publications, 1973.

Khamit-Kush, Indus. *What They Never Told You in History Class.* Bronx, NY: Luxor Publications, 1983.

Kirkwood, Byron, comp. *Mary's Message to the World: As sent by Mary, the Mother of Jesus to Her Messenger Annie Kirkwood.* New York City, CA: Blue Dolphin Publishing.

Kloss, Jethro. *Back to Eden.* 5th ed. Santa Barbara, CA: Woodbridge Press Publishing, 1981.

Landsburg, Alan, and Sally Landsburg. *In Search of Ancient Mysteries.* London: Cogi Books, 1974.

Leadbeater, C. W. *Man Visible and Invisible.* Wheaton: Quest Books.

Levi. *The Aquarian Gospel of Jesus the Christ.* Marina Del Rey, CA: DeVorss & Co., 1979.

Lewis, H. Spencer. *Mansions of the Soul.* San Jose, CA: Supreme Grand Lodge of AMORC, 1986.

————. *The Secret Doctrine of Jesus.* San Jose, CA: Supreme Grand Lodge of AMORC, 1995.

Lindsey, Hal, with C. C. Carlson. *The Late Great Planet Earth.* London: Marshall Pickering, an imprint of HarperCollins Publishers, 1970.

Lindsey, Hal. *The 1980's: Countdown to Armageddon.* New York: Bantam Books, 1983.

Lust, John. *The Herb Book.* Simi Valley, CA: Benedict Lust Publications, 2001.

Maglangbay, Shawna. *Garvey, Lumumba, Malcolm: Black Nationalist Separatists.* Chicago: Third World Press, 1972.

Manning, Junior "Ista J". *Members of a New Race: Teachings of H.I.M. Haile Selassie I.* Blantyre, Malawi: A Rastaman Vibration/Clarity Production.

Mascaro, Juan, trans. *Dhammapada: The Path of Perfection* Middlesex, England: Penguin Books.

Massey, Gerald. *Ancient Egypt: The Light of the World.* New York, 1932.

———. *Book of the Beginnings.* 2 vols. 1930. Reprint, Kessinger Publishing Co., 1992.

Means, Sterling M. *Ethiopia and the Missing Link in African History.* Harrisburg, PA: Atlantis Publishing Co.

Montgomery, Ruth. *The World Before.* New York: Fawcett Crest Books, 1990.

Narayanananda, Swami. *Brahmacharya for Boys and Girls.* Gyling, Denmark: N.U. Yoga Trust and Ashrama.

———. *Sex Sublimation.* Gyling, Denmark: N.U. Yoga Trust and Ashrama, 1979.

Nettleford, Rex. *Mirror Mirror: Identity, Race and Protest in Jamaica.* Kingston: Collins and Sangster's Book Stores, 1970.

New American Library. *The Lost Books of the Bible and the Forgotten Books of Eden: Gospel of the Infancy of Jesus Christ.* A Meridian Book, New American Library.

Owens, Joseph. *Dread: The Rastafarians of Jamaica.* Kingston: Sangster's Book Stores, 1976.

Pentecost, J. Dwight. *Prophecy for Today.* Grand Rapids: Zondervan Publishing House, 1984.

Rama, Swami. *Meditation and Its Practice.* Honesdale, PA: The Himalayan Institute Press, 1998.

Ramacharaka, Yogi. *The Hindu: Yogi Science of Breath.* London: L. N. Fowler & Co., 1960.

Rampa, T. Lobsang. *Wisdom of the Ancients.* London: Corgi Books.

———. *You Forever.* London: Corgi Books.

Relfe, Mary Stewart. *When Your Money Fails.* Montgomery: Ministries, Inc., 1981.

Riley, Frank L. *Biblical Allegorism: A Key to the Mysteries of the Kingdom of God.* Los Angeles: Phillips Printing Co. Reprint, Mokelumne Hill, CA: Health Research.

Rogers, Robert Athlyi. *The Holy Piby.* With a foreword by Ras Sekou Tafari and an introduction by Miguel Lorne. 1924. Reprint, Chicago: Research Associates School Times Publications and Frontline Distribution Int'l Inc., 2000.

Sarkar, P. R. *The Thoughts of P. R. Sarkar.* Edited by Avadhutika Anandamitra, Acarya. Tiljala, Calcutta: Ananda Marga Publications, 1981.

Scott, John P. *The Hidden Bible: Genesis.*

Sewell, Tony. *Garvey's Children: The Legacy of Marcus Garvey.* London: Macmillan Publishers, 1990.

Shinn, Florence Scovel. *The Game of Life and How to Play It.* 36th ed. Romford Essex: L. N. Fowler & Co., 1984.

Shook, Dr. Edward E. *Advanced Treaties in Herbology.* Mokelumne Hill, CA: Health Research.

Stearn, Jess. *Yoga, Youth, and Reincarnation.* New York: Bantam Books, 1981.

Tompkins, Peter. *The Secrets of the Great Pyramid.* New York: HarperCollins, 1978.

Van Sertima, Ivan. *They Came Before Columbus.* New York: Random House, 1976.

Vishnudevananda, Swami. *The Complete Illustrated Book of Yoga.* New York: Pocket Books, 1985.

Volney, Count C. F. *Ruins of Empires.* France, 1792.

Weor, Samael Aun. *The Perfect Couple.* New York: American Institute of Universal Charities.

Williams, Chancellor. *The Destruction of Black Civilization: Great Issues of A Race From 4500 B.C. to 2000 A.D.* Chicago: Third World Press, 1974.

Williams, Joseph J. *Hebrewism of West Africa.* 2nd ed. New York: Dial Press, 1931.

Windsor, Rudolph R. *From Babylon to Timbuktu: A History of the Ancient Black Races Including the Black Hebrews.* New York: Exposition Press, 1969.

Woldben, A. *After Nostradamus: Great Prophecies for the Future of Mankind.* Granada
    Publishing. Reprint, Frogmore, St. Albans, Herts: Mayflower Books, 1975.
Yoganada, Paramahansa. *Autobiography of a Yogi.* Los Angeles: Self-Realization
    Fellowship, 1979.

INDEX